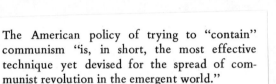

The American policy of trying to "contain" communism "is, in short, the most effective technique yet devised for the spread of communist revolution in the emergent world."

Finally Kiernan calls for a redefinition of national interest: "Can we not use our power and wealth to *support* revolutionary change in the emergent world, and smooth the path of modernizing transformation," by providing capital and technical aid without demanding a political, economic, or military *quid pro quo?* By so doing we would avoid destructive international tensions, and lay the foundations of a world in which we can safely pursue our own way of life.

BERNARD P. KIERNAN, Professor of Social Sciences at Concord College, is author of articles appearing in the *Yale Review, American Scholar,* and other journals.

The United States, Communism,

and the Emergent World

The United States,

and the

Communism,

Emergent World

BERNARD P. KIERNAN

INDIANA UNIVERSITY PRESS

Bloomington / London

Grateful acknowledgment is made to the Yale Review
in whose pages some of the material in Chapter 1
originally appeared.

Published in Canada by Fitzhenry & Whiteside Limited, Don Mills, Ontario

Library of Congress catalog card number: 72-75636

ISBN: 0-255-19009-6

Manufactured in the United States of America

Contents

1

Communism: the Revolution

of Modernization

1 · *The Nature of Communism*
in the Emergent World

ONE OF THE CRITICAL ISSUES OF CONTEMPORARY POLITICS IS THE
turmoil of revolutionary unrest which, since 1945, has been agitat-
ing the peoples of the underdeveloped world: Asia, Africa, Latin
America; those nations which comprise what the French call the
Third World (*Tiers-Monde*), and which might be described, in the
context of this essay, as the emergent world. The aspect of this revolutionary turmoil which has been viewed with particular anxiety in
the United States has been the development of communism,
defined here as any form of authoritarian socialism, not necessarily
that of an official Communist Party. The United States has assumed that communism, in the emergent world, is an alien political
force, motivated simply by hostility and hatred of the so-called free
world, and bent on spreading political tyranny. Consequently, the
United States has interpreted its role in the emergent world as one
of steadfast opposition to the development of such an odious political system. When related to the international pressures of the Cold
War which developed after 1945, the goal of American foreign pol-

icy in the emergent world has been the containment of communism.

The chief purpose of this essay is to challenge the basic assumptions behind American foreign policy in the emergent world, particularly those assumptions which justify the containment of communism. It argues that this policy is misconceived, and based on a misreading of the significance of the revolution of the underdeveloped world. The argument of this essay is based on a rejection of conventional definitions of communism in this country, definitions related to Marxist ideology, to the existence of a Soviet directed international communist movement, which appear to have limited relevance to the revolutionary phenemenon of the emergent world. Instead, this essay redefines communism as a process of change, of transformation, as a form of nationalism, a stage in the internal restructuring of what we consider backward societies. It argues that the functional ideology of the emergent world is national development, and that communism is a means of satisfying that ideology.

The United States has not been blind to the connection between communism and conditions of poverty, ignorance, disease, hunger, and social unrest in the emergent world. But we have assumed that the solution of these problems of underdevelopment did not have to take a communist form; that under the tutelage of the United States, the emergent world could overcome its backwardness without incurring the "bad" features of communism. In containing communism, we have sought to force the emergent world into the kind of mold we have deemed suitable to its interests, as well as the kind of pattern which is compatible with our own interests. Further, we have assumed that communism is not a legitimate response to the problems of the emergent world, that communists cynically "exploit" the problems of the emergent world in order to promote their own interests, which are the interests of an international ideological movement concerned with the destruction of the "free" world, and the spread of a noxious, totalitarian system.

The great weakness of our view of communism in the emergent world is that it tends to substitute moral fervor for understanding. We have developed a very righteous pose of moral indignation toward communism, but we have made little effort to see its nature clearly, in relation to objective conditions. In fact, our strong emotional response to communism tends to obscure rather than illuminate the nature of the revolutionary upheaval in the emergent world. For we have refused to view communism as a meaningful, rational policy, deliberately chosen for presumably sufficient reasons, as a possible response to the challenges confronting the emergent societies. We have sought the explanation for communism in a wholly inadequate conspiracy theory of revolutionary ferment in the emergent world. We have sought the clue to the development not only of communism, but of a whole range of left-wing revolutionary ideologies in Asia, Africa, Latin America, in the activities of an international conspiracy, rather than in the conditions and circumstances of the peoples and societies which produce these revolutionary movements. We view communism in such places as Cuba, or China, for instance, almost exclusively as an alien political force, thrust upon an unwilling population from the outside, by agents of an international conspiracy motivated entirely by morally sinister purposes. As a result, we have failed to define communism as a native response, shaped and defined by the needs and problems of those societies themselves, in the emergent world, which have turned to communism and to radical, left-wing ideologies.

We have clung to this conspiratorial theory of communism even in the face of the obvious lack of unity among various independent communist states. And we have failed to account for the success of this "conspiracy" in enlisting considerable support from the political leadership of the emergent world, or in winning allegiance from its native populations, beyond a rather vague "explanation" concerning the poverty and misery of the peoples of Asia, Africa, and Latin America; this misery presumably focuses their concern on problems of sheer survival, as a result of which, for not very clear reasons, they become receptive to communist "propaganda." As a result, we have concentrated almost exclusively on the techniques of that propaganda to account for the success of communism, and have gone so far as to develop a whole barrage of countervailing techniques of propaganda, of counterinsurgency, created, presumably, after communist models, of which the Special Forces in Vietnam, the so-called Green Berets, were the climactic example; as if the success or failure of political movements was wholly unrelated to their appropriateness in meeting real problems, and depended solely on propaganda trickery. The fact that Vietnamese communists have a success with the Vietnamese people which our own personnel, with all of our highly complex technical apparatus, cannot even begin to approximate, has failed to penetrate this wall of deliberate obtuseness. It has only convinced us that somehow, our "techniques" were at fault.

As a result, we do not see communists in quite the same way as we would the advocates of any other political system or ideology; that is, we do not see the Viet Cong, for instance, as Vietnamese people who have *chosen* communism, who have deliberately adopted communism, voluntarily deciding that communism was *their* political answer to the problems of their society. Rather, we see them as a kind of species apart—not in the sense that we condemn them for their undemocratic political philosophy, for we have no trouble accepting political leaders who command far less support from their own people than the Viet Cong, but in the sense that we do not see them as a legitimate part of the Vietnamese population. We assume that the Vietnamese people must be saved from communists who, somehow, are not Vietnamese people themselves, or not in the same sense as "real" people; we see the Viet Cong as a kind of "non-people." Trapped in this kind of ideological framework, an otherwise perceptive and knowledgeable student of the Viet Cong movement ultimately is forced to come to the remarkable conclusion that "revolutionary guerilla warfare is not indigenous." [1] As an extreme limit to which this kind of analysis can lead, we have former Secretary of State Dean Rusk's "explanation" for our rejection of the legitimacy of the communist regime in China: "It is not the government of China. It does not pass the first test. It is not Chinese." [2]

Why is communism such a strong force in the underdeveloped world? We cannot answer that question as long as we view communism as a confidence trick played upon the leaders of the emergent world, or as long as we view it as a kind of ethical deformity. We cannot hope to explain the force of communism in the emergent world, or begin to define it with any precision, unless we make the reasonable assumption that communists are human beings, seeking practical solutions to human problems. We need not approve of these solutions. We may be convinced that they are erroneously conceived and inadequate. We may abhor the moral assumptions upon which these solutions are based. But we need not justify communism in order to understand it; and to understand it, we must assume that the leaders of the emergent world do not adopt communism because they are morally depraved, or because they are "evil." Men, after all, are not born communists. Communism is not a biological condition, or a metaphysical characteristic. It should be possible to explain why certain leaders of the emergent world *adopt* communism; not because they have been "duped" by agents of an international conspiracy, but on the assumption that they have chosen communism deliberately.

An examination of communist movements in the emergent world suggests that communism has become a means by which an underdeveloped society attempts to undergo, very rapidly, the process of modernization, to transform itself politically, economically, socially, and intellectually. Under communism, such a transformation is achieved through the leadership of an elite party which applies stringent mass discipline, a totalitarian straitjacket, to force the population, by a combination of coercion and exhortation, to transform itself, to modernize itself, out of its own resources. Such a

5

transformation is, obviously, that which Russia, under the leadership of Lenin's Bolshevik Party, achieved in becoming the modern giant we call the Soviet Union.

The example and success of the Soviet Union are crucial, for they provide the most meaningful starting point for a definition of communism in the emergent world. In practice, communism has meant reliving certain basic aspects of the Soviet experience in order to achieve a comparable success. "The Russian Revolution established a new category, the revolution of the underdeveloped countries." [3] Or, as another historian puts it: "The Bolshevik Revolution has many elements of a development revolution not unlike that underway in the underdeveloped countries." [4]

The Bolshevik Revolution has become the classic example, the model, for a new kind of communist revolution, which has been determined not by the needs of nineteenth-century Europe, but by the needs of underdeveloped societies in the twentieth century; a revolution which is not explained by Marxist theories about social injustice in advanced capitalistic societies, but which finds its roots in the problem of modernization, and the apparently successful confrontation of that problem by the Soviet Union. And its great appeal is due less to the intellectual influence of Karl Marx than to the community of experience between the Soviet Union and the emergent nations—ultimately, the community of experience among the developing nations themselves.

If the Soviet Union is the supreme exemplar for the emergent world, it is a model for the techniques of change. Russia's own model, the end product for which her communist revolution was only the means, was the status of a modern, that is, Western nation. What Russia sought to achieve by communism, and what the underdeveloped countries are trying to achieve by reliving the Russian experience, is the status of a Western society, that of a powerful, wealthy modern state. Communism, as defined by the Soviet experience, is thus a means of catching up with the West, of acquiring what a French sociologist calls "the mysterious power of the

6

creators of the machines," [5] a power which the West has hitherto monopolized.

If the ultimate model, beyond the Soviet Union, is the advanced West, why is it not as likely for the underdeveloped world to achieve its goals by the presumably democratic, liberal methods of the West as it is to do so by imitating the totalitarian techniques of Bolshevism? In short, why can we not persuade the emergent world to adopt us as an alternative model to the Soviet Union for its transformation? To a large extent, United States policy in the underdeveloped world has devoted itself to that very task. We have assumed that we were engaged in an ideological conflict, a "war for men's minds" in the emergent world, in which we sought to sell Western democracy and capitalism in competition against Soviet communism. But what we call the democratic alternative, which is the route that the West presumably traveled to its present wealth, power, and freedom, appears to be an alternative no longer open to the emergent world, which faces a configuration of circumstances much more closely resembling those faced by the Soviet Union in the 1920's than those faced by England in the seventeenth and eighteenth centuries, or by the United States in the nineteenth century.

The force of communism in the emergent world is not simply a measure of the attractiveness of the Soviet Union as a model, but results from the fact that a similar set of historical circumstances is likely to produce a similar range of responses. The pressures of modern power politics, particularly as exemplified by the extension of Western domination over non-Western societies, not only in the age of colonialism, but in the contemporary world, will compel the emergent societies to see the rapid success of modernization as taking precedence over every other consideration. Their experience will reflect the same pressures for a centrally planned, massive program of rapid development as occurred in the Soviet Union. Such a communist transformation, however, is wholly misconceived if it is viewed as the expression of an ideological movement concerned

7

with the establishment and spread of a totalitarian system for its own sake. If the ultimate goal of the emergent world is modernization, then communism, in the emergent societies, is a tool, not an end in itself. It is an arsenal of techniques for the transformation of society, rather than an ideology defining a good society. Communism does not "exploit" the problems of the emergent world for the satisfaction of its own, unrelated purposes. It *is* the response of that world to its problems.

If communism is a likely response to the experience of modernization in the emergent world, this likelihood is, in fact, partly the result of the impact of American foreign policy. For the policy of containing communism, by misreading the nature of communist revolution, aggravates the problems of the emergent world. The development since 1945 of an informal American empire dedicated to the containment of communism, and the far-flung interventions which have been produced by this policy, far from eliminating the features of communism we profess to abhor, have, on the contrary, tremendously increased the difficulties of the emergent world, and have therefore greatly increased, as this essay hopes to demonstrate, the likelihood of a communist response. For in practice, our policy of containing communism has resulted in opposing modernization altogether. More accurately, we have refused to condone development in the emergent world if it challenges our interests, our power, or our self-image as the superior guardians of the world. It is, in fact, this kind of challenge which American foreign policy finds particularly abhorrent in communism, rather than its authoritarian features.

But modernization, in the emergent world, will probably not occur without presenting, to some degree, this very kind of challenge. Communism, in fact, is one central aspect of such a challenge. The only realistic, as well as the only humane goal of American foreign policy, in the face of the emergent world, is not to seek to crush that challenge, but to readjust our definition of national interest in such a way as to accommodate it to the existence of an emergent world in the process of revolutionary transformation. By refusing to accept that revolution, including its communist ingredients, we will not only tremendously increase tensions in the world, but we will be driven into a narrow, and wholly unrealistic definition of American interests, relying solely on our ability to dominate the world militarily. The recent crisis of our society over Indochina indicates one dimension of the inadequacy of such a foreign policy.

2 · *Communism: a Definition*

The kind of revolutionary response to the modernization of the emergent world which this essay seeks to analyze goes beyond the official doctrine and practices of the Communist Party of the Soviet Union, or of China, or the official doctrine and practices of any specific Communist Party. It includes all the factors held in common by left-wing revolutionary movements; and the term communism (with a small c), is used in this essay to refer to the broad community of practices, attitudes, and values shared by a certain segment of the revolutionary leadership of the emergent world, whether or not such leadership adheres to an official Communist Party (with a capital C). These common points in the political response of the emergent world, particularly in their more extreme and radical forms, comprise a recognizable entity which is real, and which deserves a name.

The use of the term communism to refer to such left-wing revolutionary ideologies may appear ambiguous, since it is confused with the use of the term in the restricted sense of the doctrine of official Communist Parties. In fact, it may recall the well-known tendency of the United States government to label all revolutionaries in the emergent world as communists. When the United States intervened in the Dominican Republic in 1965, for instance, many liberals argued that the intervention was unjustified since there were only some fifty-five Communists involved in the revolutionary movement we were seeking to suppress. This intervention, in fact, was pointed to as a classic example of our hysterical overreaction to the threat of Communism, and our readiness to see Communists everywhere. The assumption behind this argument was that Communists (with a capital C), represented an element and force absolutely different in kind from all other revolutionary forces in the Dominican Republic, and that the absence of such Communists would have removed all the reasons our government might have had for intervention.

This essay disputes this assumption; it suggests that the presence or absence of people calling themselves Communists was not the decisive factor in the Dominican Republic, anymore than in Vietnam, or anywhere else in the emergent world. And our government's response was not due to any difficulty it has in distinguishing Communists from non-Communists, but to the fact that it was opposing a revolutionary ideology in the Dominican Republic which is not limited to official Communist Parties.

The belief that Communism (with a capital C), represents something distinctive and absolutely different from all other political forces in the emergent world rests on two kinds of related assumptions. We claim that Communists are not "normal" parties, because they belong to an international conspiracy. Hence their coming to power is never a legitimate expression of the political process in a society, but brings the society under the control of this international conspiracy, which exists outside any particular state. This assumption is no longer quite tenable, even in those extremist circles which are susceptible to conspiracy theories. The second assumption, which is much more widely shared, is that although the international Communist movement has disintegrated, institutionally, there still exists a more or less official Communist doctrine that all Communist Parties subscribe to, and that differentiates them absolutely from all other parties. This essay questions both assumptions. It not only questions the existence of a tightly knit international organization of Communist Parties, which acts as a monolithic unit, but it questions whether such a conspiracy, in the sense in which it is popularly conceived, ever existed, or could have existed. It questions equally the existence of a coherent international Communist ideology shared by all Communist Parties; in fact, it seeks to demonstrate that, regardless of what Communists might say about themselves, such an international Communist movement does not exist, as is constantly demonstrated by the disputes between Communist Parties, and that, given the political facts of the twentieth century, it cannot exist.

There is one other way in which we see Communist Parties as a special breed apart, and that is their presumed special link with the Soviet Union. The coming to power of a Communist Party is inevitably accompanied, we believe, by some form of Soviet penetration, which we have to contain because of the demands of our own big-power conflict with the Soviet Union. Such a conclusion appears to turn the matter upside down. The factors which determine the possibility of Soviet intervention seem to have little to do with the existence or absence of official Communist Parties; witness, for instance, the extensive Soviet aid to an Egyptian government which has never been very sympathetic to its Communist Party. Conversely, witness the rapid liquidation of Soviet assistance to a Chinese government ruled by an official Communist Party. In other words, the possibility of Soviet intervention is premised on the facts of the international situation, and determined by the pressures of international power politics; it has little to do with the existence or absence of official Communist Parties. We shall return to this question in more detail.

If there does not exist an international Communist movement, held together by either institutional or ideological ties, if various Communist Parties are frequently at considerable divergence from one another, there does exist, on the other hand, a considerable range of identities among revolutionary, modernizing leaders in the emergent world. These identities do not result from the fact that these men have adopted a common ideology, but from the fact that they share common problems, common circumstances, seek common goals, and adopt common methods. It is this real community of experience which I feel can be described by the term communism (with a small c).

This is not to say that *all* revolutionary, modernizing leaders in the emergent world are alike. There are differences among them, and very real differences. But these differences are not meaningfully described by adherence or non-adherence to an official Communist Party. Such adherence is not decisive because official Communist Parties do not necessarily share a common ideology. On the other hand, there are very meaningful identities and similarities among revolutionary forces in the emergent world, and these identities cut across the question of membership in an official Communist Party.

The value of the term communism in referring to this common range of revolutionary experience is that it points to everything so many Americans dislike about these revolutionary attitudes, which most Americans have identified with the label communist. The usefulness of the term is that it reminds us that what these revolutionary ideologies have in common are all those traits which we claim to oppose in Communism (with a capital C); so that the tendency of our government to lump various kinds of revolutionaries under the rubric communist, whether or not they subscribe to an official Communist Party, is functional, and reflects in no way a semantic confusion. When we combat communism in the emergent world, we are not simply combating Communist Parties; we are combating all those characteristics in the revolution of the emergent world which we oppose in official Communist Parties, all those characteristics which we associate with the Soviet system, and which are the source of our dislike for that system. We oppose these characteristics regardless of the names used by the parties which exhibit them, and we tend to call such parties communist because of their association with the Soviet system and its ruling Communist Party.

The use of the term communism to identify certain common

characteristics of this revolutionary transformation not only identifies the nature of the process which our government is opposing in the emergent world, but finds the historical roots of that process in the experience of the Soviet Union. In other words, the label communism, in this essay, is used to describe a historical process which recalls the experience of the Soviet Union under the rule of the Soviet Communist Party. In the same way the various totalitarian responses to the problems of post-World War I Europe which bore some similarity to the Italian experience, and which were to some degree modeled deliberately after that experience, came to be labelled fascism, whether or not these political movements called themselves fascist parties.

This use of the term communism helps to pinpoint the real weakness in the foreign policy of the United States. The error of that policy does not lie in any tendency to confuse Communists and non-Communists. It lies, first of all, in the assumption that the methods of the communist transformation of the emergent world, as defined in this essay, can be eschewed, and that it is to our interest, as well as those of the peoples of the emergent world, to prevent this kind of revolution. It lies secondly in our misapprehension of the *nature* of the revolutionary transformation of the emergent world. The United States, as the most powerful state on earth, can have a profound impact on the experience of modernization in the emergent world. This impact can only take the form, however, of mitigating the conditions which produce extreme responses in the emergent world; it cannot eliminate altogether conditions which are rooted in the history of the non-Western world, nor can it prevent altogether those aspects of communism which it considers "evil." Modernization is not only an inevitable process in the emergent world, but one which will partake, to some degree or another, of "communist" features.

For that reason, our intervention in the Dominican Republic was not mistaken because there were only fifty-five Communists. It would have been equally mistaken if there had been 5,500 Communists. For the error lay in the goal of our intervention, and the assumptions on which this goal rested. It was mistaken because the goal of our intervention was to prevent a certain kind of revolutionary transformation, and it was based on the assumption that preventing such transformation by force would serve our interests. Given the real nature of our goal, the precise number of official Communists was not decisive to our government's action. Given the logic of that policy, this essay argues that it would have been equally mistaken if the revolution had been entirely in the hands of official Communists.

Inevitably, our government plays up the existence of official Communist Parties among revolutionaries in the emergent world, for such a presence guarantees the automatic support of our people for policies opposing such revolutionaries. This tendency, however, does not represent any real deception; our government is not using a Communist bogey-man to frighten the American people into supporting a policy they would otherwise reject. For although the hostility of the American people toward certain aspects of revolution in the emergent world has attached to the term communism, that hostility is not simply a word fetish; it is a hostility to actual things our government opposes in the emergent world. Most of us are no more willing than our State Department to see certain kinds of revolutionary transformations in the emergent world. We oppose the reality of that transformation, rather than the word communism; in fact, it is the American people who have given the term communism that kind of currency, for the same reason that our government uses the term communism to define and express our attitudes toward those things we dislike about the revolutionary transformation of the emergent world.

In summary, communism, in this essay, is defined as a historical process, determined by historical circumstances. Communism, in the emergent world, is a movement which exhibits the following characteristics. It is authoritarian, in fact, to some degree totalitarian. It is committed to economic development through large-scale government planning. It is committed to a transformation of society through a revolution from above. It seeks rapid modernization, and is willing to extensively harass its own people in forcing them to change their way of life. Most important of all, perhaps, it is radically anti-Western; that is, it hopes to achieve modernization without falling under the permanent tutelage, particularly economic tutelage, of the West. It views the advanced Western nations as a chief obstacle to its goals of national development, and it is willing to risk a confrontation with these nations, rather than accommodation, in achieving national development. These characteristics will appear if conditions produce them; that is, whether, or to what degree, an emergent society adopts a communist response will not be a "free" choice made by political leaders on the basis of subjective considerations; it will be determined by the conditions of that society. There is no way in which the nature of the response of any particular emerging society can be determined by propaganda, by "winning" political leaders to our side, or the Soviet side. The only way in which the nature of that response can be affected is by altering the real conditions confronting that society. Our interventions, as in Vietnam, have usually changed conditions in such ways as to *increase* the radicalism, the communism, of that response.

3 · *Modernization and Political Power*

The most significant change brought about through modernization in the West has been the tremendously increased power of modern societies vis-à-vis less developed ones; and the inescapability of modernization has resulted from the pressures of Western power politics. It is in this sense, primarily, that the experience of the Soviet Union, and the experience of China, represent particularly significant examples for the emergent world.

The pressure for modernization in nineteenth-century Russia resulted, as T. H. Von Laue remarks, from the gap between her ambitions and her resources.[6] She wanted to be a major power, but her backwardness prevented her. The status of a major power was defined by the advanced Western societies. The gap between ambition and resources had to be closed, not because Russia's ambitions were unrealistic, or because her leaders suffered from megalomania, but because, politically, Russia had to meet the challenge of Western power. Security, if nothing else, demanded it. And if Russia failed to close the gap, the result would be political catastrophe. Nor was the Russian czarist regime the only one to be destroyed by its inability to close this gap. The Hapsburg and Ottoman regimes were also destroyed, at the same time and for the same reason.

The Russian rulers realized their dilemma long before the Crimean War, or the Russo-Japanese War. In that sense, the redefinition of Peter the Great in Soviet historiography, as the first Bolshevik, is completely accurate. Peter the Great was the first czar to realize clearly the political dangers posed for Russia's survival as an independent political state by contact with the much more powerful Western states. Russia's ambitions resulted from the simple realization that in the world of Western politics into which she was being drawn, power was the only currency. She sought the status of a first-class power in response to the challenge of the West.

It is true that certain societies, such as Switzerland or Denmark, have been able to enjoy all the advantages of modernization without achieving a great deal of military or political power. Whatever special factors have permitted these countries to ignore, to a large extent, the pressures of power politics, such direct military threats as those of Poland, of Turkey, of Sweden, of Napoleonic France, of Germany's Second and Third Reichs demonstrated very clearly to Russia, historically, that she herself could not ignore power politics. The response to this challenge of power politics was the upheaval of 1917: the czarist regime was not overthrown primarily because of its oppressive political atmosphere, but because it failed to adjust Russian society to the realities of modern power politics. And the success of the Communists in Russia depended primarily on their ability to make such an adjustment, to close the traditional gap between ambition and resources. Molotov made the point very clearly in a speech in February, 1946, celebrating the Soviet victory in World War II: "The Soviet Union achieved victory first in the West, then in the East, something of which pre-Soviet Russia had been incapable." [7] Or, as Stalin put it, "The backward are beaten." [8]

Colonialism and imperialism demonstrated even more drastically to the emergent world that it ignored power politics at its own peril. For the emergent world, the colonial experience was the clearest proof of the need for rapid modernization. If these societies had not been so weak, so helpless, they would not have been so easily exploited and humiliated by the powerful West. Inevitably, the leaders of the emergent world seek modernization primarily as a means of throwing off a humiliating Western yoke, the existence of which proves to them that the rapid achievement of power must be their overriding political goal. China is a model for modernization in the emergent world because it has sought, through this transformation, the kind of power which all the backward societies seek in their confrontation with the advanced world; because it exemplifies, as does the Soviet Union, what W. W. Rostow calls "the demonstration effect of the relation between modernization and military power." [9]

The relation between modernization and power is crucial, because modernization, by its very nature, is not a democratic process. Nowhere has the transition from a traditional to a modern society been carried out spontaneously, or even voluntarily, from below. In offering ourselves as a democratic alternative to communism, we overlook the fact that coercion has been an inescapable factor in all the processes of modernization; that the peasant populations of traditional societies have seldom been willing to accept change and development. Modernization has been everywhere a coercive process, dependent on authoritarian techniques, even in the "democratic" West. Democracy, liberalism, and the open society, although they are related to modernization, are possible consequences of such a process rather than its preconditions.

The community of experience among the emergent societies, and between them on the one hand and the Soviet Union and China on the other, is crucial to the argument of this essay, which contends that the nature of the response of the emergent world to the challenge of modernization will be determined by historical conditions and contemporary circumstances. Not only does there exist a considerable community of beliefs and practices among left-wing revolutionary leaders in the emergent world, a community which cuts across adherence to official Communist Parties, but the numerous historical experiences shared by most emerging societies mean that the kind of response which is defined in this essay as communist will be itself a radical, extreme version of what most emerging societies are likely to experience. Further, this communist response is itself an intensification, an acceleration of the modernization which occurred in the West; in this sense, communism, or left-wing revolution in the emergent world, cannot be seen as an ideology that stands in any fundamental opposition to the ideologies of the western world. If the communist path to modernization is more authoritarian and more brutal than that of the West, the Western experience cannot present itself as a fundamentally opposed one. Communism is a process of nation-building, of political centralization, of state-building, of economic growth, of social organization, of intellectual awakening, which parallels, in a speeded-up version, the modernization of the West.

Communism is a stage in the natural evolution of many emergent nations, in the evolution of nationalism and the creation of modern nation-states in the emergent world. It is a "résumé of the revolutions that make up modernization and it offers a method of applying them speedily to societies caught fast in the dilemmas of transition." [10]

Note that using the Soviet Union as a meaningful model for

the techniques of modernization is not the same thing as either accepting Soviet political domination or even as viewing the Soviet Union, *today,* as a meaningful example. Communists wish to relive the revolutionary experience and modernization of the Soviet Union. They do not necessarily wish to create a society which duplicates the details of the Soviet Union as it exists today; nor do they wish to become satellites of the Soviet Union, a status which would defeat the goal of modernization. For that reason, although the example of the Soviet Union continues to be important, China, for obvious reasons, is today a more meaningful model for the emergent world.

Communism in the emergent world is not, and cannot be, a fixed, rigid, absolute ideological system. It continues to be defined by innumerable political leaders in their day-to-day response to the challenge of political necessities. Communism, like any other system, did not spring full-blown out of an individual's head; it was shaped and hammered by the pressures of actual circumstances. In other words, communism in the emergent world cannot be explained by reference to the theories of Karl Marx, or Stalin, or Mao Tse-tung, or Castro, or any other single individual; not because there exists somewhere a "true" communism, which has been "distorted" by the Soviet, or Chinese, or Cuban leadership, but because each society develops its own ideological response, appropriate to its own circumstances.

If communism is a modernizing revolution, it will take as many forms as there are emergent societies, each confronting modernization in its own unique conditions, and the single label communist may not be able to cover all these differences.

Not only are the totalitarian tendencies of the emergent world functional, related to perceived social needs, but the totalitarian pressures of communist transformation are themselves part of the larger pressure of new disciplines, new organizational authorities, which are inherent in the modernization process itself. As George

Lichtheim says, "this problem is not peculiar to the Soviet regime, the Bolshevik party being evidently a variant of the characteristically modern phenomenon known as totalitarianism." [11]

The totalitarian character of communism in the Soviet Union is but one expression of the gradual emergence of totalitarianism throughout the advanced world in the twentieth century, largely as a result of the pressures of total war, and the total mobilization of society which the two world wars produced. Modernization has meant, whether Europeans viewed it consciously that way or not, a process of increasing mobilization of resources for the purpose of maximizing the collective power of the society. Totalitarianism is a phenomenon peculiar to modernized societies, and can be defined simply as the process of mobilizing a society for total war. Not only was World War I the model for the totalitarian systems of the twentieth century, but the Soviet techniques of modernization owe much more to the war economies of the belligerents of World War I than to the theories of Karl Marx.

The problem of communist authoritarianism, in short, is the problem of authoritarianism and totalitarian organization inherent in a modernization which has developed essentially in response to the pressures of war and international power politics. The totalitarian system of the Soviet Union itself is the product, to a considerable extent, of these pressures. "Economic development and industrialization . . . do not necessarily lead either to democracy or to left-wing social democracy . . . Rather, they do lead as Max Weber long ago pointed out, to a bureaucratized society that may or may not be democratic." [12] Modernization does not guarantee a liberal democratic society, which is only a possible consequence of this process. Modernization only guarantees bureaucratized societies which, even in the liberal West, seriously undermine and contradict the democratic potential of modernization.

Since means determine ends, a legitimate question is whether the emergent world, if it uses Soviet means for its development, can avoid becoming the kind of conservative, institutionalized totalitarianism that the Soviet Union has become. Can the emergent world transcend the totalitarianism it creates to achieve national development? This question is related to the whole issue of totalitarianism and modernization. The moral issues posed by modernization go far beyond the scope of this essay. What will be suggested, in conclusion, is that the real ideological question of the modern world is not whether communism will triumph over something called the free world, but whether the new disciplines imposed by modernization, the totalitarian tendencies shared by all modernized societies, can be transcended, and whether modernization can finally be made to function for the genuine liberation of all men.

2

Modernization in the West

1 · *Peasant Attitudes Toward Modernization*

VIEWING THE WORLD THROUGH THE MONOCHROME LENSES OF ANTI-communism, we have assumed that the undeveloped worldfaces a simple choice between democracy and communism. But the same conditions of backwardness which make communism a plausible alternative in the emergent world also make democracy equally unlikely. The lack of freedom of traditional peasant societies stems from their lack of power to control events, to effect meaningful improvement. A traditional peasant society lacks freedom because alternative choices to the dictates of custom do not appear possible. Modernization, in fact, is essentially the attempt to overcome the impotence of peasant societies, an impotence which results from the belief of peasants that they are incapable of altering their environment.

The paradox of modernization, however, is that peasants, who would seem to be its chief beneficiaries, have everywhere resisted such a transformation. Peasants, who would seem to gain most, in the long run, from development, are also the people least capable, intellectually and psychologically, of supporting an organized movement for progressive change. The peasants in a traditional society cannot perceive the connection between their own wretched conditions and the structure of their society. Their lack of perception, in fact, is one of the chief ways of defining such a society as backward. Although the desirability of modernization appears so obvious to us that we take it for granted, nowhere have the majority of the members of traditional societies accepted this "liberation" spontaneously, or even willingly. In fact, "there is no evidence that the mass of the population anywhere has wanted an industrial society, and plenty of evidence that they did not. At bottom all forms of industrialization so far have been revolutions from above, the work of a ruthless minority." [1]

Modernization has everywhere been carried out by "a ruthless minority," an educated elite, against the will of the masses. It is not a democratic process. Peasants, by their very condition, the very limitation of their outlook, are not likely either to produce a leadership attuned to change or to respond favorably to exhortations to change. Modernizing leadership comes from elements which are not part of the traditional peasant culture, but which are part, instead, of an urban culture, viewed by itself, as well as by the peasants, as superior. Modernization has everywhere been carried out by a small handful of progressive people, a minority who have detached themselves from the traditional society. This modernizing leadership has had to overcome the resistance of peasant masses, who have been viewed by this "enlightened" minority as "backward," and whose resistance, or inertia, therefore, has not been considered justifiable.

The peasant resistance to modernization is due partly to intellectual and moral attitudes derived from the objective conditions of their life, conditions which orient them to a traditional view of reality, and which alienate them from the beliefs and values of modernization. Peasant concepts of the good life make them suspicious of commerce and finance; merchants and bankers have been traditionally viewed as rapacious, and defined as parasites. One characteristic common to most peasant cultures is "the idea that agricultural work is good and commerce not so good." [2]

Peasant loyalties are attached to the land, to the physical locality which they inhabit, and their life is part of a tradition embedded in an environment which they experience directly. For a peasant, agriculture is a way of life. He does things a certain way, not necessarily because it is the most efficient way of maximizing the production of goods, but because it is the traditional way, the way it has been done in the past. And tradition is composed of customs which have been shaped by a multitude of human needs and desires, none of which are in any way related to the maximization of profits. Coupled with the peasant's indifference to business for monetary profit is a general passivity and apathy concerning the possibility of improving himself within the existing society: "individuals in traditional societies have little expectation of change in their status and believe that the age-old social order is divinely ordained and unchangeable." [3] This tendency to view the conditions of life as a fixed datum which cannot be improved or altered to one's benefit is what defines the peasant as "backward"; this kind of apathy was greatly reinforced, in medieval Europe, by the intellectual influence of the Christian Church, which did not teach peasants how to prosper, but how to endure. Nor does the peasant envisage the possibility of changing the society and reorganizing it for his own benefit. His mental outlook is fatalistic, and he cannot conceive of a different ordering of society, more beneficial to his own interest.

It is this political negativism and fatalism which accounts for the nihilistic character of peasant revolts. Revolts have been in the past the typical peasant expression of dissatisfaction with their conditions. Such peasant revolts are blind, disorganized acts of destruction, expressing only rage, frustration and despair, and therefore without any positive or constructive goals. In that sense, peasant revolts are close to acts of individual criminality; the riots which have

24

gripped the Negro ghettos of our urban centers in recent years are analogous to peasant revolts. Revolutions, on the other hand, are organized movements by sophisticated and educated elites, motivated by a conviction that the society can be changed for the benefit of the revolutionaries.

The political inertia of peasants, their political negativism, is derived from the insulation of the peasant community, which is cut off, physically and intellectually, from contact with other societies. The conservatism of peasant societies derives partly from the lack of possible alternatives, from the fact that their physical and intellectual isolation deprives them of alternative models. Karl Marx summarized the limitations of peasant existence in a famous passage: "the great mass of the French nation is formed by simple addition of homologous magnitudes, much as potatoes in a sack form a sack of potatoes." [4] John Kautsky summarizes this limitation in these words: "The peasants, then, are not only unorganized but unorganizable." [5]

The peasant opposition to change is rooted also in material conditions; for the peasant tends to live at the margin of existence. Change means experimentation; and the peasant cannot afford unsuccessful experiments. He clings to the traditional, the tried and true, even if such methods only provide a meager existence; for he cannot afford any setbacks. "Individualism is discouraged because of the crises that the unusual person creates in the daily routine. People prefer a dead uniformity." [6] The only kind of change the peasant is likely to know is the catastrophic change of natural calamities, wars, disease, death. "Rigidity is increased if a society has little surplus energy or resources for experimentation—if it lives from hand to mouth and can run no risks." [7] Innovations are luxuries, gambles, and only those who are already secure can afford to take chances; which is why conscious, planned change aimed at deliberate improvement of society, the kind of change implied by modernization, usually comes from those already in positions of wealth and power.

25

The peasant's resistance to change is also related to his traditional hostility toward the city, which is the source of modernizing impulse. M. J. Herskovits, in describing urban attitudes toward villagers in Africa, speaks of "the arrogant manner of the people of Abomey when they visit the villages, while, on the other hand, the villagers show all the typical reactions of European peasants toward city dwellers—they are suspicious, evasive, non-responsive." [8]

The peasant hates the city dweller because he resents his superiority; he resents his wealth, his cleverness, his education; at the same time, he recognizes the superiority of these achievements, a recognition which humiliates him, and which he seeks to compensate by emphasizing the values and virtues of hard work and of a simple life. In short, peasants' recognition of the superior world of the city intensifies their resentment and rejection of urban values, at the same time that it forces them to accept the obvious inferiority of their own conditions, which they come to accept as a reflection of their own inferior nature, much as the American blacks had to fight the white man's definition of them as inferior before they could contemplate the possibility of change.

2 · *Modernization and Civilization*

Peasant attitudes not only reflect the fact that modernization has been a coercive process, carried out against their will; they also reflect the fact that modernization and urbanization, despite the liberating potential of these forces, have been, historically, the source of new and increasingly crushing disciplines.

The development of the city, at the dawn of civilization, was the first significant achievement of a modernizing leadership, the first conscious and deliberate attempt by a ruling elite to bring about large-scale change and improvement in the organization of society. But the city, from the beginning, organized rural people against their will, and for purposes unrelated to peasant desires or welfare. The organization of civilization compelled rural workers to accept a dependent, subservient relationship toward the city. It saddled them with an oppressive discipline and forced them into a kind of human machine which functioned only for the benefit of the creators of the city, parasites who could not have survived without the support of the rural society which they were reorganizing. For the city, by definition, is not economically self-sufficient, while rural dwellers could very well support themselves without city organization. The peasants were now subjected to a coercive police power, to a mechanical and regimented authority, emanating from the city: "they were reduced to subjects, whose lives were supervised and directed by military and civil officers, governors, viziers, tax-gatherers, soldiers." [9]

Modernization is but the latest chapter in a story which began with civilization itself, and which has been animated primarily by the quest for organized power. In this quest, peasants have been unwilling instruments, for the power of civilization has not been sought to satisfy humanitarian impulses toward the masses. Civilization did not emerge spontaneously of the people, was not created by the people, and does not yet exist anywhere primarily for the people. It was the creation of self-appointed elites who had detached themselves from the primitive rural culture, and who became a ruling minority of priests, warrior kings, hereditary aristocrats. "What does modernization mean for the peasants beyond the simple and brutal fact that sooner or later they are its victims?" [10]

Peasant hostility toward modernization can be explained by the fact that the city, even if it transformed peasant culture in ways that ultimately might become advantageous to individual peasants, did not appear, initially, as an institution designed for their benefit. In fact, peasant attitudes reflect the profoundly ambiguous character of the whole enterprise of civilization, of which our contemporary, urban societies are the latest product. "From the beginning . . . the city exhibited an ambivalent character it has never wholly lost: it combined the maximum amount of protection with the greatest incentives to aggression: it offered the widest possible freedom and diversity, yet imposed a drastic system of compulsion and regimentation which, along with its military aggression and destruction, has become 'second nature' to civilized man and is often erroneously identified with his original biological proclivities." [11]

The history of civilization is the history of the cumulative increase of organized power. Less civilized, that is, less organized, hence less powerful, traditional societies discover, at their own peril, that their mode of life, no matter how it may be judged ethically, cannot withstand competition with more powerful, more civilized societies. The "quaint," charming denizens of peasant societies whom city tourists view with such nostalgia are usually the helpless victims of the superior organization of that city culture which the tourist represents; their "quaintness" is an expression of their weakness and vulnerability. Advanced societies become models, establish standards of achievement for backward societies seeking to redress the balance of power; as a result, we tend to assume that civilization must represent a "superior" way of life since its advantages are being sought all over the world. But the appeal of civilization is related primarily to its capacity to organize power efficiently rather than to any ethical superiority which it can demonstrate in structuring the good life.

The paradox of modernization, like that of civilization, is that it increases, through organization, the power available to society, a power which liberates individual man from the impotence of peasants in traditional societies in the face of their environment; but it does so at the cost of subjecting the individual to an even more closely meshed network of organizational controls and disciplines. Not only must the individual submit to an increasingly complex social organization, but the added power which is gained by the discipline of organized civilization, of modernization, has rarely, if ever, been made available to the majority of the members of a modern society.

Our contemporary societies still exhibit all the ambivalence

28

which Mumford identifies with civilization. They are still marked by considerable authoritarianism, by what Mumford calls class regimentation and compulsion. The disciplines of modernization are neither accidental by-products, nor remnants of earlier stages of modernization; they are an integral part, the authoritarian half of the coin of civilization. We accept these disciplines partly because we make them voluntary, internalize them, and convince ourselves that they function to our advantage. Modernization, in other words, implies a self-discipline which, for us, has become second nature, and which, as Mumford points out, we assume erroneously to be an inevitable part of human nature, or at least of "superior" civilized people.

3 · *The Political Disciplines of the Modern State*

Modernization is related, first of all, to the process of state-building, the creation of a centralized political structure, the chief characteristic of which is sovereignty: that is, the claim to final authority over the lives of individuals. Political modernization has meant the development of an increasingly omnivorous state apparatus. All other aspects of modernization occur within the context of the state, and partake of its coercive nature. The state, in fact, is the institution which provides the framework for that mobilization and organization of people implied by modernization.

Political mobilization, in Europe, was initially launched by those European monarchs who between the fifteenth and seventeenth centuries began the process of creating modern states. Nation-building, or state-building, has meant the political mobilization of increasingly large masses of people under the authority of a centralized and increasingly inescapable political authority.

The most fundamental and dynamic character of modern European political history has been the growing power and centralization of the state and its apparatus of control. The political history

29

of Europe since the Middle Ages has been the history of the conflict between the integrating authority of the sovereign state, originally embodied in the monarchy, working for the political mobilization and unification of large societies, and the disintegrating forces of local authority, local aristocratic privilege, local sovereignty, derived from medieval feudalism. The enemies of political centralization were not originally, or chiefly, the peasants, but the possessors of aristocratic privilege, the feudal nobility and the clergy of that universal Christian church which looked to the Roman papacy for its ultimate authority. The example of France is illustrative. Throughout the Middle Ages, the French kings steadily beat down the political independence of the feudal nobility, forcing them to accept the sovereignty of a king who was identified with the centralized state and, ultimately, with the politically mobilized nation. At the same time, he compelled the church to sever its political dependence on the papacy, and to recognize his own sovereignty. Much the same process was taking place in other parts of Europe, and its significance is indicated by the fact that the activities of all these European monarchs are commonly referred to as state-building, while the inability to achieve effective centralized political authority and the political mobilization of the society prevented the creation of a German or of a Polish state. This failure is viewed as the clearest reason for the backwardness of these societies.

This failure also points to the fact that the process of state-building was not only coercive, but motivated primarily by a desire for increased political power. "The will of the people was not taken into consideration. The only goals were increased *power for the ruling dynasty.*" [12] In other words, state-building, political mobilization, and the creation of an efficient, rational, centralized political structure were sought primarily as instruments of increased organized power. The kings, it is true, were able to enlist considerable support in this coercive task, for everywhere, the centralized monarchy was allied with the forces of progress, of modernization. The king was everywhere supported in his fight against aristocratic privilege, against feudal disintegration, by the progressive, integrating force of the bourgeoisie, which sought the greater security, the greater stability, the order and unity of a society politically mobilized under a single, sovereign authority. This political evolution culminated in the monarchy of Louis XIV, which became the classic model of absolutism throughout Europe.

The French Revolution, far from halting this process of centralization, political mobilization, and increased political power of the state, accelerated it. The Revolution, in fact, completed the task left incomplete by Louis XIV, of creating a modern, unified, political system. Through the Revolution, the absolute sovereignty and power of the state were transferred from the king to the people; more accurately, to some of the people, specifically, the bourgeoisie; but that power, and its absolute character, were in no way diminished.

The opposition to the monarchy which culminated in the French Revolution was not an opposition to the centralized, unitary aspects of that monarchy; quite the contrary, it was an opposition to its aristocratic, corporative character, to that structure of privilege which prevented the state from functioning in the interests of its own people. France emerged from the Revolution more centralized politically than ever before. The French Revolution was the great leveler, destroying the whole edifice of aristocratic privilege, the corporate structure of society, dissolving the traditional, local centers of power and allegiance, creating a network of purely administrative departments to replace the historic provinces, and paving the way for the consummation of centralized political power under Napoleon. And through the great, dynamic force of nationalism, the French Revolution achieved a degree of political mobilization, of political integration and collectivization, which the old dynastic monarchy could not approximate.

The French Revolution transferred the potentially tremendous authority of the centralized state from the king to the nation, the collective people. Not only did the French Revolution demonstrate that nationalism could be a vital force in the political mobilization of people, but nationalism was itself, to a great extent, the product of this political mobilization. Frenchmen developed a sense of national identity, a common nationalism, as did Englishmen at roughly the same time, as a result of having lived for several centuries under a common political sovereignty, having shared a common political experience. The French and English monarchies, by imposing on their subjects a common language, a common set of administrative procedures, a common law, a common religion, in short a common culture, began the process of creating, in both societies, a national identity.

This process of political mobilization was tremendously accelerated, after the French Revolution, because the modern state could depend on the sense of national identity of its own people to maintain a high degree of political integration. It is this sense of nationalism which provides not only the most powerful cement of modern states, but the chief justification for the extension of state power. Carried to its extreme limit, the political mobilization of modernization creates totalitarianism; and totalitarianism has everywhere been accompanied by a sense of militant nationalism. Totalitarianism may be seen as a process by which the political mobilization of the state is pushed to its furthest extent by demands that each citizen surrender himself completely to the greater good of the entire society, the collective will of the people, identified in the state, the political institution which *is* the nation.

Nationalism, the myth of the collective will of the nation, provides a functional link between state and citizens, in a modern society, which was considerably weaker under the absolutism of the Old Regime. Modernization implies the full development of the potential resources of society and the greatest resource of any society is its own people; so that modernization creates a direct and inescapable relation between state power and the welfare of society. Such a relation did not exist between the feudal aristocracy and the peasants, and was still incomplete under the absolute monarchies of the Old Regime, for "the power of the old authoritarian regime was relatively independent of the mass of the population." [13] Louis XIV could be indifferent to the fate of his subjects. A modern state cannot.

The modern national state transforms its own people, educates them, "modernizes" them; conversely, the modern national state is itself the product of this social transformation of people. The reciprocity of the process is summed up in these words: "to 'modernize' implies an investment in people which simultaneously allows society to expect more of them." [14] A modern citizen not only attaches his primary allegiance to the nation rather than to the local community, but he is capable of perceiving the connection between his own welfare and the policies of his government. Central political authority is no longer viewed, as it is viewed by peasants in traditional societies, as one of the uncontrollable and incomprehensible forces of nature, as the expression of a distant authority, exacting a tribute which the individual peasant cannot resist, but which bears no relation to his own fate. Rather, central political authority is viewed as a rational activity, aimed at creating a society which will be beneficial to its own citizens. This is not to say that modern citizens assume that all government is benevolent, but that they conceive of the possibility of its benevolence, and understand how the central power of modern government, which mobilizes the collective political power of all its citizens, can be employed in their welfare. Conversely, modern state authorities are aware of the need to promote this welfare in order to enlist commitment and consent, and in order to promote the power of the total society which the state represents.

A modern state is one based on a "mutual interest" between ruler and ruled, and a conviction on the part of the ruled that the state functions for his welfare and benefit. As a result, the modern state can mobilize its resources with far greater efficiency than the monarchies of the Ancien Régime ever could, and "the desire . . . of modernizing leaders is . . . to mobilize and rationalize the resources of society with a view to achieving greater control, efficiency, and production." [15] This rationalization of resources, this efficient mobilization, and the possibility for increasing political control are all made possible by the functional link between the modern citizen and the modern state.

In this sense, every modern state is a welfare state. The observation, for instance, that the Russian people, through the Bolshevik Revolution, traded one form of dictatorship for another misses the point. The Communist system is much more oppressive politically than the czarist system; but unlike its predecessor, it works to improve the conditions of Russian society; in fact, this desire to transform the society, to "modernize" it, was the whole point, as we have already noted, of the Soviet Communist system. The Soviet citizen, like his Western counterpart, perceives an inevitable connection between his own welfare and the success, survival, and power of the political apparatus of his society.

The benevolent aspects of the modern welfare state, however, simply increase its authoritarian tendencies. Its increasing welfare functions, as we know from experience, are one chief reason for the extension of its political power. The modern state may be more benevolent than the monarchies of the Old Regime, or may claim to be more benevolent, but it is also considerably more coercive; it is, in fact, omnipresent.

Even in democratic societies, the modern citizen stands naked and alone before the power of the central state apparatus. The coercive power of that government is infinitely greater than that of any individual noble, and the capacity of a modern citizen to escape its coercive power considerably less than that of a subject of Louis XIV. That authority is no less great for the fact that it claims to function for the welfare of the people. Although modernization establishes a functional relation of mutual interest between the state and the citizen, the terms of that relationship are defined primarily by the state. In the relationship of mutual interest, it is almost always the individual citizen who must adjust to the state bureaucracy, and accept that bureaucracy's definition of his needs, wants, and responsibilities. Although the state can ignore neither the welfare nor the demands of its citizens, its great powers of control and organization make the adjustment of mutual interest between government and governed essentially a one-way process. To become "modernized" means, among other things, to internalize, and to cheerfully accept the authority of the state, on the ground that its authority is beneficial. The current popular slogan in America, "Love it or leave it," indicates to what degree the modernization of people implies the internalization of state authority, the voluntary acceptance of government power, and the consequent condemnation of those brash enough to suggest that the omnipotent state may not necessarily be a benevolent institution.

The fundamental political task of communist leadership in the emergent world has not been substantially different from that which confronted the modernizing leadership of the west in earlier centuries: the task of creating a centralized political structure, of building a modern nation. The authoritarianism of the communists, their political mobilization of the masses, are an intensification, an acceleration of the processes carried out in Europe; their political goals are essentially the same as those of the state builders of early modern Europe. "One could argue that the centrally-minded, nation-building elites of emergent Asia and Africa are but the present day counter-parts of the centralizing monarchs of early modern Europe." [16]

The communist leaders in the emergent world are attracted to the Soviet experience not only as a model for economic modernization, but as a model for the disciplined political mobilization of a backward society prior to modernization. Lenin's own techniques for the political mobilization of Russian society were themselves derived from the techniques of political modernization developed in Western society, and were not related to some esoteric, "Marxist" way of doing things. The political role of communism, in China, for instance, has consisted primarily of creating a political framework

35

which finally brought all the Chinese people into a common political structure, to which a sense of national identity could be attached—a task of political mobilization in which the rulers of ancient China had failed. The role of Tito and the Partisans in Yugoslavia is an even clearer example of the function of communism in political mobilization, nation-building, and state-building, in a society with a notorious record of historical divisions. In each case, communism is an intensification and speeding-up of the processes by which feudal dispersion in the West was overcome and mastered by central political absolutism.

The coercive implications of all political modernization, both "liberal" and communist, can be seen most clearly in the fact that the modern state, despite its tremendous power and comparative efficiency, with all the authoritarian controls it commands, is by no means accepted, even in a relatively democratic and open society such as ours. The contemporary crisis of confidence in our society, the increasing combination of political apathy and revolutionary attitudes, indicates an increasing rejection of the political authoritarianism of the modern state. Whether the coercive modern state is a viable institution is a question this essay cannot answer. But this political crisis suggests that the authoritarian and coercive implications of communist nation-building in the emergent world are not peculiar to that political philosophy, or to the experience of these societies.

4 · *Modern Capitalism and Industrial Growth*

The greatest apparent benefit of modernization, the one for which we are willing to accept the considerable political discipline of the centralized modern state, consists of the tremendously increased productivity of a modern economy. The greatest advantage of modernization appears to be material wealth. The enjoyment of a modern economy seems to provide an adequate compensation for the stringent political discipline which we must accept in our highly complex and bureaucratic society. Our standard of living makes the game worth the candle; as George Lichtheim puts it: "the working class, so far from generating a spontaneous drive toward socialist democracy, has shown an alarming tendency to acquiesce in patterns of socio-political domination which promise to guarantee economic advance and full employment at the cost of freedom." [17]

Economic wealth is, of course, an important dimension of human freedom; and we need not be Marxists to realize that the formal, legal freedoms defined in the political realm do not summarize the totality of individual freedom. A wealthy person is obviously freer, in a real sense, than a poor one. And a wealthy society is more powerful, hence has more options, than a poor one. Upon examination, however, the economic liberation of modernization is as full of ambiguities, of ambivalence, as its political counterpart. Economic modernization has meant the imposition of a discipline of work, the transformation of traditional economic relationships, and forcing unwilling peasants into a pattern of economic expansion and individual competition which they have everywhere resisted.

Nicolas Spulber summarizes the character of economic modernization in these terms: "High rates of growth in total and per capita product; a sharp increase in both output capacity and in efficiency; a rise in the relative shares of manufacture and public utilities and a decrease in the share of agriculture in total product; changes in the patterns of final demand and in import-export opportunities; and diversification of a population's skills and an increase in its mobility." [18] Without the economic jargon, economic modernization requires the production of a greater volume of goods, a greater efficiency in the production of these goods, the development of industry, and increased economic specialization; in short, the development of a modern industrial economy. Such a development, however, is by no means self-generating. In the West the creation of a modern economy required a tremendous effort of economic mobilization for the accumulation of surplus capital, before economic growth could reach what Rostow calls the take-off stage, and become self-sustaining. It required an acceleration of the process described by Mumford in the creation of city cultures, the transformation of the society into an increasingly organized mechanism, closely and complexly integrated; in short, the transformation of society into a gigantic machine.

Before this Herculean task of economic growth could be effected, a considerable change in economic attitudes was required, a change in the direction of increased regimentation, conformity, compulsion, and order. The individual had to submit to an intense discipline of work, he had to postpone the satisfaction of immediate desires in favor of long-range development, he had to accept the rationalization of economic life; in short, he had to submit to the well-known and well-noted capitalistic ethic of hard work, frugality, and intensive self-discipline.

Today, one of the chief tasks confronting modernizing leadership in the emergent world is to overcome traditional resistance to modern work disciplines. One explanation for this resistance, of course, is that the economic advantages of modernization are long-range advantages not immediately apparent. Before the masses of the emergent world can overcome their resistance to modern work disciplines, they must not only see a clearer connection between economic modernization and their own material welfare, they must effect a reorientation of basic values necessary to an ethic of economic growth and productivity. The creation of a modern economy requires the creation of a whole new set of values among traditional peoples, the transformation of cultural attitudes, and the enforced imposition of new and regimented work habits.

The benevolent aspects of economic modernization are put in question not only by the nature of our present economic environment, but by the fact that the new values associated with modern capitalism, and the ordering of modern economic life, were everywhere resisted by the peasant masses in the West. If modern industrialism creates an economy of abundance which increases our sense of material freedom, the development of this modern, industrial economy was in no sense a democratic process. English capitalism, in the eighteenth and nineteenth centuries, liberated the peasants from the customary restrictions and confined economic horizons of their traditional rural environment, by driving them off the land. Not too surprisingly, these rural masses did not want this kind of liberation. Enclosure was viewed as a calamity by the rural yeomen.

Throughout the Western world the speed-up and rationalization of work produced by a machine economy, the need to accept a discipline of work in competition with the machine, produced considerable and widespread dissatisfaction among those transplanted peasants driven into the unwelcome embrace of a factory existence. English domestic textile workers did not welcome the opportunity to exchange their traditional occupation for the chance to work in factories and help create, presumably, a more productive economy. In France, the most violent reactions of the Vendée, in 1793 and 1794, came from those regions which were closest to a traditional economy, and which bitterly resisted the rationalization of economic life promoted by the bourgeois leaders of the Jacobin Republic.[19]

Today, it is a cliché that because the harsh conditions of nineteenth-century industrialism have been alleviated in the West by welfare measures, and because the benefits of industrialism have trickled down to the working class, which today, in the Western world, enjoys a comfortable standard of living, this working class is no longer bitterly alienated against industrialism. But it is also true that today we take our urban, industrial environment for granted; and the first generations of industrial proletariat opposed economic modernization so much more bitterly than today's workers not only because of the harshness of their working and living conditions, but because of their proximity to an earlier, more relaxed economic

39

regime; the industrial proletariat of the early nineteenth century was but recently displaced from a traditional rural economy, and less willing to adapt to the new economic disciplines of the factory.

The liberation of economic modernization is paradoxical in another way. The values associated with capitalism emphasize economic individualism; but this individualism increases considerably our psychological sense of economic insecurity. The advantage of a modern society is that it liberates man from traditional poverty by creating an economy of abundance. But this abundance is not readily or equally available to all members of society. The increased freedom which the material wealth of modern society should provide is eroded by the sense of anxiety and insecurity of the individual living in a competitive environment, in which a share of society's abundance of goods is dependent on success in the "rat race"; and in which defeat in that race spells economic frustration, envy, and despair, in a society which keeps its abundance tantalizingly out of reach of life's economic failures. The individual is liberated from traditional restrictions which chained him to poverty. But he loses the sense of shared experience, the security of communal confidence, the expectation of social support which enables him to accept his meager standard of living, and which may be one reason for peasant apathy toward notions of progress.

The individualism associated with modernization, which is a chief source of the insecurity and anxiety of modern life, turns out, upon examination, to be largely illusory in other ways; for economic modernization increases the individual's dependence on the total economic environment. The individual in a modern economy is unable to survive without the entire economic community. For his survival depends on the successful functioning of an incredibly complex economic machine, spanning large portions of the world. The citizen of a modern economy provides virtually none of his needs directly. A modern economy depends on a very high degree of economic specialization, what Spulber calls a diversification of skills. The peasant of a traditional society enjoys a meager standard of living, but he satisfies his very limited needs directly, depending on the market primarily for luxuries. In this sense the peasant is more independent, more directly in touch with his economic life, less dependent on distant economic forces over which he has no control, than the citizen of a modern economy. Our economy of growth, of ever rising standards of living, of ever expanding economic possibilities, requires that we become securely tied to an increasingly complex mechanism of markets. The modern citizen confronts economic catastrophes which are akin to the devastations of nature in a peasant economy: inflation, business slumps, depression, and worst of all, unemployment; that is, forces which destroy his welfare, but which appear to him as incomprehensible and uncontrollable as floods, locusts, or famines.

All these bureaucratic intrusions into the economic life of a modern society, which so hamstring individual enterprise, which so control every aspect of individual economic activity, which are the despair of economic "conservatives," that is, of those who still believe in the possibility of an unregulated, liberal economy; all those evidences of bureaucratic red tape, big government, and "creeping socialism" have their roots in the need for guaranteeing the proper functioning of a complex modern economy. And the experience which provided the model for this large-scale economic planning was World War I. That war demonstrated that the government could regulate the economy, and plan it for certain desirable wartime goals; the great depression of the 1930's provided the opportunity to attempt this planning and regulation for the realization of desirable peacetime goals: that is, price stability, full employment, and economic growth. As a result a modern economy depends on the coercive regulatory powers of the modern state in a sense which is not true of traditional societies.

In fact, the coercive implications of a modern economy are most clearly evident in its relation with political modernization. For the creation of a modern economy was, of course, directly related to the development of state power. The relation between eco-

41

nomic power and state power was seen clearly as early as the Middle Ages, when the European kings came to realize that a prosperous population could provide greater financial resources for their increasing military needs. This relation was summed up by the French eighteenth-century physiocrat, Quesnay, in the phrase "poor peasants mean a poor kingdom." [20] The philosophy of mercantilism, which dominated the practice of European rulers in the seventeenth and eighteenth centuries, was based on the assumption that the state, that is, the king and his officials, should regulate the economy in such a way as would serve the military needs of the kingdom, not only by encouraging the creation of taxable wealth within the kingdom, but by directly supporting and subsidizing the growth of those areas of the economy which had a strategic significance for the state: helping merchants corner the supply of overseas materials needed by the domestic economy; developing and using a naval establishment to serve the mercantile interests of its own subjects; establishing strategic bases and centers of power overseas.

The creation of a modern economy was directly linked to the creation of the modern political state, and the processes of political and economic mobilization reinforced each other. For this reason mercantilism has been described as the economic side of state-building.[21] By stressing the definition of capitalism found in classical economics, we have obscured the tremendous role played by the state in the development of the modern industrial system. The state organized the society, created a political framework within which large-scale economic mobilization could be organized. The state enforced contracts, coined money, guaranteed currency, and supported the use of credit upon which the modern economy increasingly depended. Ultimately, through the creation of a system of national banks, the state became, in effect, the guarantor of the entire credit structure of advanced economies. The state provided military protection for the economic activities of its subjects and citizens abroad. It used its naval resources to promote the commercial activities of its people, and to protect their overseas commercial investments. The integrated nation made possible by the state became a national market, protected by state-enforced tariffs, for the development of the economy. In this functional link between economic and political modernization, the emphasis, in every case, was upon state power: "mercantilism was economic étatisme or the search for *control* . . . mercantilism is the search for *power*. Each national state wanted to make itself strong and prosperous." [22]

The communist concern for economic development in order to promote the state and political power of backward societies is not different from a similar concern among advanced societies. Benjamin Schwartz speaks of "the Leninist abhorrence of 'backwardness' as well as the extravagant Marxist-Leninist belief in the potentialities of industrialization." [23] This comment reflects a widespread belief in this country that the communists are cynical, power-hungry exploiters; that their concern for economic development is an expression of gross materialism, of a search for power for its own sake, of a lack of appreciation for spiritual or religious values; that they are overanxious to achieve an industrialization which they seek for purposes of political and state power, whether or not such industrialization is for the benefit of the people. But Lenin's "abhorrence of 'backwardness' " was learned from the advanced Western world, with its contempt for "backward" people, and its arrogant stance of superiority toward the indolent, "mañana" psychology of the "natives." It would be hard to find a more extravagant faith in the potentialities of industrialization than in the "liberal" United States, and that faith has always been firmly related to an increase in the political power of the United States: a concern which we have viewed as neither cynical nor materialistic.

5 · *Social Mobilization: The Politics of Consensus*

C. E. Black summarizes the social transformation of modernization as follows: urbanization, a leveling of incomes, made necessary by the demands of mass consumption in a modern economy, the extension of literacy and education, a change in the status of women, the growth of a network of communications, improvements in health and public hygiene, and finally, a social mobilization which "promotes the formation of a consensus at the national level by encouraging nationalism and economic and social integration, strengthening, in the process, the hold of the national community over all of its citizens." [24] In short, modernization implies the creation of a new social type, a new kind of man. Modernization means that peasants must be changed into beings other than peasants; it is not really surprising that peasants have resisted this process, and that modernization has everywhere proceeded to "socialize," to "civilize" the peasant class against its wishes.

There is no doubt that despite strenuous peasant resistance, the achievements catalogued by Black represent a genuine liberation, a liberation primarily from the social restrictions of custom and tradition. But despite these liberating implications, social modernization partakes of the same coercive aspects which we noted in political and economic modernization. Social mobilization is a process of training and taming people, of forcing them into a docile acceptance, through the internalization of discipline, of the superior authority of the collective will of the organized national state, and the desirability of modern culture. Social modernization means, in fact, the imposition of a common, uniform culture which, despite its claims to rationality, objectivity, and efficiency, is in many ways, even more rigorously compulsive than traditional culture.

The ambiguous and ultimately coercive character of social mobilization is nowhere seen more clearly than in two of Black's categories: the extension of literacy and education, and the growth of a network of communications. These categories are particularly significant because they have been viewed, in the liberal tradition, as two of the most basic liberating forces in modern society. Education, literacy, and modern communications, however, have proved to be among the most useful devices for the "training" and "civilizing" of modern man.

It has been generally assumed, in the liberal tradition, that knowledge will make man free; that education will liberate man from his most confining shackle, ignorance; that is, education will grant him the ability to understand his own environment, to make intelligent choices, to run his own affairs, to think for himself. In the United States, it has been generally assumed that the right to vote would be meaningless unless people were sufficiently well educated to exercise that right intelligently, and to make rational choices.

Although it may be theoretically possible to establish a genuinely liberal education, that is, an exercise in teaching people how to think freely for themselves, its realization is fraught with dilemmas. Our concept of education begins with the assumption, contained in the etymology of the word, that an educator, a teacher, is leading an uneducated person, a pupil; that is, that someone already in possession of the secret of education shows the way to an uninitiated person, who is thus incapable of judging the validity of the direction in which he is being led. One of the arguments against student control of the curriculum in universities is that the student, by the very fact of being a student, does not know what he needs to be taught; if he did, he would no longer be a student requiring an education. And, in fact, one of the chief purposes of the school system, in any modern society, is indoctrination; to inculcate its students with the proper respect for the established order, with love of the society, called the nation, with the beliefs, values, and attitudes requisite for an acceptance of the existing order, and a willingness to adjust to its demands. The purpose of our school system includes teaching children the rightness of the organization of national life, and the superior qualities associated with that national life. Only marginally, and with exceptional teachers, is education in modern societies a genuinely *liberating* experience.

45

One of the purposes of modern education, generally accepted by most people, is the coercive process of indoctrinating children with a patriotic sense of nationalism. It is largely through public education that we become acquainted with the symbols, the legends, the heroes, the myths, that define the nation, which together comprise a national identity, shared first of all through the school experience. The sense of national identity, of national pride, of patriotism, created by our common educational experiences provides the greatest binding force in a national culture. These national attitudes and values are part of our "learned" self, the part of our personality which we acquire through schooling.

The education of the masses implicit in modernization is analogous to the training of children in schools. Uneducated peasant masses have been "civilized," "socialized"; that is, they have been indoctrinated, like children, by their superior urban "parents" with the values and attitudes necessary to accept, and function smoothly in, a modern, urban society. And it is the educated, modern urban minority which then determines who is "ready," in the sense of correctly educated, to participate in modern national life. In the West, various layers of each national society were admitted to participation in national life once they had been deemed fit by the leaders of these societies for such participation; this meant, in practice, that they had demonstrated their willingness to accept the social disciplines and values which they were being taught in the schools—in short, when they had been properly trained. Such a process of education of peasant masses reflects inevitably the same coercive features found in the training of children. By the time they become adults, these children have been well enough trained that they internalize, and thereby take for granted, a social discipline which appears as naked, brutal, and external among the less developed societies of the emergent world.

Intimately linked to this process of educational indoctrination, and equally central to "socialization" and social mobilization, is the growth of a modern network of communications. A free press, as we frequently remind ourselves, is a basic necessity to a free society. And the assumption of liberalism, of such thinkers as Voltaire, Jefferson, or John Stuart Mill, was that free access to ideas would enable the individual to understand current issues, to manage his own political affairs; truth would emerge from the free competition of ideas. Intellectual freedom would be guaranteed in the market place of ideas, through a free system of modern communications. The liberating possibilities of modern communications have proved as difficult to achieve as the liberating possibilities of modern education; mass communications, like mass education, have become one chief device for the social mobilization, training, and disciplining of modern citizens.

One function of the mass media, comparable to the function of education, and equally accepted by most people, is to "socialize" us by providing a common picture of our national life, a life which we cannot experience directly, and the reality of which exists for us only through news media, entertainment, etc. For most of us, our nation is whatever our mass media of communications tell us it is, or show it to be. Modern mass communications tie us together by providing us with a common picture of reality, by creating a common culture which we commonly share. We are all Americans partly because we all watch the same television programs, the same movies, read the same syndicated columns, the same picture magazines. The mass media are criticized not for their failure to present "hard" news, but for their failure to "bring us together," in the same way that educators are found wanting if they merely seek to describe the world objectively, and fail to function as indoctrinators of American cultural values and national identity. The common culture we acquire through modern education and modern mass communications is, of course, a fabricated "communications" culture, which we are usually incapable of verifying against the reality of our nation.

The citizen of a modern society is, paradoxically, less capable, in many ways, of knowing his world than the inhabitant of a tradi-

47

tional community. For his world is one which he cannot experience directly. He has no way of verifying the picture of the national life which he can only obtain through the indirect and abstract devices of newsprint and television picture. We are all aware, to some degree, of the artificial nature of this "communications" world. In one way, our mass media "train" us, "socialize" us, like our education, into accepting the character of our modern national life. In another way, they cause us to doubt the validity of any information they provide, or the possibility of really knowing what is happening in our national life. In order to verify the picture we obtain from the mass media, we would have to scrutinize it much more thoroughly, and with far greater attention to detail than most of us are prepared to give. Such verification requires considerable training in the methods of historical research and scientific validation. Finally, it is difficult for us to maintain sufficient interest in our national life, unless events impinge directly upon us, because it does not exist in the world of our direct experience. Lack of time, of skills, of training, and of interest makes it impossible for us to verify the picture provided by the mass media. Since we have no way of making an objective evaluation of this picture, we are compelled to fall back on purely subjective criteria. We accept the picture of our national life provided by the mass media as long as it reinforces the prejudices we have about what it should be; but when it fails to satisfy our prejudices, when the picture of national life presented by the mass media fails to please us, we criticize the news media for "distorting" and "slanting" the news.

The national culture which we all share through our modern network of communications, which integrates us into a common national environment, is therefore highly vulnerable to manipulation. And one of the differences between modern totalitarianism and older kinds of political authoritarianism is the capacity of modern governments to manipulate and recreate the shape of our national culture in such ways that we accept the absolute authority of the government in the name of a national life the reality of which

48

we cannot question. When the President makes a report on Indochina, few of us are in a position to verify the reality behind his description; and we all naturally tend to give that reality whatever content satisfies our own prejudices. The chief purpose of President Nixon's television addresses, for instance, has not been to redefine United States policy, or foreign policy goals, or to explain to us what he is doing, or what is happening in the world, but to redefine the very content of the political picture of southeast Asia, to make it fit whatever domestic political needs he requires. "It is as though . . . the President . . . has decided that he could create new characters, phase out old characters, invent thrilling new episodes, and move the plot in almost any direction his imagination might take him." [25] In other words, the situation in Indochina is not an "objective reality" in the conventional sense, but a kind of dramatization, virtually created out of whole cloth, to suit whatever political purpose the President wishes it to serve. This process is much more obvious in the United States than in the Soviet Union, not because we are a more totalitarian society, but for the opposite reason: *because* our society is still relatively open we can see to what degree the reality of Southeast Asia, and the conflict occurring there, has become an almost infinitely malleable artifact in the hands of the government, which periodically redefines its nature and content.

The training and "civilizing" of modern citizens, the demand for consensus, for social integration, means, in practice, that everyone must conform to the standards and values of the ruling classes, of that part of society which was responsible, historically, for the process of social mobilization. The consensus of modernization is rarely the result of compromise, of give and take, the blending of cultures. It is to a great extent a process by which one part of society imposes its way of life on everyone else. National identity is seldom a melting pot, not even in the United States; it is the identity of a dominant cultural group which forces its values on the rest of society, and uses its own cultural characteristics as justification for its monopoly of political power. Numerous traditional historical

49

conflicts have their roots in this process of social coercion: whites against blacks in this country; the English against the Irish in Ireland; the English against the French in Canada; the Germans against the Slavs in Central Europe. In each case, the measure of success of the individual, his worth and dignity as a human being, be he black, or Irish Catholic, or French Canadian, is determined by the identity of the superior culture; so that social modernization means giving up one's own cultural identity, and taking on the colorations of the "master race." The white American, or the Englishman, defines social acceptability by his own standards; to have arrived is to be accepted by the more advanced culture, to cross the "color" line. Such a process inevitably breeds resentment and conflict, and a stubborn determination to cling to one's own cultural identity, to exaggerate its difference from that of the domineering culture, to refuse a "socializing" process which is based on the humiliating assumption of one's own inferiority. Irishmen do not hate Englishmen because they have different religions. Rather, the Irish cling stubbornly and defiantly to Catholicism because they hate the English. And they hate them because the English traditionally have used this difference as justification for oppressing the "inferior" Irish.

The degree to which we have been conditioned to accept a coercive social integration and mobilization as desirable, and at the same time, the persistence with which cultural minorities resist this process of social "integration" are reflected by the constant outbursts of defiance on the part of cultural minorities, and the predictable surprise and amazement with which we invariably greet fresh evidence of the unwillingness of so many people to be "trained," "civilized," and "socialized" into an integrated society. Despite our faith in the benevolence and liberating implications of modernization, people all over the world are still resisting a coercive process of social integration which involves not only the imposition of the culture of one group on the rest of society, but the assumption that certain cultural characteristics justify the domination of one group over another.

To summarize: through social mobilization and modernization, people are made into obedient, cooperative, socially oriented citizens, expected to make their maximum contribution to the smooth functioning of modern society, and able to adjust to this social discipline voluntarily, almost cheerfully. Such social modernization is an immensely difficult and painful process, and it is that pain and difficulty which we encounter in the emergent world, rather than any specifically communist authoritarianism. We are closer to the truth when we say that social modernization makes communist discipline necessary, rather than that communism imposes a gratuitous and unnecessary social discipline. In seeking this kind of social mobilization, this kind of modernization of the social structure, the communists are pursuing the same goals that were pursued in the history of Western development; and communist discipline in this process of social mobilization is not fundamentally different, although much more intensively coercive, from the methods of socialization used in the "liberal" West.

6 · *Modern Science and the Rule of the Technocrats*

Intellectual modernization would appear to achieve the most fundamental liberation of man, not only by giving him the tools to understand and master his own fate, but by introducing the ideas of change and progress. Man is only free, in short, if he can imagine alternative ways of doing things; if he has a genuine capacity for making rational choices. The key to modernization has been the search for innovation. Modernization has been intimately associated with liberalism, because it found its intellectual support in the assumptions of the philosophy of the Enlightenment, particularly the belief in what Peter Gay calls "the omnicompetence of criticism." [26] This critical approach rejects the traditional notion that a particular way of doing things is justified simply by the fact that it has been done that way for a very long time; or that certain aspects of a culture are taboo, not to be questioned, and beyond criticism. In this process, the great obstacle to modernization has been tradition, or custom. A modern society is, by its very nature, anti-traditional, and the institutions which have particularly suffered through modernization have been the great bulwarks of tradition, the family and the church.

In the emergent world, we criticize communism for destroying customary ways of life, for attacking the church, for dissolving the traditional bonds of family; we attribute to communism characteristics which are more particularly related to modernization, and to the new modes of thought associated with this change. The communists have certainly advocated a rational mobilization of resources; they have certainly emphasized scientific objectivity; and they have certainly criticized the superstition of traditional religion; but so have all modernizing reformers.

The family and the church are frequently the focus of attack of communist leadership in the emergent world, for they are the carriers of traditional values, the obstacle to that rationalization of the environment which is the crux of modernization. The individual must be "liberated" from family ties, and ties to the traditional church, and his allegiances must be attached to national life. He must seek self-improvement, and identify that self-improvement with the national state and the ruling elite, the communist party. This liberation from church and family, however, also occurred in the West; the rise of secularism, the separation of church and state, the decline of religious values, loss of respect for organized churches, the fight for women's rights, all were aspects of this process. As conservatives constantly bemoan, the decline of the family was an inevitable consequence of the atomized, "liberated" society of the modern world. In the emergent world, this attack on traditional church and family has occurred wherever the leadership, communist or not, has sought modernization. Habib Bourguiba, for instance, the President of Tunisia, and no Communist, has attempted to persuade his people to abandon the traditional religious feast of Ramadan, observance of which, he feels, is unsuitable to the needs of a modernizing nation.[27]

The communists are accused of being materialists, and secularists, but modernization is a materialistic, secular enterprise; and the concern of communist leadership with efficiency, with a critical approach to the problems of modernization, its matter-of-fact disregard for traditional modes, including religious values, is no more materialistic, no more secular, than similar changes associated with modernization in the intellectual values of any Western society. "We may even attribute the success of atheistic communism in promoting economic development and the movement toward postcivilized society not so much to its specific dogmas as to the fact that it is an instrument for undermining primitive animism and for replacing a belief in the arbitrary and willful nature of the material world by a belief in its stability and orderliness." [28] A similar faith, a similar belief, was the source of the success of liberal modernization in the West. Liberalism was equally opposed to the traditional influence of the church in western Europe, and the greatest pride of Western societies has been the power and wealth produced by modernization. It was that material wealth and power, in fact, which enabled the West to treat the religiously and traditionally oriented societies of China and India with such cavalier contempt.

The United States, which would like to view itself as the ideological enemy of "godless" communism, is the most anti-traditional, secular, and materialist society in the world. It was long a commonplace in Europe that Americans were boors and barbarians because they disdained tradition, were willing to ignore age-old ways of doing things, scorned the "good old days," and old-fashioned methods, and were obsessively concerned with the acquisition of wealth. Until the recent invention of an American "tradition" by conservatives, we were impervious to such criticism because we took it for what it was, as more perceptive Europeans themselves realized: envy of the superior wealth and material resources of the United States. Today, the pride of this country is focused primarily on our wealth and power; and our concern with material achievement has become so great that it has almost become a religion, a sort of ideal of productivity which we worship. We condemn the communists as materialists and godless atheists when they stress the importance of overcoming material misery in the emergent world, and scorn so-called "higher" values; but one chief criticism we make of communism in the Soviet Union is its failure to produce a material standard of life which compares with ours.

Although the intellectual revolution of modernization has been presumably its most liberating aspect, it has also favored the internalization of all the disciplines which are necessary for modern life. It is, in fact, primarily through intellectual modernization that we convince ourselves that these disciplines are rational, benevolent, scientific, and progressive. Modern society is in some ways even more intolerant of deviant behavior, of eccentricity, than traditional society, for it views challenges to the establishment not as demands for freedom, but as signs of social maladjustment. And the effectiveness of modern society in blocking such challenges to the establishment derives from our faith in its rationality and benevolence, our belief that it is based on scientific objectivity, instead of traditional habit. This leads us to assume that dissident behavior is unjustifiable on the grounds of reason. The rebel, in modern society, is the person who fails to adjust. His rebelliousness is a sign of shame, not of heroism; an indication that he is not enlightened, that he fails to understand the need for voluntarily internalizing the myriad disciplines of a modern society. The individual who questions the established order of society is more than maladjusted. He is ignorant, irresponsible. Intellectual modernization, in short, robs the individual of the ideological justification for criticizing the established order. The tyranny of modern society is not the arbitrary tryanny of personal whim and caprice. It is the rational, im-

54

personal tyranny of a computerized bureaucracy which rules benevolently in the name of science.

Our modern intellectual attitudes not only force us to accept modern disciplines voluntarily, but they justify the fact that these disciplines are not, and need not be, the free expression of the will of the people. The criterion by which we judge the disciplines of modern society is not whether they are what people want, but whether they are rational, based on objective knowledge, and determined scientifically. In our increasingly complex societies, such determinations cannot really be left to the uninformed and unsophisticated masses; they must be made, ultimately, by experts. The modern world is increasingly managed, administered, by professional experts. Intellectual modernization, in short, leads to the rule of technocrats, specialized experts whose right to make our choices for us is justified by their ability to manage the complex and technical structure of modern societies.

It is not only that the average layman is increasingly incapable of understanding and mastering his technological environment, but that he is increasingly willing to let the expert run things for him. At all levels, in modern society, man abdicates his freedom because he becomes convinced that experts can manage the affairs of society better than he can. This assumption has been at the center of the argument in support of the Vietnam War. Our government bureaucrats, we are told, our military experts, know infinitely better than we deluded and uninformed citizens what is best to satisfy the needs of the military security of our society. How could the average, amateur citizen be expected to provide intelligent guidance for the foreign policy and military decisions of a government staffed by experts who have access to a vast body of complicated and secret information which we are not expected to understand anyway? Former French President de Gaulle summarized this elitist, technocratic philosophy in a striking image during a televised speech to the French nation, reporting on his efforts to conclude the Algerian War: "The pilot holds the wheel, the crew performs its functions, the duty of the passengers is to remain in their seats." [29] If President Nixon had the late General de Gaulle's gift for language, he would express precisely the same sentiment about his conduct of the war in Indochina, and a vast number of Americans would accept such a definition of his role. The pilot is the political leader; the crew is the government, the team of professional experts who know how to run the ship; and the duty of the passengers, the people, the ordinary citizens, you and me, that is, is to sit still, shut up, and let the professionals, who could not possibly be in need of our advice or guidance, run the ship for us. Such a notion of the functions of government is obviously very popular in this country today. While it is true that communism imposes this elitist rule with infinitely greater stringency than is true in Western societies, the communist notion of elitist leadership, the concept of a cadre of professional experts, whose responsibility is to carry through and manage modernization from above for the unenlightened masses is derived from the same dependence on, and faith in, the technological expertise of managers which has developed in the West.

7 · *Communism as a Stage in Modernization*

This excursion into the history of Western modernization was not taken to discredit liberalism, or the positive, liberating achievements of modernization in the West; nor was it taken to justify communist authoritarianism, or to suggest that the freedoms of the open society in the West are illusory. The point, rather, is to suggest that communism in the emergent world can be explained more meaningfully by relating it to the process of modernization itself than by viewing it as an alien phenomenon, existing in deliberate hostility to Western, liberal values. If communism in the underdeveloped world is a coercive force, it is because modernization is a coercive process. Communism is a stage in the modernizing development of the emergent world, analogous to a similar development in Western societies. The goals and methods of communism, in the emergent world, can be related most meaningfully to similar goals and methods in the history of Western modernization. The methods are more brutal, more radical, but the goals are essentially similar. Modernization has not been a peaceful, spontaneous, democratic process, not even in the West, which had numerous advantages denied the emergent world.

At the political level, the goal of the communists is state-building, the creation of a centralized political structure, the development of a sense of identity with the political community at the national level. Communism may be seen as a stage in the development of nationalism in the emergent world. Communism, in fact, *is* nationalism in the emergent world; that is, it is a process, in China, in Vietnam, as it was in Russia itself, of political mobilization, of nation-building, of state-building, analogous to similar processes in Western history. The transformation of Chinese peasants into citizens of a modern, communist Chinese state is not essentially different, although apparently more brutal and ruthless, from the transformation of French peasants into French citizens.

Economically, the goal of communism is rapid growth, development, and industrialization. Such a process is parallel to Western economic modernization. It is not necessary to posit a special "communist" way of doing things to explain the drive for economic development in the emergent world, or the dependence on authority from above. Patterns of large-scale economic planning in the emergent world, particularly in communist societies, are not radically different from Western patterns of economic development; in fact, in turning to the state as a major weapon of economic growth, the emergent world is simply borrowing from a very common and very pervasive practice in Western economic development. Communist economic modernization is an intensification and acceleration of Western processes, rather than a basically opposed economic ideology.

The socialization of the peasant masses of the emergent world is analogous to a similar process of social mobilization which occurred in the West. In fact, communist emphasis on a sense of shared, communal experience, of collective working together, may make social mobilization easier, in some respects, than comparable experiences in the West. Finally, communist concern with the intellectual transformation of the backward peasants of the emergent world is not basically different from the kind of intellectual transformation experienced in the West. Our resentment at the intellectual awakening associated with communism and other forms of emergent nationalism in the underdeveloped world is rooted in notions of racial superiority, and a complacent view of a Western-dominated world. In other words, communism in the emergent world upsets us because it is associated with the intellectual awakening of "colored" peoples who had been expected to accept Western paternalism and keep their place.

If communist coercion appears so much more brutal and oppressive to us, it is partly because we have left behind us similar stages of forced transformation in our own history: the creation of a powerful central state, and the overawing of local centers of authority, as in our own Civil War; the forcible transformation of the Industrial Revolution, the exploitation of the sweatshops, the conditions of factory life and slums in the English Midlands of the nineteenth century; the violent uprooting of peasants from traditional social patterns through enclosure in eighteenth-century England, and the enforced socialization and "civilization" of masses of immigrants in our society in the late nineteenth century; the painful readjustment to a modern, technological, secular environment, severed from the psychological security of a traditional world. We conveniently forget the degree to which modernization, in our own past, depended on violence, force, and coercion. Most important, of course, Western transformation was much slower, and voluntary adjustments to new conditions much easier to achieve. The rapid pace of modernization in the emergent world, the imperative need to produce rapid results, will make voluntary adjustments and internalization of the new values and disciplines of modernization much more difficult to achieve. In fact, the rest of this essay will seek to demonstrate how the configuration of circumstances in the emergent world will produce an accelerated version of the modernization which occurred in the West, an intensified and radical exaggeration comparable to the communist experience of the Soviet Union.

3

Communism and

Peasant Mobilization

I · *The Revolution of Rising Expectations*

MODERNIZATION MEANS, IN EFFECT, THE DESTRUCTION OF PEASANT
society, the transformation of peasants into new kinds of social
beings. It is not surprising that peasants have resisted a process
which will destroy their culture, transform their way of life, and
end their identity as peasants. David Mitrany has argued that
Marxist communism, although it often appeals to the peasants for
revolutionary support, is essentially anti-peasant, since the goal of
communism includes ultimately the elimination of the peasants as
a class. It is true, as Mitrany says, that "Marx was filled with undis-
guised contempt for the peasant";[1] and in one of his classic sen-
tences, Marx refers to "the idiocy of rural life." [2] But the elimination of this "idiocy," the elimination of the peasant class, has been
the goal of all modernization; and if Marxism encompasses such a
goal, it is because Marxism is rooted in the necessity for creating a
modern society; because it is, in fact, a theory of modernization.
Marx's contempt for the peasant is part of that general contempt
found in urban civilization toward "backward" rural peasants. It is
not Marx who is against the peasant; it is the process of moderniza-

tion itself. And if the goal of communist leadership in the emergent world includes the elimination of the peasants as a class, that goal is implicit in all modernizing processes; one could as easily, and as accurately, say that modern capitalism has been against the peasant. Everywhere, for obvious reasons, peasants have been the great obstacle to the creation of a modern society. "In every part of the world, generally speaking, peasantry have been a conservative factor in social change, a brake on revolution, a check on that disintegration of local society which often comes with rapid technological change." [3]

Today, however, this observation must be qualified. For in the twentieth century, in the emergent world, we are witnessing a new kind of political phenomenon, a revolutionary peasantry, a peasant nationalism, a peasant communism. We are witnessing the successful mobilization of large peasant masses for revolutionary purposes. We are witnessing the first successful organization of peasant masses for their own modernization. The classic model for this kind of peasant revolution has been, of course, China; and the Chinese experience has become both an inspiration and a working model for peasant revolution and peasant nationalism in Asia, Africa, and Latin America. The success of the Chinese Communist Party has not invalidated the Soviet experience, or the significance of the Bolshevik Revolution; it has demonstrated that the peasants could be drawn into this revolutionary process; that it was not necessary to ignore them, or to work against them, as Lenin and Stalin had assumed they would have to do in Russia. In fact, the Chinese experience seems to demonstrate that successful modernization, in the emergent world, *depends* on the active participation and support of the peasant masses.

Peasant hostility to change and peasant devotion to tradition should not be interpreted as a sign of peasant contentment or satisfaction with the conditions of a traditional rural environment. The long history in the Western world of peasant revolts, *jacqueries*, outbursts of rural anarchy, points to the fact that the content of peasant life has not been considered idyllic by the peasants themselves. One of the chief obstacles in the past to the development among the peasants of positive revolutionary attitudes and structured revolutionary organization has been their lack of awareness of the possibilities of change; or of the possibility that change could be controlled and directed for their own benefit. It is this isolation, this lack of perception which defines a peasant.

The emergence of the affluent, powerful Western societies, and the global spread, during the age of imperialism, of Western values, Western ideas, most important, Western power, began a process of breaking down the isolation, both psychological and physical, of traditional peasant masses in the emergent world. If peasant opposition to change has resulted partly from the lack of attractive or possible alternatives, the impact of Western expansion provided a nearly irresistible alternative; not because the Western way of life was viewed as so much more attractive, but because the Western impact was so powerful that the emergent world found it impossible to resist Western intrusion. It was *powerless* to resist the West, even when such intrusion was viewed, as it was in China in the nineteenth century, as intolerable. It was this sense of *powerlessness* which had the greatest impact in jolting the people of the emergent world from their traditional apathy; at the same time Western influence, whether so intended or not, was more corrosive of traditional values than the influence of any other outside forces to which the emergent world had been hitherto subjected.

Adlai Stevenson coined a phrase to describe this transformation of the masses of Africa, Asia, and Latin America, the revolution of rising expectations. That phrase points accurately to the positive content of change in peasant attitudes in the emergent world. Overwhelmed by the fantastic wealth and power of Western material culture, peasants are no longer immune to the forces of change, and no longer insensitive to the possibilities of modernization. Peasants are now very much aware of the material benefits of modernization. The direct experience of immensely wealthy Westerners in their midst and the destructive influence of Western values and techniques have provided a motivation for change which no amount of Soviet propaganda could have created out of theoretical Marxist arguments.

Gunnar Myrdal calls this revolution of attitudes the Great Awakening.[4] Such a revolution is truly a Great Awakening, that is, an irreversible psychological process. Once the humble and dispossessed of the world have glimpsed the sugar plum vision of the affluent society, once they have been awakened to the meaning of power as an escape from poverty, they cannot be put back to sleep. Once expectations have been raised, they can no longer be lowered, which is but another way of saying that poverty is relative. Awareness of the wealth and power of the West renders intolerable, in the emergent world, patterns of living which had once been accepted as part of inescapable tradition. Peasants are increasingly aware of the possible benefits of modernization, particularly its material benefits; and they are increasingly convinced that the traditional conditions of rural poverty are not part of a divinely ordained plan which cannot be questioned. "Latin America's angry millions know that the twentieth century exists; they have a passionate determination to partake of its benefits." [5]

It was the impact of Western colonialism which provided the impetus for this awakening of the masses of the emergent world. The gap between the Western world and that of traditional societies in the underdeveloped world was much greater than any similar gap between rural and urban classes in Europe; the cultural shock produced by the meeting of such disparate cultures was infinitely more disruptive in the emergent world; and the Western influence on the peoples of Asia, Africa, and Latin America was imposed with such brutality, such ruthlessness, this influence became so completely pervasive, that it produced a shock of awakening among the emergent masses not comparable to any experience of European peasants in the past.

Whether or not peasants are willing to pay the price of modernization may be irrelevant. Or at least, the problem may never present itself in those terms to the emergent world. For the overwhelming fact in the lives of the people of Africa, Asia, and Latin America has been their complete powerlessness in the face of Western intrusion. This sense of powerlessness has been particularly difficult to tolerate because it exists in relation to a foreign invader whose presence has no trace of legitimacy either in tradition or in morality. The peasants of Europe, even when they resented their feudal masters, had come to accept the legitimacy of their position. They lived in a world of dues, obligations, responsibilities. Peasants never conceived of substituting their own political leadership for that of existing rulers; their revolutionary attitudes were basically fatalistic.

The colonial conquerors of the emergent world, on the other hand, came as aliens, destroyers of the traditional culture. The Western conqueror could only be a source of permanent anxiety and insecurity; for he destroyed the traditional order, and substituted for it his own unlimited and, in the eyes of the peasant masses of the emergent world, completely arbitrary and therefore devastating rule. The presence of this Western invader in China became an overwhelming burden, a burden which European peasants never experienced in the same way or to the same degree. In this sense, the goals of the Taiping Rebellion, in the 1850's, of the Boxer uprising in 1899 and 1900, of the Kuomintang, and of the Communist Party have all been alike in one fundamental respect; they have all been concerned with restoring the independence of China and the integrity of Chinese society: "the revolutionary upheaval which has been chronic in China during the past century has been largely a reaction of resurgent Chinese nationalism against western encroachments and influences." [6]

Such appeals to a sense of moral outrage at Western desecration of traditional values, of injured national pride, the very concept of nationalism, for that matter, were restricted in the emergent world, for a long time, to an educated minority of intellectuals. But eventually, the necessity for organizing the society against foreign domination reached down to affect even the peasant masses, who were drawn into the process, for the first time, of supporting a program of political organization, social mobilization, and modernization, for the purpose of terminating foreign control. The classic case of this peasant awakening against foreign domination was China, and China is the model for the development of that revolutionary peasant nationalism which we call communism.

2 · *Revolutionary War and Peasant Mobilization*

In *Peasant Nationalism and Communist Power,* Chalmers Johnson describes the process by which the experience of Japanese military occupation of China provided the necessary catalyst to mobilize the Chinese peasant masses into support of an active, revolutionary nationalist movement.[7] He argues that it was the experience of the war against Japan, and the brutal fact of an alien, foreign military occupation, which brought home to every Chinese peasant what had become obvious to the intelligentsia for some time, the need for common, organized political action among the Chinese people, and the creation of a strong national state. Johnson emphasizes the way in which the war produced, *created,* in fact, a new kind of revolutionary, nationalist, peasant communism. "The politically illiterate masses of China were awakened by the Japanese invasion and its aftermath; wartime conditions made them receptive to a new kind of political appeal—namely, the defense of the fatherland." [8]

The experience of the Japanese occupation produced a peasant nationalist movement which recognized the need for new ideas and institutions to mobilize the energies of the Chinese people for the task of ridding their country of this latest and most devastating product of Western imperialism. For even if Japan was not a Western nation, its military power and efficacy were derived from successful copying of Western models, from having adopted those ideas and institutions which Chinese society had hitherto resisted. In short, the Japanese occupation of China was a particularly brutal version of the process by which emergent societies were compelled, because of their backwardness and consequent weakness, to accept tutelage and domination by advanced societies. This brutal intensification brought home to every Chinese peasant the paramount importance of creating new institutions and techniques of modernization which he had previously resisted. "The Japanese . . . took ruthless action against the rural population, action that resulted in the depopulation of several areas. The effect of this policy—as in Yugoslavia under similar circumstances—was to arouse even the most parochial of village dwellers to the fact that politics could no longer be ignored." [9]

Johnson suggests the possibility that similar experiences might produce parallel peasant responses in other places: "the hypothesis of social mobilization via a guerilla resistance movement may be extended to such cases as Cuba, Malaya, Greece, and Algeria." [10] Johnson has chosen not to attempt to pursue the parallel beyond one case, that of Tito's Partisans in Yugoslavia. The parallel, however, is very real. The impact of war, of foreign military invasion, the development of guerilla resistance movements, either during World War II or in colonial wars following World War II, have all produced a peasant mobilization, a peasant nationalism, a peasant communism very similar to the Chinese experience; in many cases, patterned deliberately after the Chinese model, not only in places listed by Johnson, but also in Indonesia, in the Philippines, most importantly, in Vietnam, which bears the closest resemblance to the Chinese model. Even before the revolutionary struggle against the French, the Japanese occupation had accelerated the development of nationalism under communist leadership in Indochina, where Ho Chi Minh played a role precisely analogous to that of Mao Tse-tung.

In all these societies what Rostow calls "the demonstration effect of the relation between modernization and military power" was made vividly; in all these societies the great mass of rural people were awakened politically, and forced by the brutal experience of alien military rule to recognize the paramount necessity for organized action at the national level. "Before the Japanese invasion the Chinese peasantry was indifferent to 'Chinese' politics, being wholly absorbed in local affairs. The war totally destroyed the traditional rural social order and sensitized the Chinese peasantry to a new spectrum of possible associations, identities, and purposes." [11] In this process of revolutionary mobilization in the emergent world, the example of China, and of Mao Tse-tung, played a decisive role as a model and as an inspiration. Although such revolutionary leadership in the emergent world did not invariably adhere to official Communist Parties, it developed the whole panoply of techniques and attitudes which had succeeded in China: a collective discipline, a virulent anti-imperialism, which meant a violent hostility toward the arrogant West, as well as ruthless totalitarian techniques for the organization of a successful national movement. In that sense, the Algerian FLN, which never acquired the label Communist, bears a precise parallel to the Vietnamese FLN, as their identical names indicate. What all these societies demonstrated was that the one fundamental problem which the entire underdeveloped world would have to confront sooner or later was the problem of its powerlessness in the face of the modernized nations of the world.

War played a role in peasant mobilization in several ways. It destroyed traditional patterns in a particularly violent and sudden way, and deprived the peasants of the security which the traditional conservative order, despite its exploitative nature, had provided. At the same time, war discredited the traditional ruling classes, which were unable to perform their own self-appointed tasks of protecting the integrity of the society from destruction. In some cases, these ruling classes were destroyed physically by the occupying forces; more often they were destroyed morally by their collaboration with the foreign invader. War radicalized the peasants, forced them out of their apathy, confronted them with a brutal and violent situation, and brought home to them in unmistakably clear terms the necessity for accepting political leadership and discipline in a polarized context. "Japanese military reprisals against the peasantry under the guise of eliminating Communism . . . awakened the peasantry to the personal danger posed by the 'foreign invader.' The peasant's participation in the war effort . . . caused him, for the first time, to equate personal danger with national danger. National consciousness entered the thinking of the war mobilized peasants." [12] Peasants, in short, were politicized in a context which did not afford the luxury of political pluralism, in which monolithic support of a disciplined, totalitarian, military leadership was extremely likely.

These resistance movements established for the first time a sense of communal interests among the peasants; for the first time, the peasants ceased to be "unorganizable," and for the first time, they engaged in common political action, seeking common, national, political goals. This peasant nationalism differed from European nationalism in the nineteenth century. It arose as a response to a direct challenge, a direct physical threat against the traditional order of society. It was motivated more by what it was against, alien, foreign rule, than what it was for. A sense of nationalism developed out of a shared sense of danger in the face of great, destructive military power. It was the experience of war itself which created among the peasant masses this new sense of nationalism. David A. Wilson observes that "the process of revolutionary war . . . has been notably successful in China and Vietnam . . . in advancing the process of mobilizing the societies of these states toward nationhood. . . . Revolutionary war . . . can be considered a concrete example of nation-building in process." [13]

Not only did revolutionary leaders like Luis Taruc, Ho Chi Minh, Mao Tse-tung, Belkacem Krim, Tito, and others stress a collective discipline based on a sense of national identity, but this sense of national identity was itself created by the war experience.

In Yugoslavia, "the key element in the Communist victory was the ability of the Partisans to identify themselves with a true Yugoslav nationalism, one which seemed to offer an alternative to the bloody ethnic war which had been the outcome of King Alexander's pan-Serb Yugoslavia." [14]

We would make a great error, however, if we concluded that revolutionary peasant communism is an accident born of the fortuitous circumstances of guerilla movements during or after World War II. For the war situations which produced these communist movements were no more than an intensification, in the emergent world, of the whole process of colonialism, and its tendency to destroy the traditional order. The process of Western intrusion and colonial domination had exposed the peasants to a cultural dislocation, and revealed their powerlessness to resist this process, in such a way that sooner or later, these peasants would have been compelled to recognize that "politics could no longer be ignored." Foreign military occupation brought home to the peasant in an unmistakable way the basic condition which had been created, not by the accident of World War II, but by the juxtaposition of the weak, backward, and powerless cultures of the emergent world with the violent world of Western power politics. The mobilization of peasant masses in guerilla resistance movements is but the extreme instance of a process of peasant mobilization which has been a reaction to an unwanted Western intrusion, a reaction which is intensified and accelerated by revolutionary war.

W. W. Rostow, in trying to justify the American imperial adventure in the Philippines at the turn of the century, provides, unwittingly, the most incisive reason for the development of that radical, revolutionary, communist nationalism which he condemns in the emergent world. The weakness and backwardness of the Philippines made it impossible, he asserts, for that society to escape colonial status in 1898: "there was no way of relinquishing a colony which had not modernized its society, without turning it over to another colonial power." [15] It was this growing realization that their societies could never escape colonial status until they had achieved the necessary power to resist alien, Western intrusion which gradually converted the leadership of the emergent world to radical, revolutionary programs, and which impressed the peasant masses with the need for unified support of such programs.

3 · *Communism and Peasant Nationalism*

The revolutionary transformation of the peasantry of the emergent world, its violent political awakening in wars of colonial independence, is a process unparalleled in Western experience. Communism, in the emergent world, is partly a process of revolutionary mobilization of the peasantry in a struggle against backwardness and its attendant political weakness. Modernization, in many parts of the emergent world, rests on a peasant base in a way which never occurred in the West. This phenomenon is in no way "explained" by saying that such communist leaders as Mao Tsetung deliberately decided to exploit peasant unrest and enlist peasant support.

The development of radical, revolutionary, left-wing national movements among the peasant masses of the underdeveloped world has been viewed to a large extent in official United States policy as a triumph of communist propaganda, and has been attributed primarily to the cleverness of Mao Tse-tung in developing a doctrine with peasant appeal. As a result, the strategy of Mao Tse-tung tends to be viewed as no more than another example of a successful exploitation and take-over by the communists of a popular movement. But it was not Mao Tse-tung who created the revolutionary potential of peasant masses in Asia; nor did he invent the possibility of peasant nationalism. The explanation for the revolutionary transformation of the peasantry in the emergent world must be sought in the conditions and experiences of that world itself. The role of Mao Tse-tung was to recognize the political reality he confronted, to give it leadership, and to provide it with an intellectual expression and explanation. In short, Mao Tse-tung enunciated a doctrine for a developing peasant revolution in China which he did not create, which no single individual could have created, a peasant awakening which would have occurred even if Mao Tse-tung had never lived. This is not to underestimate the importance of the political and intellectual leadership which Mao provided for this peasant revolution in China. One need not assume that every revolutionary situation will work itself out automatically, according to some kind of inflexible historical law. The role of individual leadership is obviously crucial, and without Mao Tse-tung the Chinese Revolution might well have become a different event. The facts of the revolution itself, however, and of the peasant transformation underlying it, are not to be explained by the influence of Mao's doctrines. Nor is the claim that Mao and the Communists "exploited" and "took over" a popular, national, peasant revolt very enlightening; for the communist leadership of Mao Tse-tung was itself a part of that national awakening in China in the 1930's.

Not only was the new peasant, national communism of China created by the circumstances of increasing resentment against foreign domination, culminating in the conflict with Japan, but Mao's own conversion to this new concept of communism was itself the result of the same experience which he shared with his fellow Chinese. Mao did not create this new brand of peasant communism out of theoretical materials. Chinese communism was not the product of abstract meditations upon the merits of Marxism, Leninism, or socialism; nor was it the product of Soviet ideological influence. It was a reaction of which Mao himself was a part. We tend to assume that a communist leader like Mao Tse-tung has no personal identity as a Chinese, no personal commitment to the future of China; that he acted in a purely cynical manner; that he deliberately chose a peasant base for his communist movement as an act of sheer political expediency, governed solely by considerations of personal power. We conclude, therefore, that the communists "exploited" cleverly for their own sinister purposes conditions of peasant unrest in China. The opposite would be more accurate. Mao Tse-tung discovered among the Chinese peasants a growing commitment to a sense of Chinese national identity, a growing sense of personal anxiety as a result of the political weakness of Chinese society, a growing resentment against foreign intrusion, and consequently an increasing willingness to submit themselves to the collective discipline of a political organization; all of which paralleled his own feelings of national humiliation, feelings which had existed before he became a communist, which had been, in fact, the original motive for his joining to help create the Chinese Communist Party. Mao, after all, was not born a Communist, anymore than Ho Chi Minh, or Tito, or Castro. He became one, not as a result of some kind of spiritual deformity or moral taint, not because he was the dupe of some kind of diabolical conspiracy, but because he became convinced that communism was the *means* that could satisfy his goals of national fulfillment for China. What motives of personal ambition and personal power played a role in his decisions would be impossible to disentangle from the total configuration of his political career; but whatever role such personal motives played, they were no more nor less important than similar motives in the career of any political leader. Mao's "communism" no more disqualifies him as a legitimate expression of one aspect of Chinese political life than Spiro Agnew's so-called "conservatism" would disqualify him from his role as an American political figure.

Further, in joining the Chinese Communist Party, Mao did not simply accept a complete, finished system, to guide forever and ever all of his future political actions. He helped to define, *to redefine,* that is, to *create* Chinese Communism, through the experiences which he shared with his peasant followers in the 1930's and 1940's. That the kind of communism which emerged from that experience was considerably different from so-called orthodox Soviet Communism has become a commonplace. But it is hardly surprising that the Chinese revolution would differ from the Bolshevik revolution in Russia. It is only surprising to people who insist on viewing communist revolution as an external phenomenon foisted upon the society from the outside. "It is rather a misnomer to describe the adaptation of Communism to national circumstances as 'revisionism', since the orthodox Communism that is allegedly being revised is actually Soviet national Communist ideology." [16]

Chinese communism differed from Soviet communism not because Mao was a heretic who strayed from "true" communism, but because his political philosophy reflected, as does the political philosophy of any political leader, the nature of the circumstances which he confronted, and the range of solutions applicable to the specific problems of his society. Mao's communism was, in short, a *means* for the satisfaction of *national* aspirations. Johnson's term, "peasant nationalism," summarizes most accurately the nature of that phenomenon born out of revolutionary warfare which he labels communism. The point is not that communism in the non-Western world has acquired a "national" character, which runs contrary to its "communist" character, or that some strange hybrid has emerged, called "national communism"; the point is that communism in the emergent world *is* nationalism. Communism is an ideology in the emergent world used to explain and justify a national movement, a national awakening, the primary aim of which is to create a national state, that is, to solve the political problem of backwardness. "The Chinese Communist Party was from the beginning an indigenous phenomenon . . . composed of men who had become largely convinced of the value of soviet theories and methods for solving China's problems." [17]

The appeal of communist ideology derived primarily from the successful *example* of the Soviet Union, as the successful example of China would later influence the conversion to communism of other non-Western leaders. The examples of the Soviet Union, later of China, pointed the way to the solution of *national* problems, the problem of preserving the integrity of the society, of achieving national independence, of liberating it from foreign political control,

73

of overcoming its backwardness and powerlessness. The Chinese Communist leaders adopted Soviet methods, adopted communism, as an *instrument* for solving their own, that is, *China's* problems. Benjamin Schwartz, no supporter of communism, concludes that "the gravitation of power into the hands of Mao Tse-tung and Chu-Teh was the result of circumstances and power relations existing within the Chinese Communist movement rather than of any decision made in Moscow." [18] It was Mao's communist movement which provided the framework for the peasant nationalism awakened by the turmoils of the 1930's; and the success of Mao's movement was due to his ability to satisfy the *national* aspirations of the Chinese people.

The same point can be made for Castro, Ho Chi Minh, Tito, Taruc, or any of the other revolutionary leaders of the emergent world who turned to communism. In Cuba, many people were willing to support Castro because he promised basic reforms, and an end to the special, dependent relation of Cuba to the United States, because he appealed to a sense of "jingoistic nationalism." [19] The Cuban people demanded a kind of political solution to their problems, including the satisfaction of long-suppressed anti-American frustration, which inevitably recalled the kind of solution which the Soviet Union and China had developed. And when Castro "came to put his ideas and hopes into practice, he found himself driven, as he thought, into the Communist position." [20]

In Yugoslavia, Tito's Partisan movement became the great instrument and carrier of national unification. "For those who joined Tito's movement, communism, replacing traditional faiths, became in a sense the hallmark of Yugoslav nationality." [21] Communism overcame the religious, cultural, and historical divisions which had left Serbs, Croats, and Bosnians at each other's throats in the past, and subsumed their differences under Yugoslav nationalism. The same point is made by Fitzroy Maclean, who headed the British Military Mission to the Partisans during World War II, and who speaks of the Partisans' fiercely proprietary attitude toward "*their*

74

Revolution, *their* War of National Liberation, *their* struggle against the invader, *their* victories, *their* sacrifices." [22] He then quotes Tito as follows: "The Jugoslav brand of Communism was not something imported from Moscow but had its origin in the forests and mountains of Jugoslavia." [23]

Our view of revolutionary communism in the emergent world may become clearer if we reverse it. Instead of viewing communism as a kind of abstract idea, or total system, existing prior to and outside the conditions of the emerging societies, we might view communism more realistically as *itself* the expression of the reaction of the peasants to the revolutionary conditions we have described; we might view communism, in the emergent world, as the ideology of a revolutionary "peasant nationalism." Every nationalism develops an "ideology" to justify and explain a sense of national unity which *ought* to rally the people together; to explain and justify the pursuit of common goals and common interests; to explain and justify a sense not only of separateness from, but frequently of superiority over, other peoples, whose difference is emphasized, and whose inferiority is explained, partly by their failure to share in the true ideology, the superior way of life identified with one's own national consciousness.

In the Dutch Revolution against Spanish rule in the sixteenth century, for instance, Calvinism provided the ideological foundation for Dutch nationalism. The victory of the rebels, however, did not signal the victory of an international Calvinist conspiracy, which had duped and captured Dutch patriots to work against the interests of the Dutch people; the victory of the rebels was not due to the superior propaganda techniques, and organizational skill of the Calvinists. Nor was the Calvinism of the Dutch rebels opposed to their nationalism. Quite the contrary: their Calvinism became a mark of identification, a badge of their Dutchness, a way of demonstrating their differences from the Spanish, and the superiority of that "Dutchness" over the Catholic oppressor. Calvinism and Dutch nationalism reinforced each other; they became, in fact, identical; and the more patriotic, the more anti-Spanish, the more devoted to the superior burgher way of life of the Netherlands, the more likely one was to be a fanatical Calvinist.

One need not doubt the sincerity, or even fanaticism and devotion, of the Soviet leaders to what they call communism, any more than we need doubt the sincerity or fanatical devotion of those Americans who declare their allegiance to the principles of free enterprise capitalism. These ideological convictions are in no way incompatible with nationalism; quite the contrary, in every case it is national patriotism which gives strength and meaning to the ideological myth. Soviet Communism provides justification for Soviet nationalism; but more than that, the validity of Soviet Communism itself derives from its identification with the Soviet Union. Communism is the superior way of life *for* the Russians, because it is the superior way of life *of* the Russians. In the same way capitalism and democracy are superior ideologies *for* Americans, because they are practiced *by* Americans. Chinese Communism is not only different from Soviet Communism, but it is the ideological justification for *Chinese* nationalism; the Chinese Communists cannot accept a position subservient to Moscow, because they cannot accept that a *Chinese* national ideology would be inferior to a Russian one.

Nationalism is a process of asserting the rightness, in many cases the superiority, of one's own way of life. Every nationalism, therefore, contains an ideological dimension which describes the content of that way of life, which defines those aspects of the national life in which people take pride. Communism is such an ideology. In former times, such ideologies were defined in religious terms. Today they tend to be defined primarily in secular terms. This transformation in no way reduces the intensity, the fanaticism which once attached to the religious implications of nationalism, and which now attach to its secular implications. Nationalism, in fact, has been described, most accurately, as a secular religion. "If we ask ourselves what provides the operational connection between

76

Communist ideology and Yugoslav nationalism we must answer from the evidence available that it is probably the religious character of Communism." [24] This religious character *is* its national expression. The political leaders of China are communists *because* they are nationalists. Communism itself is the ideological base of their nationalism.

4 · *Revolutionary War and Totalitarian Communism*

Nationalism and national ideology are, of course, defined more rigidly and fanatically in communist states than in the United States. This ideological rigidity is typical of all totalitarian states. In any given society, national interest will be defined differently by different individuals. There does not exist one single, absolute, objectively true national interest: not only because individuals will differ in their theoretical interpretations; not only because an objective national interest can never be proven, or demonstrated scientifically; but because every nation is composed of diverse groups, diverse individuals, whose group and individual interests genuinely differ from one another. A definition of the national interest which will serve the interests of large industrial corporations may not serve those of small farmers; neither definition is "right" or "wrong." Differences in concepts of national interest reflect not only different theoretical interpretations, but the fact that the group and individual interests which together compose the nation may not always be compatible. In a pluralistic society such as ours is supposed to be, everyone is presumed to have the right to make his own interpretation of the national interest, and to express it freely; and the national policies of our government are supposed to represent a compromise between conflicting interests. Totalitarian states, on the other hand, insist on a single definition of the national interest which everyone must accept. Complete consensus is institutionalized in one-party states, where everyone must rally behind the official definition of the national interest, that is, the official ideology.

The willingness of people to accept a totalitarian definition of national interest is greatly enhanced in times of war or national emergency, because at such times there does appear to exist one overriding concern which submerges all individual differences. That is the physical survival of the nation itself, which is insured, presumably, through military victory. The need for military victory creates the conditions for a fanatical and rigid definition of national interest, as occurred during the French Revolution with the *levée en masse,* and the concept of the *nation en armes.*

The kind of revolutionary wars we have been describing in this chapter will be, in and of themselves, conducive to a totalitarian definition of national interest, for the one overriding goal of success in the revolutionary struggle submerges all individual differences. In such places as Algeria and Vietnam, where the wars of revolutionary liberation became, in fact, wars of national survival, totalitarianism becomes the response to the needs of a total war for survival. Nationalism, in the throes of creating itself through violence and revolution, will be pushed in the direction of totalitarian organization, for it will be faced with a totalitarian definition of its own nature. We tend to assume that war and totalitarianism in the emergent world are created by communism. The reverse is closer to the truth. Revolutionary war produces a totalitarian, communist definition of national identity. Julius Nyerere, President of Tanzania, makes the point, and twits his American critics, in these words: "I would not have been surprised if America had had only one party in the beginning. You would have said, 'We've got to win the war and get this stupid King George out! The most important thing is unity!'" [25] The struggle for national independence, particularly when accompanied by violent war, as in Vietnam, puts such a premium on unity as to create irresistible pressures for a totalitarian organization of the society.

Because of its totalitarian tendencies, revolutionary war has an attraction to those leaders of the emergent world bent upon the revolutionary transformation and modernization of their society. Mao Tse-tung was one of the first revolutionary leaders of the emergent world to note not only the potential strength of peasant nationalism in effecting a successful revolution, but the usefulness of revolutionary violence in developing a shared sense of national identity and national purpose. Revolutionary violence is attractive not so much because leaders like Mao Tse-tung are "totalitarian" by nature as because a collective, organized, unified political movement, in which the individual differences, as well as the innate conservatism of the peasant masses, are submerged within the struggle for victory in a revolutionary war, greatly simplifies the task of modernizing political leadership.

War is the great unifier. It rallies the peasants to the common task and the common cause of nationalism and national identity. It is this emphasis on the importance of revolutionary violence as a means of building a modern nation which makes Mao Tse-tung the great prophet of revolutionary warfare in the emergent world; and it is the task of revolutionary warfare which creates and rallies peasant movements most successfully. The great contribution of Mao Tse-tung was to develop a theory of revolutionary warfare, not only as the means to overthrow colonial, imperial domination, but as the very instrument for forging a united nation, and for creating a political system capable of modernization, capable of national development. As Irving Horowitz, the great sociologist of the emergent world, expresses it, "the national liberation front has been the major stimulus to successful popular reform . . . in the Third World." [26]

The experience of war creates a bond of comradeship among the leaders, submerging differences between individual plans, individual ideas, individual personalities, within the common, shared experience of the fight against the foreign enemy; and between the leaders and the masses, who accept a disciplined, totalitarian leadership, because it is exercised by men who have earned the right to be such leaders in a national, revolutionary war. "The mobilization of the masses, when it arises out of the war of liberation, introduces into each man's consciousness the ideas of a common cause, of a national destiny and of a collective history. In the same way the second phase, that of the building up of the nation, is helped on by the existence of this element which has been mixed with blood and anger." [27]

The sense of nationalism created by such a revolutionary experience will stress unity, a collective purpose, since this shared experience, this common destiny *defines* the new national identity. In a society where all will be destroyed together, or all will be saved together, concepts related to liberal individualism, the open society, and a democratic system of compromise between conflicting interests will be meaningless. Such a realization, of course, leads to the fairly obvious conclusion that one way to spare the emergent societies the more intense and violent collective disciplines created by revolutionary violence, one way to reduce the pains of modernization in the emergent world, and to reduce the intensity of communism in a real way, is not to provoke such societies into wars of national liberation from Western domination; to avoid pushing these societies into conflicts like the Vietnam War, which certainly does more to build communist totalitarianism in the emergent world than almost any other policy we have pursued.

One consequence of revolutionary war is that the wartime leader, the guerilla chieftain, becomes the political leader, the personal, popular dictator who unifies in his person the experience of the revolutionary war, which justifies his unquestioned leadership since the experience of that war provides, at that point, the only genuine experience of national unity, of national identity. Mao Tse-tung is again the supreme model and the foremost theorist of this concept of revolutionary leadership. The strength and coherence of the Chinese Communist Party leadership derived primarily from their shared experience of such ordeals as the Long March.

"Most of the Communist cadres which govern China today are drawn from these 'Yenan graduates,' with their deeply rooted memories of heroic days." [28] In Yugoslavia the strength and coherence of the Partisan leadership derive from the shared experience of the ordeal against the Nazis, and Tito's unquestioned leadership of the Communist Party derives from the authority and legitimacy he acquired as leader of the Partisans, not from his talents as a "communist agent." Ho Chi Minh, of course, achieved this kind of charisma, and the Viet Minh organization established the same grip on Vietnamese society as a result of the long colonial war against the French. Luis Taruc and the Huks in the Philippines, Fidel Castro and the 26th of July movement in Cuba, and the leadership of the Algerian FLN are all cast from the same pattern.

The same process of nation-building through revolutionary war can be seen in our own revolution. That the War of the American Revolution did not create a permanent institutionalized totalitarianism is due partly to the relative ease with which it succeeded; colonial society never experienced the kind of devastation and threats to its very survival experienced by Vietnamese society. It is also due to the fact that once British political domination was overthrown, the task of building a modern nation was extremely easy for the United States, as will be demonstrated in the next chapter.

In short, the kind of authoritarian rule which we find in the emergent world, the totalitarian dictatorships built around a leader like Mao Tse-tung, are the result of the experience of revolutionary war itself. Such revolutionary movements as developed in China, Cuba, and North Vietnam did not become totalitarian dictatorships *because* they were communist. They became communist dictatorships because the revolutionary war created the need for such a leadership. Our own Revolutionary War, because it was so much less desperate, never pushed us to this kind of extreme. Communism, in the emergent world, with its collective organization and its cult of the strong leader, is the *functional* response of that world to the demands of revolutionary warfare. Mao Tse-tung is the symbol and inspiration of such movements, not because of the cleverness of Maoist agents in "exploiting" conditions, but because other emergent societies find in the Chinese experience a model for the revolutionary transformation they are themselves experiencing.

Communism in the emergent world would then appear to be what Johnson calls "a particularly virulent form of nationalism." [29] This virulence results from pushing the conditions of weakness and powerlessness in the emergent world to their utmost limits. Communism is a national response to the problems of the underdeveloped world, the intensity of which is directly proportional to the difficulties and violence accompanying the struggle for nationhood; as sheer physical survival becomes the paramount issue, as it is in Vietnam, national interest is defined increasingly in totalitarian terms. Such societies do not become totalitarian because they are communist, they are communist because such a totalitarian response appears appropriate to the conditions of their existence.

4

The Telescoped Revolution

1 · *The Liberal Character of*
Modernization in the West

MODERNIZATION IN THE LIBERAL WEST, THAT IS, IN SUCH PLACES
as France, England, and the United States, was a unique experience, and it does not appear that the emergent world can reproduce its relaxed and "liberal" character. The main reason why the
Western experience of modernization appears to be an alternative
not open to the emergent world is the success of the Western world
itself. That world, by its presence and its experience, has spoiled,
unintentionally, the possibility of a peaceful, evolutionary transformation in the emergent world. This reason is basic, for most of the
other factors hindering a more liberal modernization of emerging
societies derive in one way or another from this primary one. The
existence of the Western world, and knowledge of the experience of
that world, represent two factors which Western societies themselves did not confront in their development, and which radically
alter the conditions of development in the emergent world.

The existence of an already developed world was a factor
which the West did not confront, and which creates tremendous

pressures for a rapid, planned development, pressures which did not exist in the West. The underdeveloped world has a model to which it can compare itself; it knows what it wants very concretely, since that goal is embodied in the wealth and power of the West. The modernization of such societies as France and England was, by comparison, unplanned. The transformation of the Western societies could not be planned in the same way that development in the emergent world will be planned, since the modern nations being created were new and unprecedented phenomena. Development in the emergent world is almost certain to be planned on a grand scale, for a model now exists. The leaders of the emergent world cannot help rationalizing their actions in reference to a clearly perceived goal. Consequently, the leadership of the emergent world is in a hurry. This contrast between the rapid, hurried, urgent development of the emergent world and the gradual, evolutionary, unplanned process of Western development is crucial, for the "liberal" character of the Western experience was not so much that modernization was willed, democratically, from below, and accepted cheerfully by the majority of Western peoples, as that it took place gradually, over a long period of time, permitting a constant internal readjustment to changing conditions.

Nor was Western development free of violence. Our conviction that Western modernization was a peaceful experience, a good kind of "civilized" development, and that our example is proof that revolution and radical violence are unnecessary excesses in the emergent world, caused by the evil influence of communism, results from a convenient lapse of memory. We forget such successful "wars of national liberation" and modernization against a traditional pattern of rule as the Dutch Revolution against Spain in the sixteenth century, the Puritan Revolution against the English monarch in the seventeenth century, the French Revolution against the Old Regime in the eighteenth century, and our own American Revolution. In fact the modernization of every major

Western society has been accompanied at some time, and to some degree, by revolution and violence; even in "conservative" societies, which sought to accommodate modernization without changing the basic political structure and distribution of power, that is, without revolution, the elimination of traditional sectors in Germany and Japan, for instance, not only involved considerable violence and coercion but created internal crises which were resolved partly through the international violence of the two World Wars. Democracy and a liberal open society may be the possible products of modernization after the traditional Ancien Regime has been destroyed, but the destruction of that traditional social structure was not itself a peaceful or democratic experience in the West, any more than in the emergent world.

The slow, gradual, and unplanned character of modernization influenced Western development in several ways. Most obviously, this slow pace allowed time for the internal readjustment and social rearrangements necessitated by modernization. People were weaned away from traditional patterns over several generations; "the countries that modernized first were not under the pressure of more advanced models and had many generations in which to make their experiments." [1] Today, modernization must telescope into one generation tremendous and tremendously disruptive changes. "The developing countries of Asia, Africa and parts of Latin America may have to accomplish . . . within a few decades a process of political change which in the history of Western Europe and North America took at least as many generations." [2] Even more important, modernization grew inside the Western societies, developed, as it were, within them, and in response to internal changes. It was not an import, a change associated with a foreign culture. Hence it was much easier to absorb than has been true in the emergent world. In non-Western societies, by contrast, the machine age is much more disruptive because such modernization is an alien force thrust upon these societies from the outside. In western Europe, since modernization was itself a European creation, development was not only gradual, but was able to fit itself much more successfully into the existing patterns of society.

As a result, much of the institutional structure of modernization, in politics and economics, was erected before the age of mass politics. Political centralization, nation-building, the creation of modern administrative organizations was begun, and in some places, notably England, developed considerably long before mass participation in the political process. The institutional structure of modern politics and economics was the work of an elite that did not have to concern itself with the management of a large political audience. It was not necessary, as a result, to impose rigid, mass disciplines, and force people into the rapid mobilization which modernization requires until much preliminary institutional change had been achieved. In such countries as England the great masses of the people did not become meaningful political factors until after the process of political modernization had been considerably advanced, or, in some cases, virtually completed. The distinguishing characteristic of totalitarianism is the attempt to mobilize the entire population into the political process within an authoritarian system. The kings who created the national states of France and England had no need for this kind of collective discipline. The age of mass politics, in these societies, did not come until after a centralized and modernized political system had already been established in the struggle against the feudal aristocracy.

Not only were the kings of early modern Europe able to ignore the masses in their task of state-building, but the fight between king and feudal aristocracy, which marked the creation of every monarchical state, left a legacy of aristocratic privilege which is the basis for the concept of individual rights and liberties in the West. This legacy is the result of the long struggle between aristocratic privilege and royal power, with its roots in the conflicts between the monarchy and the feudal aristocracy in the Middle Ages, and of which the Magna Carta is a typical example. Traditionally, in

England, liberty and privilege were viewed as synonymous; that is, liberty was an aristocratic privilege, not shared by the mass of the people. A concept of traditional rights and privileges, limiting the state authority, and forming the basis of the modern notion of constitutional and civil rights, is a legacy that was made possible by the aristocratic context in which modernized, central political structures were created in certain countries in the West, and by the association that developed in the West between liberty and aristocratic privilege.

This link between political liberty and aristocratic privilege has been, in fact, the besetting weakness of conservatism in the West. For liberty as a privilege means not only that certain people enjoy rights which the state cannot arbitrarily encroach upon, but that they enjoy these rights at the expense of unprivileged individuals within the society. Conservative critics of democracy have argued, since Burke's *Reflections on the French Revolution,* that by leveling centers of aristocratic privilege the democratic supporters of the modern centralized state have greatly weakened the capacity of society to resist its all-powerful authority. What Burkean conservatives conveniently overlook, of course, is that the capacity to resist sovereign authority in an aristocratic society was limited to the privileged classes, and extended to commoners only if one makes the assumption that the traditional aristocracy acted as a shield, protecting peasant and burgher from the arbitrary rule of an oppressive monarchy. The opposite, in fact, is precisely what took place. The French commoners supported the centralized authority of the monarchy to liberate themselves from the harsh and arbitrary oppression of the privileged orders. As long as the aristocracy bitterly resisted sharing its rights, or abolishing the privileges it enjoyed at the expense of commoners, the masses willingly supported the growth of a centralized state power which could be used to destroy the edifice of aristocratic privilege, as occurred during the French Revolution. For the masses were more concerned with the aristocratic exercise of privilege at their own expense than with the

87

extension of state power against rights and privileges which existed only for the aristocracy.

Despite the selfishness, and, eventually, the blind stupidity of its motivations, it was the aristocracy of the Western societies which traditionally established the principle of legal and constitutional restrictions to the central authority of the state. A long history of aristocratic privilege before the advent of mass politics created a structure of individual rights which, although limited originally to a privileged few, restricted central state authority; and when this structure of rights was extended to the mass of the people, when it ceased to exist as a system of privileges, this structure of individual rights, despite its aristocratic roots, formed a very real bulwark against the pressures of totalitarianism created by modernization and mass politics.

In the same way, modern economic and social structures and a modern intellectual point of view developed gradually within Western societies before the age of mass politics, permitting considerable time for internal readjustments. It was not necessary to change overnight the work habits of the entire population, and transform peasants into factory workers in one generation; nor was it necessary to develop within one generation a sense of social allegiance to larger units of organization than the local community. The modern populations of the Western world grew up inside a gradually modernized, capitalistic economic system; they were "trained" and "civilized" over a period of time, within modern economic and social institutions which had been created by members of their own society, within the environment of their own culture. In the emergent nations, mass political awakening, the development of mass politics, and the creation of modern political and economic institutions must all take place simultaneously. In addition, the new economic and social institutions of modernization must not only be absorbed very quickly, not only must these people adjust to their new conditions much more rapidly than their Western counterparts, but the institutions of modernization emanate from an alien, Western culture. As a result the adjustment to modernization in the emergent world will be much more painful, much more difficult than it was in the West; it will produce much more coercion than occurred in the West; and it will create much more severe cultural dislocations, in which the luxury of an open society and democratic processes will be far less likely.

The sense of urgency which grips the emergent world in the face of modernization stems also from the pressure of international competition, a pressure which makes it mandatory for these societies to catch up with the West if they are to survive and maintain their integrity. International competition was a major factor in the modernization of the West; it may well have been the single most important factor; but the pressure of such competition was extremely mild for the first modern nations, as compared to the pressures confronting the emergent world today. The international conflicts of the sixteenth, seventeenth, and eighteenth centuries were not only greatly limited in scope, but they were not accompanied by the extreme insecurity which the present international state system inevitably creates among the emergent societies. These societies must modernize in the context of already existing major powers with infinitely greater destructive capacities than they themselves possess.

Such major powers as France and England did not confront an international state system already dominated by other states infinitely greater in power than themselves. England's economic leadership, her great wealth, coupled with her fortunate island position, which made her, in the past, virtually invulnerable to outside attack, combined to create a feeling of great security, hence of great self-confidence. England, the most powerful nation in the West, protected by her navy, was free of the pressures of militancy, mass mobilization, and war hysteria which have helped produce totalitarian conditions not only among the struggling societies of the emergent world, but in such states as modern Germany. The relaxed, liberal character of modernization in a society like England resulted partly from the absence of those feelings of panic which accompany the realization that one's society is falling hopelessly behind in international competition, and becoming completely dependent upon the mercy of much more powerful states. All the emerging societies feel inferior, in terms of military power, to all the advanced societies, because all of them have been subjected, in varying degrees, to the domination of the advanced world.

The pioneers of Western modernization, England, France, the Netherlands, were the most successful European societies in creating a liberal, open political tradition; such late comers as Germany and Italy faced the problem of modernization out of a legacy of international competition in which, traditionally, they had been powerless in the face of the great powers. The Italian wars of the fifteenth and sixteenth centuries produced a national reaction on the part of Machiavelli which in bitterness and virulence was a Renaissance version of the fanatical nationalism of men like Ho Chi Minh or Castro, confronting modernization within a legacy of powerlessness in relation to the modern nations. The Thirty Years' War and the Wars of Napoleon, among others, produced conditions in Germany where the creation of a powerful national state became as much more important than the question of individual liberties as it is in contemporary China. The defeat of World War I created a virulent national reaction in Germany, culminating in the Nazi regime of Hitler, a totalitarian imposition which the Germans accepted as the price to pay to end the powerlessness which they believed had been forced upon them by the Versailles settlement. Such a nationalistic reaction was analogous to the "jingoism" of the Cuban people under Castro, or the wounded feelings of national humiliation which China has sought to redress under Mao.

The United States provides a particularly suitable illustration and summary of these themes. W. W. Rostow, borrowing a phrase from the work of Louis Hartz, refers to this country as one that was born free;[3] that is, without going through all the painful processes of readjustment and internal reallocation of resources associated with many of the phases of modernization. The United States, Rostow says, was "created mainly out of a Britain already far along in the transitional process." [4] Rostow is concerned primarily with economic development. But the fact that the United States was "born free" eased all the processes of modernization, and largely explains the comparative success of this country in combining modernization with a tradition of liberalism and a relatively open society.

The United States inherited from Great Britain an already considerably advanced economy, a tradition of individual rights unencumbered by the legacy of feudal traditions and aristocratic privilege which reduced the effectiveness of this tradition in Europe. Further, the United States had no problem of peasant mobilization and peasant modernization; hence it avoided totally one of the chief sources of tension in modernizing societies, the reactionary resistance of conservative rural masses. The commercial revolution in agriculture was already well advanced in England by the time the United States was founded, and in the United States the social cleavage between a landed upper class and a peasant mass did not exist, except in the southern states; although the peculiar institution of slavery, our version of the peasant problem, created an explosive conflict between progressive and backward forces in the society of such magnitude as to demonstrate that the success of liberalism, in the United States, was due to unusually fortunate circumstances, rather than to any "genius" of the "Anglo-Saxon" peoples, or any "racial" adaptability of white people to democratic institutions. In short, the United States was a society considerably advanced along the road to modernization by the time it was founded, simply because it was created largely by emigrants from the most advanced society in Europe, England, which placed the stamp of its culture and institutions on the new nation. The United States, in fact, was an overseas England, with all the modernizing achievements and accomplishments of the old country, but free of most of the burdens and complications caused by traditional residues undissolved in the old society. The United States was unique in being a society virtually unfettered by traditions.

The good fortune of the United States extended, in fact, even further; for not only was the United States "born free," it was also born rich. The United States had available an entire continent, full of natural resources virtually untapped by organized civilization. This rich wilderness made its products available to a people who were Europeans, and therefore possessed of all the skills and organizational talents necessary for the exploitation of these resources. The United States confronted modernization with less economic pressure of mass poverty and mass unrest than any other society. Further, the United States was even more isolated from the pressures of international competition than Great Britain. This isolation was not so much a deliberate policy as the fact that, until 1941, we did not believe, and indeed, we had no reason to believe, that the competitive world of power politics posed a threat to our survival, to our independence, or even to our wealth, power, and freedom. Through most of our history we were protected by a natural moat even more impassable than the English Channel, the Atlantic Ocean; we developed in a context even freer of pressures from powerful neighbors than had been true of England. At no time in our history did we feel that the race of international competition was a matter of life and death for our society. The open character of American society in the past has been the consequence of the good fortune of being born free and being born rich; the absence, with the exception of the institution of slavery, of irreconcilable political conflicts between traditional and modernizing forces; the absence of overwhelming economic pressures, of mass want and mass poverty; the absence of excessive pressures of overcrowding; most important of all, the absence of dangerous pressures of international competition. The United States had its share of political, economic, and social problems; but they have been far less serious, in the past, than those of other modernizing societies. This unique character of American society means not only that modernization created fewer problems in our society than in any other, but that the United States is a particularly poor model for other modernizing societies; for today's emergent nations cannot hope to duplicate America's good fortune.

On the other hand, such problems as the great depression of the 1930's and the exigencies of the Cold War have resulted in a rapid shrinking of our civil liberties, as well as a considerable deterioration of the open character of American society, suggesting the link between our ability to avoid authoritarianism in the past and our relative ease in confronting modernization. In recent years, American politics have become embittered partly because questions involving the very survival of the nation appear to be at stake. Only as a result of the division over slavery had we ever confronted, in the past, such a sense of national emergency.

In summary, certain Western societies were able to avoid the extremes of totalitarian mobilization in their struggle to modernize, and acquired a relatively liberal and open character as a result of the slow pace of change, which enabled more successful adjustment to the conditions of modernization, and the creation of modern institutions before the emergence of mass politics. In this process, certain aristocratic legacies from the Middle Ages played a role in establishing a tradition of individual rights; the slow pace of modernization also reduced the pressure of international competition; and in the United States, most of the problems of modernization were considerably attenuated as a result of a configuration of unusually fortunate circumstances unlikely ever to be repeated in the emergent world.

2 · *The Role of the Intelligentsia*

The underdeveloped world cannot duplicate the West's gradualism, for it cannot duplicate the West's ignorance, the West's innocence. The gap between dream and reality could never be, in the

West, the source of frustration which it is bound to be for the leaders of the underdeveloped world today. This gap between wish and reality becomes a source of intense frustration and impatience, encouraging forcing methods.

This point is well illustrated in an interview with the Shah of Iran, who describes himself "as a revolutionary head of state. The decision to bring about a profound revolution came to me with the certainty that a country such as ours must force the pace and skip stages in order to achieve a modern technology and a higher standard of living." [5] The sense of hurry, of planning in relation to already existing models, of striving to catch up with the already developed nations is a characteristic which will be found among many leaders of the emergent world, whether or not they are communists. The point is that the kind of forced pace and revolution from above we associate with the communists does not result from the peculiar political views of communists, but from the needs and conditions of modernizing societies, and from the problems of leadership in such a society.

Although the leadership that transformed the West was not democratic, it had evolved gradually within the society. As a result, some organic relation, some continuity, existed between Western leadership and the masses. The character of leadership in the emergent world has been considerably different. The leadership of that world is best defined by the term intelligentsia. The word intelligentsia was coined in Russia in the nineteenth century. An intelligentsia, in this sense, is produced when a backward society is exposed to an advanced one, and to its sophisticated system of education. Exposure to Western education has produced a class whose education alienates it from its own people, drives a wedge between the masses and the educated minority. "The best education available at the most modern schools and universities in Eastern Europe, Asia, and Latin America has been little inferior to that available at the same time in the Western world." [6] Members of the intelligentsia are provided with an advanced Western education ill suited for adaptation to their own undeveloped societies; further, this education allows them to perceive the backwardness of their own societies in a way which was never true of Western leadership. Such perception alienates the intelligentsia from its own people, and creates among this educated minority a sense of frustration and impatience.

This dilemma could not have existed in the Western world, where modernization, inevitably, always ran ahead of the traditional educational institutions. There were no modern societies already existing, in the history of the development of the West, which could provide Westerners with a training in excess of the level of development of their own society. Further, the modernizing process, occurring over a long period of time, and developing from inside the society, was able to gradually absorb an increasing percentage of the total society.

All of the problems confronting the intelligentsia in the emergent world are enormously exaggerated by the crippling ambivalence created by the experience of colonialism. The emergent world must cope with the challenge of modernization in the shadow of colonialism, an experience which is the result of the prior modernization of the West, and to which the West itself was never subjected. The memory of colonialism creates a disturbing ambiguity in the attitudes of the intelligentsia. It was the colonial experience that first triggered the process of transformation in the emergent world; that is, it was the impact of the advanced Western cultures which first began the process of dissolution of the traditional societies of Asia, Africa, and Latin America. That experience produced a profound resentment against Western domination; but at the same time, the Western world is the source of much that the emergent peoples want and need to escape that domination.

The emergent nations seek the status of modern, Western nations, but the very pressure for modernization is a constant reminder to the intelligentsia that their traditional cultures were inadequate to the challenge of the West. Modernization means rejection of their traditional societies, of all the symbols of their traditional cultural identity. Modernization creates a cruel paradox which intensifies anti-Western feelings. For modernization is a tacit admission of the inferiority of non-Western cultures, and the superior power of Western models. One by-product of this ambivalence will be a sense of exaggerated and aggressive nationalism, masking feelings of cultural inadequacy and inferiority. To the extent that the advanced civilization of the West acts as a magnet, an irresistible lure to the intellectuals of the emergent world, to that same extent it is a crushing reminder of the poverty and backwardness of their own societies; in short of how much catching up they have to do. Such awareness, inevitably, is a source of envy and resentment, at the same time that it produces frustration and despair. The greater the determination of the intelligentsia to catch up with the advanced nations, the more likely it is to be consumed with hostility toward the West; for the attempt to catch up is itself a reminder of backwardness, a reminder that pride has difficulty acknowledging. "When the goal is to do what others are already doing, the haunting fears of failure are related not to the disappointment of broken dreams but to disturbing doubts about the worth of the self." [7] The emergent societies are seeking a status already achieved by the advanced nations, and their success in achieving that status is related to considerations of the worth of the societies themselves.

The intellectuals of the emergent world, in confronting modernization, are animated by a sense of inferiority, of self-doubt, which in itself creates hostility toward the Western world, whose achievements are the source of this inferiority—a crippling dilemma which never plagued the modernizing leaders of the West, and which prevents the emergent world from embracing the culture and techniques of the West in an attitude of confident acceptance. This ambiguity creates further pressure for rapid results to still the self-doubts created by the attempt to catch up with the developed world. The West is not only the ultimate model for the intelligentsia, it can also be viewed, as in fact the West tends to view itself, as a kind of benevolent fairy godmother, come to help the poor peoples of the world, a superior moral order which introduced into the benighted ignorance of non-civilized people notions of change, of progress, of political freedom, of material opportunities, of social mobility. Not only did Westerners implant these ideas among the peoples of the emergent world, but they built roads, schools, hospitals, instituted programs of public hygiene—created, in short, an infrastructure of modernizing institutions. The Western world, therefore, claims the gratitude of the emergent peoples. But it is impossible for this intelligentsia to be grateful to a world which is the source of its own profound sense of inferiority.

The feelings of self-doubt of the intellectuals in the emergent world are enhanced by the memory that their societies were once ruled by that superior Western world, and by the fact that Western powers frequently continue to exercise preponderant power, particularly economic power, in their lands. If they were not animated by such feelings of inferiority, and by the realization of actual inferiority in power relationships, the intelligentsia of the emergent world would be amused rather than insulted by the arrogance of Westerners. But such arrogance cannot be overlooked because the emergent world is too aware, through the colonial experience, of the crushing weight of superiority of the Western nations.

Feelings of hypersensitive nationalism, of cultural, in fact, of racial inferiority, memories of the colonial experience, and the continued humiliation born of the realization of the comparative power and wealth of the Western world, all burden the leadership of the emergent world with psychological difficulties which distract them from the rational and objective confrontation of the problem of development and modernization. As a result, the nationalist feelings of the leaders of the emergent world are far more abrasive, and psychologically much more disabling, than comparable national sentiments in Western history. As Lucian Pye observes, colonialism becomes a convenient scapegoat for all the problems of underdeveloped societies, for it focuses the blame on "them," on the outsiders, and leaves the self blameless for the society's shortcomings.[8] The leaders of the emergent world exploit the inevitable hostility which exists between the wealthy and the poor, between the strong and the weak, reinforced, in this case, by the hostility between former colonial master and slave, and the very real resentment against the experience of Western domination. They exploit this resentment, and turn attention away from the positive, but much more difficult, problem of building a modern nation. There is no doubt that colonialism, or the semi-colonial status produced by economic imperialism, was a cruel and painful experience for the emergent societies, and that the West had a profoundly debilitating impact on these societies. Nor does one need to minimize the selfishness, greed, arrogance, and callousness of the Western powers, not only in the era of imperialism, but even today, to recognize that the task confronting the emergent world is infinitely larger than removal of Western political and economic domination. The conditions of poverty of their own societies, the lack of skills of their own people, their own backwardness, are as much of an obstacle to the achievement of this modernization as the imperial and neo-colonial activities of Western powers.

Not only is the positive task of building a modern nation as difficult as the negative goal of escaping Western domination, but it requires a hard look at, a responsible acknowledgment of, the real shortcomings of the society. The tendency of the intelligentsia to use imperialism as a scapegoat for all the problems of emergent societies simply reinforces the crippling ambivalence of their attitudes toward the developed world. The leaders of the emergent world need acts of defiance, over and above the objective needs created by deliberate Western policy, for the same reason that adolescents require acts of defiance against the adult world to affirm their own identity.

3 · *The Legacy of the White Man's Burden*

The psychological difficulties of the emergent world are further complicated by immature attitudes of "benevolent paternalism" among the Western nations, attitudes which are particularly marked in the United States. The leaders of the emergent world must define their identity in acts of defiance against a Western world which has always viewed them as inferior, even in its most benevolent moments. The paternalistic attitudes of Westerners toward the emergent world cannot be dismissed as mere hypocrisy, masking economic motives, rooted in a simple desire for economic exploitation. Even where Westerners are sincere in their desire to help the emergent world, they refuse to yield their own image of themselves as superior peoples helping benighted savages. As a result, the Western world is very reluctant to end the dependent relation of non-Westerners, and to allow its aid to eventuate in the creation of genuinely independent and equal societies.

This attitude is best expressed in Kipling's famous phrase, the white man's burden, or the French concept that their colonial activities were part of a *mission civilisatrice* to extend the benefits of French culture all over the world. As Kipling's phrase indicates, the benevolent paternalism of the West implies, in fact, a sense of racial superiority. The paternalistic attitudes of the white man toward the "lesser breeds without the law" mask a profound need for the dependency of these "lesser breeds." The white man is willing to take on the burden of a civilizing mission to the non-Western world, as long as that mission provides him with constant reminders of the inadequacies of "colored" peoples, hence of his own racial superiority, as well as magnanimity. Even where the feelings of superiority are not rooted in racial factors, as in the case of French assimilation policy, they are based on the assumption of the moral superiority of Western civilization. The philosophy of the white man's burden complements the self-doubts and feelings of inferiority of the people of the non-Western world; for it is based on the assumption that the "colored" peoples of the world are not able to take care of themselves. The struggle for modernization is viewed in the West as a kind of test of fitness, a test through which inherently inferior people demonstrate to the Western nations, acting as judges, whether they have "arrived," and are politically "mature" and capable of running their own affairs. Except that the West seldom wants to cut the umbilical cord, and seldom acknowledges that other people are ready to be free of Western interference; "colored people were somehow never ready for democracy." [9] This attitude was well expressed at a meeting of the Council of Foreign Relations attended by this writer, in which one member viewed the struggle for development in the emergent world in the image of the attempt to achieve membership in a club. Clearly, in his eyes, that club was the superior white man's world; and the ability of the rest of the world to attain membership in that world would be determined by a kind of admissions committee dominated by the United States.

The process is most clearly evident in the experience of European colonial rule in Africa, and is well described by the anthropologist, M. J. Herskovits. Speaking of the cultural shock experienced by Europeans and Africans coming together for the first time in the nineteenth century, he says that "the difference was that the European was in control. It was his system of values that framed the rules and ordinances which were established. The 'natural justice' so often referred to in earlier British statements on colonial policy, and the *mission civilisatrice* of the French, like the Belgian and Portuguese counterparts of these concepts, were implemented by legal and other conventions that from the point of view of European culture were self-evident, essential and right beyond doubt for human societies everywhere. The White Man's Burden was therefore a discipline for the African which would bring him eventually to what was firmly and sometimes fervently believed to be the better ways of life of what were considered more advanced societies." [10]

For the intelligentsia of the non-Western world, the racial prejudice upon which the colonial experience was built greatly complicates their own search for identity, and their own attempts to overcome self-doubts about their own culture. Frantz Fanon summarizes the colonial atmosphere in these words: "The first thing which the native learns is to stay in his place, and not to go beyond certain limits." [11] That lesson was learned over and over again, in China, in Vietnam, in India, in Africa, wherever the European white man came as colonial administrator, as businessman, or even as missionary; and never was the lesson clearer that the native must keep his place than when the white Westerner came to assist his inferior brother and help him out of his darkness and misery.

René Dumont, the French agronomist, who has lived and studied extensively in Africa, has described the profound feelings of racial superiority which animated many of the most sincere Christian missionaries in that continent. Some of the examples which he cites would be comic if they were not so tragic, including the story of the aging Bishop who had spent his life in missionary work in Africa, and who declared that when he died, he would ask God to open the skull of a Negro to show him whether there was anything inside; or the missionary in the Congo who concluded after forty years in Africa that the black man did not have a soul. One does not know whether to feel sorrier for the missionary or for his black victims. Such cases were admittedly extreme, but the whole missionary-colonial enterprise, Dumont makes very clear, was based on profound feelings of racial superiority, and the practice of racial segregation.[12]

The sense of Western superiority, the paternalistic conviction that the white man could judge the fitness of "colonial" populations, is well illustrated in the remarks of the British consul-general in Shanghai in 1932, commenting on the growing anti-European sentiment in China: "One cannot forget that all foreigners and especially British have suffered in recent years from utter incompetency and unjustifiable pretensions of Chinese nationalism." [13] China's "reasonableness" is measured, implicitly, by her willingness to act in ways that would make her acceptable to the West; the reverse, that the British should act in ways that would make them acceptable to the Chinese, is not even imagined. In spite of the fact that the British were intruders in China, imposing their own national tutelage on a foreign society, they dismiss Chinese nationalist reactions to such intrusion as "unjustifiable pretensions." The same point was made by the British President of the Hong Kong Chamber of Commerce in 1870: "China can in no sense be considered a country entitled to all the same rights and privileges as civilized nations which are bound by international law." [14] Perhaps the most crushing example of this insulting sense of superiority are the instructions supposedly given by a United States Senator to Assistant Secretary of State for Latin American Affairs Nelson Rockefeller, during the San Francisco Conference on the United Nations, in 1945: "Your God damned peanut nations aren't voting right. Go line them up." [15]

W. R. Crocker, an official of the British colonial bureaucracy, completes the indictment in these words: "It is difficult for easygoing Britishers at home to realize how much bitterness gets into the hearts of some of the literate minority in Asia, the Caribbean, the Pacific, and Africa. They know nothing of what it feels like to be treated, however politely, as a dressed-up ape which has been taught to ride a bicycle, of what it feels like to belong to a part of the human race that is commonly assumed to be congenitally backward, of what it feels like to be given to understand that you are a species which cannot look after itself." [16] Nationalism, in the emergent world, is naturally embittered by reactions of racial inferiority, and one of the most difficult problems of the emergent world, one not encountered by the modernizing leaders of the United States, or England, will be the ambivalent love-hate relation created among the intelligentsia by Western imperialism and Western paternalism.

4 · *The Politics of Confrontation*

Western attitudes have complemented and reinforced the self-doubts and feelings of inferiority of the emergent world; if the emergent nations play the role of defiant adolescents, this role complements the Western role of selfish and immature parent. But despite the aptness of the image, the emergent world cannot accept the role of a child, no matter how poor and backward that world is. Jean Paul Sartre defines the psychological dimensions of this problem by saying that: "We become what we are by the radical and deep seated refusal of that which others have made of us." [17] The intelligentsia of the emergent world must reject the role of inferior, childlike people into which their societies have been cast by the Western powers. They must struggle against that role to achieve their own identity, despite all the difficulties attendant upon such a demand for self-identity, for genuine political independence, for the right to make their own mistakes. And no amount of jesuitical argument by Westerners concerning the advantages and benefits of Western tutelage can alter this determination. Even to the extent that Western tutelage is helpful, that Western capital aid and technical assistance are desperately needed by the poor countries of the world, to that extent, in fact, must they insist on their independence, and reject the role of the dependent child as the price they must pay for the aid of the United States and other rich nations. The ambiguity and difficulty of this task was expressed poignantly by a Brazilian journalist: "We need, ask for, and hate foreign capital at the same time." [18] That is, the underdeveloped world needs outside assistance, but hates the fact of that need, as well as the acknowledgment of that need. "People do not like being exploited but they can put up with it. What they cannot put up with is being considered inferior." [19] What the emergent world finds intolerable is the belief that Western domination, and a tacit acceptance of its own inferiority, will be gladly accepted in return for certain material benefits deriving from the presence of Western powers, an attitude summed up in the philosophy of French colonialists: "Feed and dress the people, they say, and all will be well." [20]

The difficulties created by this psychological problem are pushed to an extreme in situations of revolutionary war. For the simplest way that the emergent societies can dissolve these ambiguities, can face the problem of the superior Western world without succumbing to crises of self-doubt, and without giving hostages to the ex-colonial masters, is by going it alone. Going it alone has a tremendous attraction for the leaders of the emergent world. It enables them to view the problem of modernization in its simplest terms, as a revolutionary struggle against Western opposition. Revolutionary wars not only push the leaders of the emergent world into radical, defiant, anti-Western, communist responses, but the desire to go it alone makes revolutionary war, the concept of political mobilization through revolutionary violence, and the ideas of Mao Tse-tung extremely attractive to a leadership which is sorely tempted to confront the West with unflinching hostility.

The usefulness of revolutionary violence, and a militant stance against the West in mobilizing peasant support for revolutionary leadership, can become a dangerous addiction, however, and the thought of Mao Tse-tung may be of less value in confronting the positive task of modernization than in managing a successful colonial revolution. The skills and abilities required for successful guerilla warfare may not necessarily be the same as those needed to build a modern nation. Yet, inevitably, the characteristics developed in conditions of revolutionary warfare will be carried over into the peacetime task of modernization. Then, the virtues of revolutionary warfare may become defects in modernizing leadership. As a French journalist notes: "Cuba is discovering today that revolutionary enthusiasm can replace neither organization nor technique, and that the laws of industrial output are inescapable." [21]

The attempt to make the revolutionary enthusiasm of a colonial war, or a guerilla resistance movement, the chief motor of modernization may have other liabilities. The kinds of charismatic leaders who have emerged from guerilla resistance movements depend heavily on a political leadership which earned its spurs through military command. In Yugoslavia, a popular joke is that the only skill of too many of the country's Communist leaders is the ability to tote a rifle. In other words, the chief criterion for advancement and positions of power in Yugoslavian politics is still one's status with the Partisans during World War II. And the Communist Party, many feel, is dominated by old men who live on the glorious memories of the old days of resistance against the Nazis, and have nothing further to contribute to the development of Yugoslavia as a modern nation. David Wilson puts the matter very tersely: "Charisma . . . is parsimonious in administrative skill." [22]

And yet it becomes very difficult for revolutionary leaders to give up these ideals of collective egalitarianism and militancy; for they are the virtues which mobilized the peasants, submerged differences, and created a practical and successful nationalism. "Personal and fragile parties need crises in order to maintain their following." [23] The temptation becomes great to maintain an atmosphere of crisis, to keep alive memories of hostility and resentment toward the Western world, to maintain a climate of rancor, to stress the existence of foreign enemies, and to use the threat of foreign domination as the continuing justification for one-party rule, for an atmosphere of totalitarian discipline, and for personal dictatorship. "A Sukarno *needs* a Dutch 'threat' in Western New Guinea; a Nasser *needs* the 'menace' of Zionism; a Castro *needs* American 'imperialism' in Latin America. At this point, nationalist unity may instead of breaking up into the disunity of democracy, be turned into the unity of totalitarianism." [24] Those leaders of the emergent world who have risen through revolutionary wars seek eagerly for a kind of politics of confrontation with the Western societies, not only because they have become convinced that such an approach will serve the development needs of their fledgling nations, but because the politics of crisis maintain the circumstances which hold the society together in the face of a common enemy. Frequently, this kind of leadership in the emergent world seems to welcome a climate of hostility toward Western nations, since these nations thereby conveniently play the role of Goldberg, the imaginary revolutionary whose fictitious depredations in Orwell's *1984* provided the justification for the continuing totalitarian rule of the single party elite. "The social tensions which modernization and industrialization produce everywhere and which in Europe were necessarily turned inward, resulting in conflicts dividing societies, are, in underdeveloped countries, largely turned outward. Instead of blaming each other for the difficulties growing out of modernization, the various social strata all blame the colonial power." [25]

Today, the West still maintains a near-monopoly of both the technical expertise and the surplus capital resources which could be used most effectively to modernize the emergent world. Memory of the colonial experience and the ambivalence of feelings of inferiority make it unlikely, however, that the emergent world can accept Western aid graciously. When that aid is granted conditionally, that is, in return for various kinds of concession to United States military and economic interests, for instance, the temptation becomes overwhelming, in the emergent world, to achieve modernization without Western aid, and without attachment to the "Western" camp in the cold war; that is, to achieve modernization out of its own resources. The classic example for such a transformation is the communist revolution in the Soviet Union, which modernized Russia without giving any hostages to the West.

5 · *The Intelligentsia's Struggle Against Western Culture*

The intelligentsia is seeking, in effect, to modernize its society, but without acknowledging any sense of inferiority, or the superiority of the modern way of life which it is adopting, and which is associated with the arrogant Westerner. The intelligentsia feels compelled to maintain a defiant attitude, not only toward the Western powers themselves, but toward Western culture and Western values. Such defiance appears necessary, not only because the West is identified as a colonial oppressor, but because an exaggerated defiance of the overwhelming power of Western civilization, an exaggerated expression of national pride, seem necessary to express a sense of self-identity. Rejection of Western culture and an insistence on reviving certain indigenous cultural characteristics, in fact, the general anti-Western climate of the underdeveloped world, is a measure of the strength of Western influence, not of its weakness; of a strength with which the emergent cultures can hardly cope. In Africa, intellectual leaders seek to eradicate the French and English languages, despite the enormous practical advantages to be derived from their use in administration and in absorbing the technical expertise of the West; despite the fact that most of these intellectuals were themselves educated in Europe, and use these languages fluently; despite the fact that the use of French or English is frequently the only common denominator among a variety of different tribes. A Turkish journalist who was a close and sympathetic observer of the Algerian revolution reminds us that "Colonel Boumedienne never speaks French." [26] Colonel Boumedienne came to power in Algeria after superseding a number of other FLN leaders. His ability to outlast his colleagues reflected his greater radicalism, that is, his greater determination to assert an Algerian identity in the face of French domination. Algeria, of course, was compelled to wage a bitter, eight-year war to wrest its national independence from France. The demand, the need, in fact, for a defiant attitude toward French culture is an inevitable product of that conflict. In 1961 when Ferhat Abbas was ousted as president of the Provisional Algerian Government, one charge made against him was that he spoke Arabic badly. Boumedienne, by contrast, was one of the few leaders of the FLN fully educated in Arabic instead of French.[27]

This rejection is more than simple pique at Western colonialism. It is *necessary* for the psychological health of leaders who need to feel an identity with their own culture, who need to resist the rootlessness which results from becoming completely Westernized, who need to believe that their African, or Moslem, or Asian identity is not worthless; who need to feel that their society has an identity of its own, and that their own existence is not simply a pale reflection of Western culture.

The reactionary tendencies created by an assertion of traditional identity, the tendency to seek modernization by revolutionary enthusiasm and anti-Western militancy, rather than by the rational application of programs of development, are further enhanced by the personal anxieties and personal insecurities of the members of the intelligentsia themselves. Intensely politicized, trained in skills and attitudes appropriate to a modern society, but living in a pre-modern world, they develop a vested interest in a modernizing process which will give their own training, their own background, their own political education, personal meaning. In Africa, in India, in Latin America, a system of modern education creates modernized elites with no opportunities in their own countries. These elites turn to politics, not only to accelerate the modernization which they have come to view as essential to their own society, not only to create a modern state in which they can function, but also for what Lucian Pye calls its "psychologically therapeutic powers." [28] That is, politics provides a means of expression for innovating talents and energies in societies where the hostility of colonial masters or the apathy of traditional rulers has effectively bottled them up. In fact, we might define a successful revolutionary leader, in the emergent world, as one whose personal anxieties, search for self-identity, whose demand for dignity and status, whose sense of outrage and shame at his personal conditions express the larger dissatisfaction of the entire society. This search for personal therapeutic powers, however, may, at times, work at cross purposes with the society's need for rational development.

The ability of the intelligentsia to identify with the needs of its society is rendered difficult by the gap which the education of the intellectuals inevitably creates between them and the masses. Even those intellectuals who have seen modernization as a weapon to be used against the West, and who therefore are capable of expressing the frustration and resentment, as well as the groping for material advancement and national dignity, of their own people, are separated by a tremendous gap from the mass of their own people. These intellectuals, aware of the need for economic growth and industrialization to solve the problems of their societies, aware of the difficulties of modernization, aware of the tremendous poverty and backwardness of their own people, ashamed of the inadequacy of their own culture, but fired by a sense of national pride and indignation, become, inevitably, the bureaucrats of an authoritarian political system, of what John Kautsky calls the totalitarianism of the intellectuals.[29]

Despite the gap between the intelligentsia and the masses, and despite the potential inertia and apathy of the peasants, the intellectual leadership of the modern emergent world cannot ignore its own people in the way that modernizing leadership could ignore the peasant masses in Europe in early modern times. In the emergent world, modernizing leadership must cope with a mass following increasingly dissatisfied with many aspects of tradition, and demanding a better life immediately. Modern communications bring awareness to the masses of the underdeveloped world of the possibilities of a richer and freer world. Knowledge of other peoples, of other ways, particularly of the wealth and power of Westerners, breaks down the sacrosanct character of tradition, and creates that revolution of rising expectations we discussed in the last chapter. Pressure for change brings to power a modernizing leadership which promises to satisfy the demands of the masses, and to break the cake of custom.

Unlike their counterparts of an earlier day in the West, the intellectual leaders of the emergent world must achieve modernization against a background of demands for immediate results from a mass following aware of the inadequacy of tradition, but not always willing or able to support a program of rapid modernization. "The first result of the drive for economic development may be a tougher lot for the very people for whom the new regime was brought into power—a fact which is unlikely to increase the masses' esteem for the regime." [30] No such pressure for immediate results was exerted on the modernizing leadership of the West. This pressure increases further the need for the leaders of the emergent world to accomplish modernization without delay.

An understanding of these various dilemmas will enable us to understand the fact that the emergent nations, in the past, have had a double standard in their relations with the United States and the Soviet Union—not so much because the Soviet Union did not engage in imperial activities, or because they believed that racial prejudice did not exist in the Soviet Union, as because, in a sense, the Soviet Union was viewed as one of *them.* The Soviet Union achieved the transformation from backwardness to modern power in conditions approximating those confronting the emergent world, in the face of a similar kind of Western hostility and Western assumption that these simple muzhiks could not possibly understand the intricacies of Western technology; and they achieved this transformation without becoming a client state of the West. The Soviet Union becomes the focal point of the dreams of glory of many of the intelligentsia in the emergent world.

What was true of the Soviet Union, of course, has become even more true of China, for the very success of the Soviet Union tends to alienate it from the struggling peoples of the poor nations. The Soviet Union has arrived, whereas China is still in the throes of transformation. The success or failure of China becomes a symbolic test of their own ability to achieve the same goal. The appeal of the two great Communist giants, however, is not to be interpreted as some kind of political or propaganda "victory" in the emergent world. The appeal of the Soviet Union and China is the product of historical circumstances which are, by their nature, irreversible.

We should err considerably if we concluded that our task was to combat the influence of the Soviet Union, and that of other Communist states, in the emergent world. For not only is that appeal rooted in historical conditions which we cannot change, but one problem of that world is an excess of Western influence, rather than a lack of it. What would simplify the task of African and Asian leaders would be more Western capital assistance and technical aid, granted with no political or military strings attached, and accompanied by a general reduction of Western presence, and of Western influence. The worst course of action we can take is to interpret the endemic anti-Western attitudes of the emergent world as an indication of the need for more Western cultural influence and penetration. For what threatens the emergent world is not an insidious, foreign "communist" take-over at the expense of the West, but the crushing weight of Western domination. The shrillness and virulence of anti-Western nationalism in the emergent world is a measure of the strength of that suffocating embrace, rather than of either the skill of Soviet agents or the ineptness of our own propaganda.

For this reason those intellectuals who seek to solve their personal problems by joining the world of Western civilization, thereby, in effect, by escaping their own world and seeking refuge in the West, cannot act effectively as leaders in the underdeveloped world, for their personal solution does not express in any way a solution possible for the mass of their own people. These intellectuals gradually become completely Westernized; that is, they come to view their own people and their own culture as inescapably inferior; they value their own individual ability to escape their background of poverty and backwardness, and shun all the characteristics which might identify them with their own inferior culture. Their cultural identity is finally transferred altogether to the Western world, and their political allegiance to the colonial power, or to a dominant Western power, whose agent, in effect, they become. In short, they cross the "color" line and attempt to join, individually, the superior Western world.

As a consequence, one might establish as a rule of thumb that a genuine, popular, national leader in the emergent world probably cannot be pro-Western to any great degree. A pro-Western leader in the underdeveloped world is very likely to be a deracinated intellectual, without effective ties to his own people. For that reason, our search for strong pro-Western national leaders in places like Vietnam tends to be unreal. Such a pro-Western orientation probably implies an acceptance of the role of the emergent society prescribed by the philosophy of the white man's burden. And in fact, the only actively "pro-Western" leaders we have been able to find in Asia, for instance, are military puppets, like the regimes in Saigon, Seoul, and Taipei, clients of the American military, whose power would collapse without American aid; military dictators with very little support from their own people, not because their rule is authoritarian, but because they are either unable or unwilling to provide a satisfactory solution to the dilemma of modernization and Western domination in their societies.

A genuine *national* leadership, expressing the needs and aspirations of the emergent societies, must establish as its chief goal not the moral imperative of becoming civilized, that is of shedding its own presumed savagery and moral inferiority, but the political imperative of becoming powerful, that is, of shedding its disorganization and weakness in order to throw out the arrogant Westerner. And it blames the weakness and powerlessness of the society not on any inherent inferiority of the people, but on the imperialism of the West, combined with the willingness of a Westernized native elite to betray its own people to the foreign invader. Although such a picture of reality is vastly oversimplified and obscures the ambiguous position of the intellectual, it is the kind of analysis likely to be made by the intelligentsia in the emergent world, and likely to rally the support of the society. This likelihood becomes certainty when the West responds to this analysis by acting the paternalistic role of imperial benefactor.

The Western world in general, and the United States in particular, must be prepared to accept a considerable amount of anti-Western nationalism for a long time to come in the emergent societies. Injured reactions of wounded national pride on our part, complaints that the people of Asia and Africa *should* love us, and are ungrateful not to do so, will merely make the dilemmas we have been examining unbearable; they will increase the anti-Western bias of the intelligentsia, force them to resolve their ambivalent attitudes through militant, anti-Western attitudes which will make the advanced world the scapegoat for all the problems of emergent nations.

In summary, the character of the intelligentsia will tend to create an authoritarian pattern of modernization, partly because of its alienation from its own people, combined with an even stronger alienation from the world of advanced nations, partly because its impatience to catch up with the West will make large-scale manipulation of people very tempting. The experience of colonialism, combined with the relative weakness of the emergent world, greatly reduces the possibility that these societies can accept modernization under Western auspices, or at the cost of accepting Western tutelage, or continued Western domination. Overt hostility from the advanced world will drive the emergent world to the desperate expedient of going it alone. Going it alone, of course, means a transformation out of the society's own resources, through a gigantic effort of mass discipline, sacrifice, and effort, in which modernization is paid for out of the hides of laboring peasant masses. Going it alone, in short, means a communist transformation of the underdeveloped world. The temptations to go it alone are enormously increased, of course, by Western paternalistic attitudes, by attempts at Western interference and domination, and become irresistible in the face of active, military opposition by the advanced nations, as occurred in Algeria, and as is now occurring in Vietnam.

5

The Struggle for

Economic Development

I · *The Burden of Imperialism*

THE PRESENCE IN THE CONTEMPORARY WORLD OF THE AD-
vanced Western societies, particularly the United States, creates
economic pressures in the emergent nations which do not permit
the luxury of a gradual, relaxed economic development; pressures
which did not exist for those Western societies which pioneered the
transformation of modernization. For the developed societies, in
pursuing their own goals, constantly and inevitably intervene in the
affairs of the less developed societies. Colonialism was the most extreme form of such intervention, but even with the gradual termi-
nation of Western political control, the continued preponderance of
economic power among the developed countries is a constant temptation to further intervention and manipulation.

Economic intervention is associated primarily with the dynamic and aggressive character of Western capitalism, particularly
of United States business enterprise. Western business, during the
great era of imperialism, established dominant economic positions
throughout the non-Western world, positions which the West is reluctant to yield. Although the Western presence produced consider-

able material advancement in the emergent societies, the economic activities of the West have always been premised on the assumption that the economic development of the emergent world would remain within confines and limits defined by the economic interests of the advanced nations. As a result, the emergent societies not only must seek economic development in an international context dominated by much more powerful economies, but are confronted, in many cases, with the basic problem of achieving independence from Western control of their economic life.

As a result, the factors of international economic life are weighted heavily against the new nations in a way which could never be true about the Western economies at the time of their development. Benjamin Higgins, in his monumental work on economic development, summarizes four factors adversely affecting the emergent world in international trade. First, "there is a long-run tendency for the *terms* of trade to turn against producers of raw materials and foodstuffs"; second, exports tend to be concentrated in one commodity; third, markets for these exports are highly unstable; fourth, "long run trends in patterns of consumption lead to a deteriorating *balance* of trade for underdeveloped countries." [1]

The economies of the underdeveloped world are, by definition, producers of raw materials and foodstuffs; it is partly this condition which defines them as underdeveloped. The Western economies were also, at one point, producers of raw materials and foodstuffs. That stage in their economic development, however, could not have the same significance that it has for the contemporary emergent world, for these societies must establish patterns of trade with societies which are already developed, highly specialized, tremendously wealthy, and largely producers of industrial and finished goods. The Western economies never faced this set of economic circumstances. Producers of raw materials and foodstuffs are at a disadvantage if they must operate in an international context of already developed economies. Such societies represent what Raul

Prebisch, the Argentinian economist, and a champion of radical economic reform in the emergent world, calls peripheral economies; as he says, "the trading of primary commodities against manufactured goods" is working increasingly against the development of backward areas.[2] Most economic observers make the same point, that the terms of trade have deteriorated steadily against the interests of the producers of primary commodities, that is, the emergent nations.

This deteriorating pattern of trade is aggravated by the fact that such primary exports tend to be concentrated in a single commodity. The classic example of this type of concentration, and the one most familiar to Americans, is the one-crop economy of the Latin American nations. Petroleum represents 98 per cent of the value of the exports of Venezuela; coffee over 70 per cent of the exports of Brazil, and from 85 to 90 per cent of the exports of El Salvador and Colombia; copper 65 per cent of the exports of Chile; bananas are virtually the only export of Guatemala, and their marketing is completely monopolized by the United Fruit Company.[3] The same was true of sugar for the Cuban economy before the Castro revolution. Dudley Seers remarks that as a consequence Cuba, in 1958, despite pockets of modernism, and the existence of a small, privileged, wealthy minority, was *not* a developed economy. "The revolutionary government took over an economy that was structurally unsound. It depended excessively on exports of a single, not very promising crop."[4] Higgins concludes: "Virtually all Latin American countries present the same picture of one to half-a-dozen commodities accounting for well over half the total value of exports."[5]

Undeveloped societies are faced with a pattern of international economic life weighted heavily against their development needs. Hla Mynt summarizes the factors in the unfavorable terms of trade for the emergent world in this way: their concentration on single commodities results in a lack of flexibility in readjusting to changes in world prices; they are unable to switch to other exports; and they lack a home market to absorb their own production, which depends almost entirely on sales in the world market.[6]

Besides unfavorable terms of trade and concentration of export markets for their commodities, the developing societies face an unfavorable balance of trade with the developed world. The demand for their primary commodities continually lags behind their need for the industrial goods of the advanced nations. As a result, the economic gap between the wealth of developed and undeveloped nations is greater today than it was twenty-five years ago.

This widening gap is crucial, for the relative economic weakness of the underdeveloped nations is one factor which prevents them from controlling their own economic destinies. In addition to being poor and weak, the economies of the emergent nations are frequently dominated by the advanced Western nations. These nations, for a number of reasons, are not willing to see the emergent world achieve genuine economic independence. As a result, one basic goal of the emergent societies must be to gain control of their own economic lives.

Despite considerable material achievements during the era of Western imperialism, the economic development of the emergent world was at best an accidental by-product of the pursuit of Western economic interests, at worst, the result of a deliberate neo-mercantilism in which the non-Western world was assigned the role of economic colony to complement the economic needs of the advanced nations. The Western powers built up an infrastructure of economic development in the emergent world, but this task was carried out primarily to facilitate their own exploitation of the economic resources of Asia, Africa, and Latin America. Even when such Western achievements as public health and education were motivated by genuine humanitarianism, Western assistance was seldom meant to end the dependent colonial relationship, or to create independent economies. "It is true enough that not one of the western colonial powers laid the foundations of self-sustaining economic growth in their dependencies." [7]

Western economic activities in the developing societies of the emergent world have been motivated primarily by a search for individual profits, rather than by any conscious plan to help the emergent societies develop modern economies. As a result, the underdeveloped world is dotted with islands of modernism, controlled by Western financial interests, which contribute very little to the economic development of the whole society; the preservation of which, in fact, actually retards economic development. In Latin America the concentration of Western financial interests in extractive operations and the development of raw materials contributed heavily to the preservation of a static social and economic pattern, impervious to change, for the control of mines and single-crop agricultural operations was in the hands of Western financial interests, allied to powerful native elites in the underdeveloped societies. This concentration of economic power prevented the development of a diversified and independent economy. Such islands of modernism contribute little to the development of the society. The existence of a highly modern oil industry in Venezuela, for instance, is no indication that any real economic development is occurring in that country, likely to transform it into a modern society, or to produce self-sustaining growth for the benefit of the society. On the contrary, these islands of modernism indicate that the economic life of the country is in alien hands.

It is because the advanced Western nations were able to gain control of the economic life of much of the emergent world during the great era of imperialism that they have been able to keep these societies under the curse of monoculture. The advanced economies have encouraged the production of single commodities which complement the economic needs of the developed world. The inability of the emergent societies to break the curse of monoculture has been due to the fact that their economies are dominated by Western nations.

A notorious example of this kind of pressure has been the United States' economic policy toward Latin America, particularly in Cuba before Castro, where "the United States dominated the economic life of the island . . . by overtly and covertly preventing any dynamic modification of the island's one-crop economy." [8] The Cuban economy became wholly dependent on the export of sugar to the American market. Further, the economic institutions of Cuba were largely owned and controlled by a combination of American businessmen and a small Cuban elite, based in Havana, whose personal political and economic fortunes were tied entirely to the fate of American business interests. Eventually, the possibility of sugar as the basis for expanding the Cuban economy was exhausted: "the problem was that after the end of the sugar boom, a structural transformation of agriculture was required if the economic resources were to be fully employed. Yet this transformation did not take place." [9]

It did not take place because the Cuban people did not control their own economy; and although Cuba's heavy dependence on sugar meant economic stagnation for the island as a whole, American business interests and their allies in the Cuban aristocracy, who controlled the economy, and who were quite satisfied with its returns to them, did not allow the kind of economic reforms which were instituted eventually by Castro. "American power was consistently deployed and used to support conservative and even reactionary Cuban governments that thwarted or repressed any and all efforts to effect fundamental social and economic changes." [10]

In Guatemala, in 1954, Jacobo Arbenz attempted to challenge this kind of economic imperialism, and instituted reforms which presaged the Castro revolution in Cuba. The United States accused the Guatemalan government of communism and, through the activities of the C.I.A., overthrew the Arbenz regime. This intervention brought the point home clearly to the Latin American countries that they would not be allowed to manage their own economies, that we reserved the right to impose our own definition on Latin America of what was good for their economic life. "Guate-mala . . . could not accept the view that any government in Latin America which touches the interests of foreign companies that con-trol basic resources in Latin America will be called Communist, will be accused of jeopardizing continental security, and thus will be threatened with foreign intervention." [11] Guatemala, of course, was compelled to accept such a view as a result of the superior power of the United States. The exercise of this superior power, however, convinces the Latin Americans that we will not tolerate the development of economic independence in their societies. To the Latin Americans, the intervention of the United States in Gua-temala had a significance quite other than the official justification provided by the government of the United States: "The real truth, as they see it, involves intervention by Washington to protect the United Fruit Company, which was undergoing nationalization." [12]

The same point can be made about the policy of all the ad-vanced nations toward the emergent world. "The underlying rea-son for French unwillingness to force change in Algeria lay in Alge-ria's economic dependence on France, and the benefits which almost everyone (except the Moslems) derived from such depend-ence: right up to 1944, the idea of Algeria's industrialization was opposed because it would provide France with unfair competi-tion." [13] And even today, when Algeria has established its political independence, France's attempt to continue to dominate its eco-nomic life led the Algerian Minister of Industry to exclaim, in a re-cent interview: "One has seen French bureaucrats attempt to direct Algerian investments into products which will not compete with French industry." [14] Throughout Africa, little effort was made be-fore World War II to promote meaningful economic development in the European colonies. A notoriously bad example was Belgian rule in the Congo, where the Belgians deliberately suppressed any attempt at economic development which would threaten their own economic interests in developing the mineral resources of this great African region.

The same colonial economic policies were pursued in Asia. "Colonial policy in most of the Asian countries did not permit development of the secondary and tertiary sectors in the colonies themselves. Where domestic entrepreneurship appeared in the 'Western' sector, it was usually discouraged." [15] French policy in Indochina offers a striking example of this practice of discouraging indigenous economic development, and of emphasizing the usefulness of the economic resources of the colonial area for the advanced economy of the mother country. "Vietnamese landowners who tried to get a foothold in industry and big business were generally kept out of the French colonial monopolies. By and large, Vietnamese were excluded from both the control and the profits of the modern economic enterprises which the French brought to Indo-China." [16]

The advanced Western nations have the capital resources, the technical expertise, and the political power to exploit the economic potential of the emergent world, as in fact they are still doing in Latin America, and in many parts of Africa and Asia. Such economic development must be inevitably for the profit and advantage of the Western economies, not only in the sense that profits are funneled away from the people and into the pockets of Western businessmen, but that the economic development of the society is distorted and twisted to fit the economic needs of the advanced nations.

Richard Barnet summarizes the way the international economy is viewed by revolutionary leaders in the emergent world in these words: "The rich nations are getting richer at the expense of the poor . . . because the developed countries, particularly the United States, have the political power to impose terms upon the underdeveloped world which are profitable for the rich and impoverishing for the poor." [17] In view of the pattern of international economics we have just described, this analysis appears difficult to challenge. The advanced societies have the economic power to freeze the underdeveloped societies into a permanent pattern of concentrated exports, retarded development, and control of their economies by foreign interests.

The determination of Western powers to keep the emergent world in a dependent economic relationship has meant not only opposition to development that might eventuate in genuine economic independence, but also opposition to internal changes of the social and political structure that would facilitate such independent development. Western businessmen, as a result, support traditional aristocratic regimes favorable to their economic interests, and oppose changes which would dissolve the traditional status quo. In Latin America American policy has opposed the kind of social revolution which would break up traditional patterns of land tenure which retard economic development. Edmundo Flores, a professor of agricultural economics at the National University of Mexico, and an expert in land reform policy, contends that the Alliance for Progress was "not designed to put into effect real, fundamental, irreversible reforms," and that American financial aid through the Alliance for Progress has had the opposite result of *preventing* the kinds of internal reforms which might produce genuinely independent economies in Latin America.[18]

Raul Prebisch, the Argentinian economist, argues that if genuine economic development is to take place in Latin America, wealth must be taken out of the hands of the privileged elites, the traditional aristocracies. These elites are not interested in economic development, and spend their share from foreign economic enterprise in patterns of extravagant consumption. What Latin America needs is investment of economic profits in Latin America itself for the development of a domestic market, and self-sustaining economic growth. Such economic development is not possible as long as profits are either remitted back to the advanced societies which control the economy, or concentrated in the hands of a privileged aristocracy which opposes social and political reforms which threaten its power and privileges.[19]

Instead of developing a class of native capitalists, Western economic interests were concerned primarily with supporting an aristocracy of luxury consumers who would not be likely to challenge Western economic domination. In many places, as a result of deliberate Western policy, "the original native distaste for commercial pursuits was reinforced by European colonial policies." [20] And when the Western nations gave up colonialism as a viable technique, they depended increasingly on the support of these indigenous elites, which shared in the profits of economic exploitation, but which neither contributed to the economic development of the society nor challenged Western domination.

2 · *The Colored Man's Burden*

Many people have argued, since the publication of Hobson's classic work on imperialism in 1902, that imperialism does not pay. And when measured against the over-all losses and gains for the societies of the Western world, perhaps this argument is valid. Whether imperialism pays or not, in purely economic terms, however, is a question which we need not answer here. For the advanced societies have believed that the kind of economic domination described in this chapter, and termed sometimes imperialism, is not only beneficial to their interests, but necessary to the kind of economic world order they desire. It is this belief, regardless of its economic validity and accuracy, which has motivated Western actions. In addition, there is no doubt that private business interests have made fortunes out of the exploitation of resources in the non-Western world; and such interests continue to exert great influence on government policy. In the United States, for instance, American business enterprise identifies the national interest with its own economic activities, declaring, in effect, that what is good for General Motors is good for the country. The governments of most advanced nations have tended to accept this definition, partly because they believe that it is part of their responsibility to promote the private economic interests of their own countrymen, partly because they feel that economic imperialism does serve the national welfare. As O. Edmund Clubb, Jr., reminds us, "there is little likelihood of the President's proposing to Congress that we should open the protected U.S. market to the competition of Indian cotton goods, Peruvian ceramics, or Venezuelan petroleum, not to mention Chinese hog bristles or Cuban sugar." [21] In fact, most so-called foreign aid consists of subsidization, by American taxpayers, of United States business interests; that is, such foreign aid is in the form of credits to emergent nations to purchase goods for which American businessmen are seeking a market. Such foreign aid, although it produces some relief from the misery of economic backwardness, does nothing to cure the disease.

In addition, Western investment in the emergent world, as we saw in the last chapter, is not exclusively an economic investment. It is also a psychological investment in the image of the white man's superiority and magnanimity, an investment even more difficult to yield than the economic one, and one which provides the moral justification for the attempt to maintain a Western economic empire throughout the world. A French colonial official expressed this attitude in 1930, in a speech celebrating the centenary of France's "civilizing" mission in Algeria, when he asserted: "The hypothesis of Algerian independence . . . is inconceivable." [22]

The advanced world cannot tolerate putting down the white man's burden because that burden was taken up, originally, in all Western countries, to satisfy some profoundly important feelings of cultural and racial superiority among Westerners, whose very sincerity in taking up that burden is what makes it so difficult for them to put it down today. It becomes very difficult for the Western world to sever its ties of authority in the emergent world, not only because of the economic value of these ties, but because of the psychological investment which the West has made into the image of the white man's burden. These ties have been just as strong for the United States, which did not build a large political colonial empire, but which established a far-flung economic empire, which was filled, perhaps more than any other Western nation, with a sense of messianic, self-righteous mission toward the rest of the world, and which established paternalistic ties, particularly in Latin America, which, as the Cuban experience demonstrates, have been extremely difficult to sever. "What was good for Americans was also good for foreigners. Humanitarian concern was thus reinforced by hard headed economic requirements." [23] Our willingness to help the emergent societies is predicated on the assumption that they can *never* get along without us, because of their essential inferiority.

Our reactions to Castro, for instance, cannot be explained simply in terms of an objective evaluation of our national interests, even defined in economic terms. Even if we can point to specific American economic interests which were injured by Castro's actions in Cuba, these interests cannot account for the tremendous popular revulsion among large masses of the American people, which is both unaware of, and unconcerned with, the economic issues between Castro and the American sugar companies. The revulsion of the American people toward Castro is not the revulsion of an injured pocketbook. It is the revulsion of a people wounded in their vanity. We cannot stand the fact that the Cuban people should no longer regard us as their indispensable tutors. Even less can we stand the idea that Cuba might succeed without us. The American press "reports only the negative aspects—the economic difficulties, the purges of individuals from the government, the exodus of Cubans to the United States—and remains silent about everything else. . . . It consistently publishes as unchallenged fact the most absurd rumors that emanate daily from the embittered Cuban exile community." [24]

Our tutelage of Cuba was never meant to produce a "free" Cuba, in the sense of an economy that could function independently in the modern world. We certainly never felt toward Batista, who was a brutal dictator, the kind of pathological hatred that we feel for Castro. Our policy toward Cuba has depended on a strong feeling among our people that Cuba *cannot* get along without our tutelage. And our hatred of Castro is a measure of our outrage; an outrage so great that we refuse to even acknowledge the objective fact of his survival.

Much the same kinds of feeling of wounded conceit motivated French President de Gaulle's reaction to the decision of Guinea's President Sékou-Touré, in 1958, to reject a dependent partnership with France within the French community, and to demand complete independence. The French, in arrogant fury, "made the break as painful as possible, taking with them archives and telephones, stripping the bank of currency and diverting a rice ship on its way to Conakry." [25] Such a reaction was motivated primarily by a determination to demonstrate that Guinea could *not* get along without France. In the same way, and for the same reasons, the French policy of assimilation was a complete failure in Algeria, for it was based on the assumption of continued French superiority over the natives. The same policy also failed in Vietnam, and simply exacerbated native demands for genuine self-rule.

Belgian policy in the Congo, which was designed specifically to prevent participation by the Congolese in the development of their society, is summed up in "the monstrous slogan, 'no *elites,* no problems.'" Higher education was closed to the natives in the Belgian Congo until 1955, five years before independence.[26] British policies in Malaya before World War II indicate the same pattern. Although the Chinese were the backbone of the indigenous economic life of Malaya, the great majority were denied citizenship by British political authorities; they were without political rights or political power, and they were prevented from obtaining positions in the civil service. These discriminations were part of a deliberate British policy to suppress Chinese influence in Malaya, because the British recognized that the Chinese were sufficiently skillful, educated, and politically alert not to accept British domination indefinitely. Nor was this British opposition motivated by some kind of moral objection to communist organization of the Chinese community, since they equally repressed the attempts of the Kuom tang to organize the Chinese in Malaya.[27]

Western paternalism is everywhere based on "the two assumptions, familiar to aristocracies everywhere, that the backward masses, incapable of administering themselves and misgoverned by their own regimes, will receive a far better deal at the hands of their advanced overlords, and that they are primarily interested only in living their lives in peace and quiet with rising standards of welfare to be provided for them from above." [28] The United States has been more reluctant, perhaps, than any other Western society to give up these dreams of superiority, which, in this country, have a frankly racial basis. The very sincerity of Americans in helping the emergent world has frequently been based on an unwillingness to admit that colored peoples can stand as equals before the mighty United States. Our hostility to communist revolution in the emergent world, in fact, is based on the fact that such revolution is aimed expressly and specifically at breaking the pattern of Western paternalism. We insist that the emergent nations must transform themselves *our* way, through *our* tutelage; we prescribe that certain forms of development in the emergent nations are acceptable, and others are not.

The most fundamental economic demand of the emergent societies is independence, the right to manage and guide their own affairs and economic destinies, motivated by their own needs and the desire to produce genuine economic growth. In the context of the international economic situation we have just described, such a policy will be, inevitably, an anti-Western policy, aimed particularly against Western economic interests. During the great era of imperialism, Western business interests established a commanding position in the economic life of Asia, Africa, and Latin America. Western capital resources, technical skill, and political power make it unlikely that non-Western businessmen can wrest these dominant positions away from their Western counterparts in open and "free" economic competition.

As a result, the emergent nations may turn against Western capital and technical assistance, and drive out foreign economic factors, even when domestic capital is not available to replace Western financial investment, even when the seizure and alienation of foreign capital, as occurred in Cuba under Castro, and in Chile under Allende, involves incurring considerable economic risks. The emergent economies may be forced into such a course of action because their own economic independence, their ability to run their own affairs, is their most important goal; for without this ability to manage their own economies, they will not be able to achieve genuine economic development for the benefit of their own people.

Not only do the conditions of the emergent societies incline them to anti-Western attitudes, but their economic needs will force them into a policy of confiscation and nationalization of Western economic interests within their own societies. The emergent societies are forced to seize the capital resources of the West in their own societies, and to sacrifice the possibility of Western technical assistance, if such assistance carries with it the heavy price of continued Western domination and tutelage. Going it alone is preferable to a position of subservience and inferiority toward the West, not only for psychological reasons, but for the economic health of the developing societies. The militant attitudes created by Western economic paternalism are well summarized by the Algerian Minister of Industry, commenting on the future of Franco-Algerian economic cooperation: "We are no longer willing that Algeria be considered a satellite of the French economy. For us, the essential point is for France to admit that Algeria has come of age. If France is only willing to accept, to a certain degree, a dependent Algeria, then it is better for us to cut all ties." [29]

The climax of this process of challenge against Western paternalism, against Western economic domination, against the self-appointed "right" of the United States to intervene in the economic affairs of the emergent societies, will be the kind of revolution we usually label communist, of which the Castro revolution in Cuba is a typical example.

Such an anti-American policy as that produced by the Castro revolution is the inevitable result of the need to secure economic independence and break a pattern of dependency on an advanced Western world unwilling to accept the right of "colored" peoples to manage their own economic affairs. Castro is not anti-American because he is a communist. He became a communist because his reading of the needs of Cuban society was necessarily anti-American. His anti-Americanism is the expression of the fact that he represents a revolution aiming at genuine economic development and independence. Whether or not Castro adopts the label Communist or Marxist is considerably less relevant than the fact that everything we dislike about him, everything which would make him, in our eyes, a "communist," is what all the leaders of the emergent world may be forced to do sooner or later, if we insist on maintaining the existing pattern of international economics. Faced with the continued hostility of the West, particularly of the United States, to its economic independence, the emergent world may be compelled to achieve economic development out of its own resources, out of the mighty collective effort of its own people, in a desperate struggle which will recall, inevitably, the development of the Soviet Union and of China. It may be compelled, in fact, to adopt communism.

3 · *The Burden of Poverty*

In addition to the formidable obstacles created by the existence of a powerful Western world unwilling to recognize the legitimacy of its economic challenge, the emergent world faces a number of other severe obstacles to development which did not exist in the West. The emergent world is denied one enormous advantage enjoyed by the Western economies during their period of modernization, the availability of a frontier. In his classic *The Great Frontier,*

Walter Webb explains the history of the dynamic economic expansion of the entire Western world since the sixteenth century by the existence of a frontier. Webb defines the frontier as all the new lands which became available for the exploitation of European societies, what he calls the Metropolis, as a result of the Age of Discovery. The frontier, as Webb defines it, embraces the entire non-Western world. The non-Western world provided surplus resources which had been either virtually untouched, as in the New World or Africa, or had been exploited only to a very limited extent, as in Asia and the Far East. Webb suggests that the great economic expansion of the West was made possible by its ability to exploit these surplus resources. In short, the West did not have to achieve economic expansion solely out of its own resources; the task of primitive capital accumulation was greatly facilitated by the possibility of accumulating enormous profits in the overseas world.[30]

Webb believes that the frontier was a windfall, an accidental good fortune, without which the Western societies could never have developed their economies in the spectacular fashion which has marked Western capitalism since the sixteenth century. The frontier was *"inherently a vast body of wealth without proprietors."*[31] More accurately, it was a vast body of wealth which its indigenous proprietors had never exploited, and which the Western nations were strong enough to wrest from their hands. Describing land, labor, and capital resources in Europe in 1500, Webb concludes: "It is inconceivable that this many people, confined to this small area, could by any stretch of their genius or by any invention they might make produce the wealth and create the boom which they enjoyed during the four following centuries . . . The frontier upset the ratios by supplying a *surplus* of land and a *surplus* of capital."[32]

These surpluses are defined as windfalls, which Webb divides into two categories, primary and secondary windfalls. Primary windfalls were economic wealth that was to be had for the asking, as it were. The most important such primary windfalls were silver, gold, furs, and finally slaves; these were commodities that Westerners could simply gather up, collect with virtually no economic investment. Secondary windfalls included agricultural commodities and other raw materials, which required some investment of effort and capital; but such windfalls as the plantation economies of the New World, the cattle ranch industry, and the great agricultural boom of the American West were based on labor and land costs infinitely lower than would have obtained in the Metropolis, that is, in Europe.[33]

Webb concludes that "this sudden, continuing, and ever-increasing flood of wealth precipitated on the Metropolis a business boom such as the world has never known before and probably never can know again." [34] For this boom was produced by a unique conjunction which the emergent world cannot hope to reproduce; that is, the societies of Europe were presented with fantastic economic opportunities at a time when they were already well organized, partly developed, and equipped with a considerable accumulation of technical skills. They were placed in contact with a world either uninhabited or ruled by cultures insufficiently well organized to resist Western penetration. In the meeting of Europe and the non-European world, from the sixteenth to the nineteenth century, the balance of power was heavily weighted in favor of Europe.

Such opportunities do not exist for the economies of the emergent nations; few weak, undeveloped societies, or open, uninhabited spaces are now available to them as a frontier. They must not only modernize out of their own resources, but these resources are already heavily mortgaged to the Western economic powers, and trade patterns, as we have seen, work against their economic development. Modernization out of their own resources means that their primary task is the transformation of their traditional agricultures. Agriculture is their primary economic activity, and it is out of agriculture that they must produce the surplus for economic growth; but a number of factors will make it very difficult for the emergent societies to use their agricultural economies as a basis for economic development. The basic economic task of underdeveloped societies, if they are to modernize out of their own resources, is to overcome agricultural poverty, to transform their traditional agricultures into modern ones. The underdeveloped nations are not only poor because they lack large modern industries; they are also poor because many of them fail to produce enough food to feed their own populations, much less create surpluses for export. The contemporary emergent nations are faced with the problem of creating a modern economic structure, including a modern industrial sector, before they have been able to transform traditional agriculture. The West had the time to develop a highly productive agriculture and break the hold of the traditional manorial economy before confronting other aspects of modernization. The need for rapid results in the emergent world precludes this kind of gradual, piecemeal economic development.

Further, the emergent world is plagued with adverse natural conditions. Much of it lies within the tropic zone, and this has been the chief cause of its agricultural poverty. Tropical soils are ill suited for organized agriculture. The soil of Africa, of India, and of many parts of Latin America is not well suited to intensive farming. The pattern of rainfall in many places is inimical to efficient agriculture, with long dry seasons alternating with heavy rains, when excessive water leaches the land of necessary nutrients. The climate of tropic zones is ill suited to a rhythm of disciplined work and individual enterprise; and the tropics have long been cursed with a high incidence of endemic diseases.

The existence of other kinds of primary resources besides agricultural commodities, such as petroleum or metal ores, is of only limited value at the stage of economic development of most of the emergent nations. They do not yet possess the skills or capital resources to develop their potential energy resources. Not only are they not yet ready to develop resources outside of agriculture, but the development of these resources is frequently in the hands of outsiders, with adverse effects we have already noted.

For all these reasons, the emergent world will be drawn to the

Soviet Union as a model, will be drawn to communism. For the Soviet Union is the classic example of the very rapid creation of a modern industrial nation, starting from a traditional agricultural base. The forcing, collective methods of Soviet communism seem more appropriate to the traditional societies of the underdeveloped world than do the techniques which obtained, for instance, in American history.

The emergent nations face yet another problem spared the Western societies during their modernization, and that is the problem of population pressure. Western development occurred in a context of population growth sufficiently slow that increased productivity was able to stay ahead of increased population, yet sufficiently large to provide an expanding labor force for an expanding economy. This happy conjunction of economic development and limited population growth in the West was no more than a fortunate economic accident; the modernizing leadership did not deliberately plan population growth in order to maximize economic development. Certain demographic conditions proved highly appropriate in the West to economic development. What produced these conditions is difficult to estimate; it certainly had nothing to do with either the superior wisdom or the wise sexual continence of white Europeans and Americans. The windfall of the frontier certainly provided a very useful safety valve in skimming off surplus population. In any case, a fortuitous set of demographic factors created circumstances highly favorable to the development of the Western economies. "In many underdeveloped countries the initial favorable impact of industrial investment . . . was swamped by population growth in a way that did not occur in the currently advanced countries." [35] Although the demographic conditions of the emergent world are also accidental in the sense that they are not the result of deliberate planning, the accident of the population explosion was caused, specifically, by the intrusion of the Western world. The population explosion was triggered when the West introduced into the emergent world public health and public hygiene, and began the elimination of numerous diseases, all of which drastically lowered the death rate, while the traditional cultural pattern of these societies continued to be oriented to very high birth rates.

Undoubtedly the pressures of population growth, and the frustration inherent in the realization that the best laid plans for economic development are going awry because of unchecked population pressure, create further strong temptations for the use of authoritarian methods. The threat of population pressure in the emergent world enormously complicates the attempt to create surpluses out of agriculture. Not only are food surpluses constantly being consumed by unchecked population growth, but this growth increases the problem of rural unemployment. One way of transforming traditional agriculture is to adopt the techniques of the agricultural revolution in the West: that is, mechanization, and the use of large-scale productive methods not dependent on the utilization of a large labor force. Population pressure not only affects the food supply and the possibility of creating surpluses in agriculture, but it aggravates the social problems resulting from the dislocation of traditional rural populations. Rural underemployment, which is one of the basic problems of a traditional agriculture, will be further aggravated by the population explosion.

Population pressure moves the leadership of the emergent world in authoritarian directions, but not in the sense that it attempts to use direct political coercion to forcibly achieve birth control, although such methods may be attempted, and have been tried in China, for instance. Rather population pressure magnifies the problems of economic development, increases dramatically the sense of urgency, and greatly intensifies the internal tensions which would already be prevalent in a society in the throes of transition from traditional to modern. In the face of such problems, and filled with the need to succeed quickly, the leaders of the emergent world will be greatly tempted to turn to the kinds of forcing methods we associate with communism.

One further problem confronting the emergent world in achieving economic development is the tremendous gap between the skills and habits of people in traditional societies and those of the advanced industrial world. "Industry has come to the countries that are or were until recently underdeveloped as an import through colonialism rather than as a native growth." [36] As a result, modern industry is an alien, disruptive force to a degree far beyond anything that occurred in the West, where the machine arrived much more gradually, and was produced by Westerners themselves. In Europe many people were able to adjust gradually to a machine age which was created out of indigenous skills and values. In the emergent world the adjustment to industry involves bridging a cultural gap between the abilities of the peoples of the traditional societies and the needs of a modern machine economy far greater than was experienced in the West.

One of Thorstein Veblen's classic essays was concerned with the advantages of the late comer in industrial technology; Germany, for instance, benefited in her economic competition with England at the end of the nineteenth century, from the fact that she could take advantage of all the technical developments which England's pioneering efforts had made possible, and build her industrial plants according to the most modern methods, while England was saddled with an increasingly obsolete industrial plant, and committed to outmoded industrial techniques which were difficult to change rapidly. For the emerging nations, unfortunately, the role of late comer, far from presenting such advantages, means overcoming a cultural, educational, and intellectual gap of enormous dimensions. Industrial technology is so far removed from the patterns of skills, achievements, and values of the peoples of the emergent world that its modernity becomes a serious obstacle to its adoption rather than an advantage.

In facing these multiple difficulties, in seeking a successful great leap forward that will enable them to achieve economic development, the emergent societies will turn naturally to the model of Russia, a backward, tradition-bound society which achieved a rapid transformation from extreme weakness and poverty to great power and industrial productivity, which broke the bonds of a traditional agriculture and forged a modern economy without yielding any economic hostages to the advanced western world. But despite the appropriateness of the Soviet Union as a model, that model embodies to a certain extent a misleading historical lesson. "Russia in 1917 was not, like many under-developed countries today, overpopulated, nor did her industrialization really proceed without western aid: it began with the foreign capital accumulated under Tsarism." [37] In other words, Russia in 1917 was considerably more advanced than most of the underdeveloped countries of today are likely to be. She had a backlog of capital accumulation, as well as a certain amount of skills and expertise, both technical and administrative, which do not exist today in Asia or Africa. Russia was not completely outside the mainstream of Western development, and the Bolshevik leaders were part of the Western world in a way which is not true of most of the intelligentsia of the emergent world. Finally, Russia did not face some of the problems, particularly that of population pressure or completely undeveloped resources, that promise to cripple so many development efforts in the emergent world. In the Soviet Union "most of the preconditions for building an industrial base on the predominantly rural agricultural underpinnings had been met by the time the Soviets took power." [38] In all these ways the Russian experience holds out hopes that may be delusive. But if they are, the frustrations of the emergent world will thereby be increased, and the possibility of an even more painful and coercive development is likely to be the result.

If the Soviet Union is a somewhat misleading model, presenting ourselves as an alternative model, on the ground that we achieved tremendous economic growth with few of the more extremely painful experiences associated with the Soviet Union, and without giving up our constitutional democratic regime, is even more misleading. For this country was, as we indicated before, born free and rich; rich in natural resources, in human skills, in all the achievements of modern organization already reached in England. The societies of the emergent world cannot even approximate an experience like that of the United States, and our historical example will be of considerably less value to them in confronting modernization than the example of the Soviet Union. China, on the other hand, will increasingly appear as the most appropriate example, not as a result of an "ideological victory" for communism, but because China's experience is closest to that of the rest of the emergent world. Julius Nyerere, the President of Tanzania, summarizes this point in these words: "I've been telling my own people, 'We've got to change; we must mechanize, we must have better tools.' . . . This is the kind of thing China is doing. An ancient people, dealing with the difficulties of feeding seven hundred million people. The *stage* of their development is relevant to us." [39]

6

The Ideology of Revolution

1 · *Political Authoritarianism and*
Revolution from Above

IN THE FACE OF NUMEROUS OBSTACLES, INFINITELY GREATER THAN
any that faced the West, many of the leaders of the underdeveloped
world will adopt authoritarian, collective, planned solutions to
their problems. This kind of revolution from above will depend on
authoritarian techniques and considerable political and economic
discipline; it will produce one-party states, of which communism is
a typical example. "In all the new states, there is, in fact and in
theory, a widespread belief in the need for a higher concentration
of authority and a stronger medicine for the cure of parochialism,
disunity, and apathy." [1] Strong government initiative is a very
likely response to the multiple difficulties confronting the emergent
world. It is the means of breaking traditional patterns, of imposing
new patterns of modernization not yet fully accepted or understood, of overcoming "parochialism, disunity, and apathy." Political authoritarianism is the means by which the leaders of the new
nations can compel their peoples to accept the sacrifices necessitated by economic development.

138

Existing economic and social patterns in the emergent societies make it unlikely that they can generate enough capital for economic growth through voluntary savings and private initiative. Voluntary savings, no matter how induced, will not be adequate for the tremendous growth problems of underdeveloped societies. Rupert Emerson notes that the struggle to "accumulate capital from a base of poverty is a difficult task under any conditions," and concludes that to depend on voluntary savings is to expect too much from the peoples of the emergent world.[2]

In Latin America private capital has traditionally been invested in real estate, and much of the wealth of these societies is either concentrated in uneconomic, that is, unproductive enterprises, or in the hands of foreigners. As a result, "capitalism cannot be expected to develop in Latin America as it has historically developed in the United States."[3] Instead, a pattern of collective enterprise, motivated by a sense of collective, national sacrifice, is more likely, a pattern much closer to the experience of the Soviet Union than to what we traditionally define as capitalism in the West. For capitalism has meant, in the emergent world, the control of the economy by foreign factors. Because of the conditions we have been examining, the development of backward economies "cannot take place through the spontaneous interplay of . . . forces, as happened in the evolution of capitalism in the advanced countries."[4] This pressure for rational, deliberate planning to instigate development makes it likely that government, rather than private initiative, will play the major role in modernization. "Only centralized state power, only collectivist organization in some form, only government financing can bring in this generation so gigantic an economic transformation."[5]

Even W. W. Rostow, a fanatical proponent of free enterprise, observes that "governments must generally play an extremely important role in the process of building social overhead capital."[6] The responsibility of government in providing this social overhead capital will be tremendously increased, in the emergent world, by the magnitude of the tasks confronted. In addition, the peoples of the emergent world, although reluctant to accept the disciplines of modernization, are very eager to enjoy its material profits. Raul Prebisch summarizes the attitudes of the leadership of the emergent world, when he concludes: "The notion . . . that development takes place spontaneously, without a rational and deliberate effort to achieve it, has proved to be an illusion." [7]

The political leadership of the emergent world is also drawn to authoritarian methods by the fragility of the society's political and economic structures. The leaders recognize that only a process of rapid economic growth is likely, in the long run, to satisfy the demands of their own people. At the same time, they are much more painfully aware of the difficulties involved in such growth than their Western counterparts, who did not have themselves as a model and reminder, ever could have been. The intellectual leadership is quick to see the reluctance of the mass of the people to pay the price of modernization, and the tendency of that inertia to become a fatal obstacle to the creation of the kind of modernized state which alone can satisfy their demands. "Resenting the current sacrifices being imposed upon it for the sake of uncertain future gains and fearing the disintegration of its familiar world, this mass might bring about a serious reversal in the drive for development." [8] The intellectual leadership of the emergent world, exposed to modern ideas and to the reality of modern societies, aware of the difficult nature of creating modern institutions, of the possible resistance of its own people to the disciplines necessary to economic growth, and of the internal weaknesses and lack of cohesion of its own societies, will have difficulty resisting a managerial revolution from above. "Alarm over the gap between polity and society, and apprehension that the 'reactionary mass' of the traditional society will drag down the movement toward modernity, are major motives for the espousal of forms of government which concentrate authority and seek to establish complete consensus." [9] Rule by single parties, by monolithic intellectual elites, by political leaders seeking "complete consensus" to achieve modernizing goals is the most likely pattern in the emergent world.

The peasant masses, awakened by the impact of the West, their traditional life disrupted, the weakness of their society exposed brutally, their existence threatened by new, unexplained forces, are more likely to be moved by the need to overcome their powerlessness, by demands for a collective effort to build the strength and power of the society, than by demands for individual rights and freedoms which had never existed in their traditional societies.

The demand for strong, authoritarian government reflects not only the political philosophy of the intelligentsia, or the traditional attitudes of peasants toward political authority, but also the fact that the drive for modernization creates the need for a single, unified, total national interest. The demand for "complete consensus," in short, reflects the need for such consensus to achieve successful economic development.

We noted earlier that the roots of totalitarianism were found, in the West, in the need to achieve total mobilization of the society for victory in total war. Total war defined a total national interest within which individual differences were smothered, individual rights and freedoms no longer relevant. Modernization, in the emergent world, creates a similar definition of national interest; it takes on many of the characteristics of total war—war, however, not against a foreign enemy, but against the backward conditions, the poverty of the society itself. Modernization, therefore, requires a totalitarian effort comparable to the totally mobilized character of a modern nation engaged in total war. Modernization in the emergent world will depend on collective hard work, a girding up of the loins, a mighty, disciplined effort by the entire society to catch up with the advanced West, a call for dedication, for sacrifices, for those qualities emphasized in periods of struggle. "To catch up with 'fully developed' societies becomes a definition of national purpose. To introduce doubt as to the value of this contest becomes a form of intolerable subversion. . . . Controversy has itself come to be viewed as a luxury which only advanced nations can afford." [10]

Cheik Anta Diop, the great West African intellectual, says of the one-party state that although it is bad when it represents selfish interests concerned only with their own power, or when it is used as a device by Western powers to maintain control in former colonial areas, "when this is the incarnation of national goals, it is a very good idea." [11] The incarnation of national goals is particularly meaningful to developing societies where modernization is, and must be, a single overriding goal. This point is stressed, as well as clearly explained, by Julius Nyerere, the President of Tanzania, who argues that the overriding concern, in a developing nation, is the need for unity, the support by the entire society of the collective goal of development.[12]

The willingness of many people in the non-Western world to accept collective discipline in order to end their conditions of backwardness, poverty, and economic dependency is well illustrated by the remarks of a young Guinean: "I don't care if it takes a hundred Stalins, a hundred Mao Tse-tungs. We'll have them if this is the way for us to get out of the dirt and stand up and be seen in the world." [13] The young Guinean sees quite clearly the authoritarian, oppressive nature of Russian or Chinese Communism; he understands very well that such men as Stalin, or Mao Tse-tung, are not idealistic heroes, but necessary scourges—necessary in the sense that they represent the path to the one goal which, for the leaders of the emergent world, must take precedence over every other goal, that is, the goal of modernization, national development, the creation of a society which can live independently in the modern world. Ch'en Tu-hsiu, one of the founders of the Chinese Communist Party, expressed this realization in these words: "Better that all our ancient culture should disappear than that our race perish by its inability to live in the modern world." [14] The likelihood of totalitarian political organization, of course, will be enormously increased in societies which have experienced military conflicts against the

West, or revolutionary uprisings against Western domination. In these societies, modernization will be viewed as an extension of the revolutionary struggle for independence, requiring the same kind of mass effort. The economic warfare of the United States against Cuba creates a siege situation and a siege mentality which is only somewhat less intense than the conditions of open warfare in Vietnam. Castro's rule, as a result, has all the features of a revolutionary, military dictatorship: that is, the kind of highly personal, charismatic leadership and one-party rule which characterizes guerilla revolutionary movements, where discipline and dedication are more important than individual freedom. "In Cuba . . . for all its problems, the government has succeeded in communicating a sense of urgency to the people as well as the feeling that the sacrifices demanded are for their own benefit, not for foreigners or their own upper classes." [15]

Not only do circumstances suggest an authoritarian program of development, a revolution from above sponsored by a strong government, but in fact, as we look over the emergent nations, we can find almost none which have escaped strong authoritarian methods, or which have established the kind of parliamentary democracy which we claim to be championing in the emergent world as an alternative to communism. Wherever a serious effort is being made to modernize, we encounter programs of reform which are defined and administered from above, imposed on society by a ruling, managerial elite, which, whether communist or not, usually views the process of political competition, as defined in the West, as a source of weakness, a way of dissipating social energies, which have to be rallied collectively behind the common goal of development. And where such modernization is not taking place, we find equally authoritarian regimes, dedicated to the preservation of the status quo by force.

In Latin America, although some effort is made to maintain a facade of parliamentary government in deference to American pressures, the typical pattern is one of strong authoritarian governments and permanent one-party rule, even where the pretense of a multi-party system is maintained, as in Mexico. Of course, in much of Latin America, dictatorship exists primarily to prevent change, or to contain change within sharply defined limits. The military play a key role in maintaining such authoritarian structures in Peru, Bolivia, Ecuador, Brazil, and Argentina. Only in the first three is there an appreciable commitment to change. Cuba, of course, is an authoritarian state. But so are Haiti and Santo Domingo, and neither shows much commitment to genuine development. Mexico is permanently ruled by the appropriately named Partido Revolucionario Institucional (Institutionalized Revolutionary Party). Only Costa Rica, Chile, Uruguay, and possibly Venezuela and Guatemala show some semblance of a genuine parliamentary democracy. The last two, however, are dominated by foreign economic interests which manipulate political life to prevent a genuine challenge to the status quo.[16]

Throughout Africa, the one-party state is not only typical, but is viewed by most African leaders, in Uganda, Tanzania, Ghana, Guinea, the Ivory Coast, Gabon, Nigeria, Kenya, and elsewhere, as more appropriate, more expressive of the collective needs of the nation than Western multi-party systems. Socialism is defined as a collective process of growth and development in which the individual neither requires nor deserves the luxury of individualism as defined in the West.[17] On the other hand, neither Ethiopia nor Liberia, which are viewed as "pro-American," is a democratic regime.

The Arab world is dominated by strong, authoritarian figures. Such men as Colonel Boumedienne, Colonel Kazafi, Anouar-el-Sadat, and the Shah of Iran reflect the determination to bring about revolution from above by strong, forcing methods. In both Turkey, where modernization was launched through a revolution from above by Mustafa Kemal, and Iraq, which still flounders in backwardness, political power is ultimately in the hands of the military. Even such milder regimes as those of Morocco and Tunisia are far from exhibiting the kind of institutionalized multi-party system, and the open, competitive play of factional interests which characterize parliamentary systems in the West. King Hassan maintains a heavy hand on Moroccan society, while the Neo-Destour party completely dominates Tunisian political life. The recent decline of Habib Bourguiba, the charismatic figure of Tunisian political independence, is a reflection of his advancing years rather than of any democratic reorientation of Tunisian society. Only such nations as Lebanon, which is dominated by a wealthy middle class, and which has not been subject to pressures for rapid modernization, or the oil-rich sheikdoms of the Persian Gulf, can afford more relaxed political regimes in the Near East.

Asia is certainly dominated by authoritarian regimes, whether communist, as in China, North Vietnam, and North Korea, or military, as in Indonesia, Pakistan, and Thailand. Malaysia has hitherto avoided collective discipline, and communist revolution failed there in the 1950's. Malaysia, however, has shown little ability, up to now, to achieve genuine development. Burma possesses valuable agricultural resources, and has been outside the arena of big power conflict. These advantages mitigate the pressures for rapid development, and Burma is somewhat of an exception in Asia, as is the regime of Lee Kuan Yew, in Singapore, a wholly mercantile society, an entrepot, in fact, which is untypical of the emergent world. The Philippines, on the other hand, has avoided the discipline of collective authority at the price of stagnation, political corruption, and an economic system which is virtually a colony of the United States. South Korea, Taiwan, Cambodia, and South Vietnam, of course, are American military protectorates, and the last three, in particular, are wholly worthless regimes. It may be too early to speculate, but it appears unlikely that the new state of Bangla Desh will avoid some form of authoritarian rule, whether in the person of Mujib Rahman or that of a more radical figure.

India, of course, is frequently pointed to as the showcase of democratic development. But India is a one-party state; political life is dominated by the Congress Party. That party is committed to a program of planned modernization through management from above. It is true that the Indian government has been far more reluctant than China to turn to drastic forcing methods, and it has moved slowly and hesitantly in overcoming such traditional obstacles to modernization as the caste system. But there is no evidence that these obstacles are disappearing spontaneously, and Indian performance suffers by comparison with that of China. In China, "communism has produced profound change in a decade, whereas the process of modernization in a non-communist country like India is mired in obsolete institutions, crippling traditions, and political malaise." [18]

Irving Horowitz summarizes the trend in the emergent world as follows: "nearly every nation in the Third World exhibits a powerful leader principle . . . in which power is seen to reside first and foremost in the leader, since he contains within his person the sum and substance of the aspirations and sentiments of the whole people." [19]

All the conditions of economic development in the emergent world, the sense of urgency, the attraction of large-scale government planning, the pressure and opposition of Western economic interests, the backwardness of the people, all tend to make the Soviet Union and China plausible economic models for the underdeveloped world. "In terms of economic development the appeal of Communism is evident since it not only offers a set of blueprints showing how the advanced countries can be overtaken but also points to the concrete achievements of the Soviet Union and China which have lifted themselves up by their bootstraps and shown that industrialization can be accomplished without surrender to the alien capitalists." [20]

The ability not to surrender to "alien capitalists" is very important for the emerging nations, who must be free to develop without a Western control which will either distort or prevent that development. Note that the determination of the emerging nations

146

not to surrender to "alien capitalists" is a reflection of their demand for independence. They are not opposed to domination by "alien capitalists" because they have been captured by anti-capitalist communists. In fact, all modernizing leaders in the emergent world, from Nasser to Castro, from the Peruvian military junta to Allende, must be committed, to some degree, to a "communist" policy of confiscation of Western economic interests.

American objections that neither of the great communist states, neither the Soviet Union nor China, can match Western standards of living has obviously no force, not only because the Western experience was so different from that of the non-Western world that the emerging nations cannot hope to duplicate it, but also because the Soviet Union and China represent very recent efforts at development, and their achievements, in relation to the extreme backwardness from which they started, appear very impressive from the perspective of the underdeveloped world. That these communist states have not yet caught up with the West is not viewed by the new nations as a sign of failure. Julius Nyerere, speaking to those who would hold up the advanced West as a model for the emergent nations, replies: "All I can say is, 'wonderful.' But it is irrelevant to what we can do in Tanzania. The assembly plants in North America and Europe are irrelevant. . . . China is different. China is a backward country trying to pull itself up. . . . You can see the steps, and you can say, 'Boy! Why didn't we think of that? We should do that!' " [21] The difficulties of the Soviet Union in the past, or of China and Cuba today, are not interpreted in the emergent world as indications of the failure of their strategy, but as the result partly of the enormity of their task, partly of a deliberate policy of opposition by the United States, an interpretation which justifies even greater forcing methods, greater militancy, and more complete submission to authority.

From the point of view of the emergent nations, the formula which was used in Russia has succeeded. "Communism has a *functional* attractiveness to the underdeveloped lands . . . it may be the political and economic system best adapted to the tasks of the backward areas." [22] This functional attractiveness is enhanced not only by the success of the formula in Russia, but by the success of the formula, or something very much like it, in places like Yugoslavia, China, and Cuba. "The broad framework of development policy under the Castro regime has been essentially that which any advisory mission with competence and objectivity would have been compelled to recommend to any Cuban government in 1958." [23]

The clearest record of the success of Castro's experiment comes from the first-hand report by Lee Lockwood, of *Life* magazine, who did not overlook the numerous shortcomings of Castro's program, but came away, not only with an extremely favorable impression of the over-all experiment, but with the clear conviction that the greatest difficulties faced by Castro's regime are caused, not by his own incompetence, or the inadequacy of the policies and ideologies he had adopted, but by the bitter hostility of the United States, particularly the economic blockade.[24]

2 · *The Appeal of Left Wing Revolution*

Many American political observers recognize that the success of such radical revolutionary movements as communism in the emergent world is related to the conditions and circumstances of that world; many reject, therefore, what Luis Taruc called, in the Philippines, the "mailed fist" policy, and seek a more positive, constructive approach to the problems of the emergent societies. Such observers, however, share the basic assumption of the "hawks," that the goal of American policy should be to prevent communist victories in the underdeveloped world. They argue against military measures, not because they wish to spare the communists, but because such measures, they believe, clearly do not work. This type of analysis shares with the "hawks" the view that communism is an alien outside force, "exploiting" the conditions of unrest of the emergent world. It views communism, in fact, as a disease. "The only effective kind of anti-communism in these areas is that which, like an antibiotic, inhibits the growth of a micro-organism by destroying the nutrients on which it feeds." [25] Communism is the micro-organism, and the nutrients are the internal problems and weaknesses of the society. Such an approach is essentially a modified, sophisticated, "dovish" version of the doctrine of containing communism. The goal of American policy remains the containment, and ultimately, the defeat of communism in the emergent world; the violent methods of direct military intervention are excluded because of their inefficiency.

Despite its more sophisticated appearance, such an analysis fails to confront clearly and accurately the problems of the emergent world. For communism, in that world, is not the micro-organism which "exploits" the unrest of the society; it is the cure to that unrest. We cannot "contain" communism in the emergent world, for communism is itself the response of that world, functionally related to the problems it confronts and the goals it seeks. It is true that modernizing leadership in the emergent world will not inevitably adhere to an official Communist Party. But that fact will not make the experience of modernization any less communist. Further, the difference between communist and other forms of modernization in the emergent world, as we noted in Chapter One, is one of degree. Communism represents a kind of extreme limit of the process of revolutionary transformation.

Our view of the communist phenomenon in the emergent world may become clearer if we view communism as an indigenous response by the people of the society themselves to the problems of that society, as a possible means of confronting their problems, and assuring the success of modernization. Communist revolution breaks out, not because the "communists" have decided that such and such a country is to be "taken over," but because conditions in that country have produced a revolutionary response which is communist in nature. And the conditions of the emergent world make it likely that they will produce such revolutionary, communist responses.

Further, communism and analogous left-wing philosophies will have a certain purely *ideological* appeal to the intelligentsia of the emergent world, for whom a communist or left-wing philosophy will seem appropriate on intellectual grounds. One obvious reason is the central fact of hostility toward the Western world. The leaders of the emergent world are all anti-imperialist, and consequently, to some degree, anti-Western. In fact, this anti-Western resentment and hostility are basic to all other attitudes. They will be drawn, therefore, to anti-imperial ideologies in their confrontation with the Western world. And communism represents the most extreme form of anti-imperialism. In the emergent world, "the bare fact of long and bitter animosity between the communist countries and the imperial west is by itself persuasive evidence to many that communism must have virtues worth investigating." [26] This communist animosity is itself an extreme and virulent version of an ideological opposition to imperialism shared by the socialists, which had its roots in left-wing thinking, in its precise, European sense, in the nineteenth century.

The anti-imperial attitudes of socialist and other left-wing thinkers in Europe make them immediately appealing to the intellectual leaders of the emergent world. Although socialism, as a nineteenth-century European phenomenon, can only have limited relevance in the emergent world of the twentieth century, its anti-colonial animus strikes an immediate responsive chord. In socialism the intelligentsia found an ideology they could use, not only to explain and justify their own position, but to rally the masses to their political programs. Socialism was a Western product, reflecting their Western education, but one which could be used against the West, or at least against its colonial activities.

Further, there are certain aspects of Marxist theory which, reinterpreted to fit the circumstances of Asia, Africa, and Latin America, have a particular appropriateness to that world. The notion of class conflict is readily applicable to the relations between the developed Western world and the underdeveloped world; the Marxist emphasis on revolution is appealing to a leadership animated by hostility toward the West, which finds it convenient, as well as plausible, to cast itself in the role of oppressed underdogs, the have-nots of the Marxist class war. Most important, perhaps, is the central significance which Marx attached to the process of modernization itself.

Lenin's theories on imperialism, carried to their logical conclusion, suggest that the Marxist class struggle is being replaced by an international conflict between the colonial powers and their former colonies; and by extension, between the underdeveloped, poor, and backward non-Western world and the dominant, powerful, and rich Western nations. To the extent that the West acts out the role of a dominant class, treating the emergent world with a mixture of contempt and patronizing tutelage, violently suppressing all political developments unsuited to its own interests, to that extent the West helps to make convincing this Leninist version of the Marxist class war.

Left-wing radicalism, including Communism, is a plausible ideology for the emergent nations because it defines the nature of their tasks. John Plamenatz has defined Bolshevism as "the distorted Marxism of a backward society exposed to the impact of the West." [27] In one way or another, the ideologies of most of the leaders of the emergent nations who seriously seek the independent modernization of their nation are variations on this definition. Whether or not they adhere to an official Communist Party, and to whatever extent they are influenced by the example of the Soviet Union, the leaders of the emergent world adopt a distorted Marxism suited to their own needs. Although revolutions of development have taken on other forms than communism, they "usually borrow some aspects of communist experience and organizational technique." [28]

The appeal of left wing-radicalism goes beyond the mechanics of economic development. It is the appeal to a sense of justice, of equality, of collective fair play, which was the source of much of the moral strength in original European socialism. Socialism means an attack, much more intense, but essentially of the same nature, as the attack in the French Revolution against privilege. Certain of the ethical and idealistic aspects of Marxism, of communism in its original sense, make a strong appeal to a sense of justice, a dream of a more equitable society, in the emergent world: the ideal of a society governed by cooperation, by mutual love, by compassion, in which people work to help each other rather than to harm each other, a society so perfectly conceived and engineered that it would be free of typical human evils and sufferings. The appeal of this kind of utopian Marxism is related to a concept of communism in its simplest and most emotional terms; that is, the appeal of a vast collective effort in which there are no pigs who are more equal than others. In different terms, it is the appeal of the moral, almost apocalyptic, content of nineteenth-century Marxism, its ethical message, as distinct from its tools of social and economic analysis, and quite distinct from the purely technical model of the Soviet Union as a developing society.

The fact that this ideal egalitarianism is more honored in the breach in the Soviet Union does not escape the attention of left-wing leaders in the emergent world, who are not only more aware, and more intelligently aware, of the shortcomings of the Soviet Union than we like to believe, but who are equally determined, in most cases, to avoid what they consider the errors of Soviet development, while enjoying the advantages of the successful Soviet model. That the Soviet Union has succumbed, in the process of modernizing, to the evils of bureaucratization, and created a new caste system, does not tarnish the appeal of its original egalitarian ideal. "The Chinese are determined that the whole nation must advance together by reducing to a minimum the inequalities which can appear in a poor country in the process of socialization; while the Soviets, on the contrary chose to use them as incentives." [29] It is this determination to reduce inequalities to a minimum, to abolish privilege, to create a system of collective cooperation, that comprises the greatest emotional appeal of communism among the masses in the emergent world.

What is a communist movement in the emergent world? More accurately, what are the ideological common points of the various revolutionary, modernizing movements in that world? Jean Daniel, a French journalist who was one of the most knowledgeable observers of the Algerian revolution against French colonial rule, offers this comment: "The revolutionary spirit leads undoubtedly to the one party state (therefore, to a weakening of democracy), to agrarian reform (therefore, to the expropriation of French colonial settlers) and to the process of nationalization (therefore, to a transformation of economic relations, particularly financial relations.)" [30] A genuine revolutionary movement in the emergent world will very probably produce the categories outlined by Jean Daniel. It will be a collective, disciplined, revolutionary transformation of the internal structure of the traditional society, aimed at mobilizing and releasing the energies of the masses for the task of building a modern nation; it will aim at a radical transformation of relations between the peoples of the emergent world and the advanced nations, and a rejection of Western tutelage and domination; it will be anti-Western, and prone to violate the property rights of the Western nations; it will carry out its program under the aegis of a disciplined, authoritarian, national leadership. In other words, the modernizing revolution of the emergent world will be a left-wing revolution, pushing toward communism as an extreme limit.

To the extent that the leaders of the emergent world adopt a Marxist ideology, it is, as Plamenatz says, a distorted Marxism, suited to the needs of modernization. This redefinition of Marxism is a "distortion" only to the extent that we accept the Soviet claim that Marxism is an absolute, absolutely valid system, which expresses a final and absolutely true insight into the mechanics of reality. We need not accept this Platonic concept of Marxism, any more than it was accepted by Marx and Engels themselves, whose "dislike of utopian blueprints prevented them from trying to envisage the political model of a socialist society." [31]

Marxism is, among other things, a technique for interpreting the processes of social and economic changes, a method the success and appeal of which have derived from its open-ended nature, from the fact that it has proved adaptable to changing circumstances and changing situations. The Marxism of the underdeveloped world cannot be similar to that of the nineteenth century, for today's Asia and Africa are noticeably different from Europe in 1850.

Further, the ideological commitment of the leaders of the emergent world is no more rigid than the Marxism which they adopt; or rather, its rigidity is related, not to Marxist ideology itself, for its own sake, but to the modernizing needs of their societies. Their overwhelming concern is the successful transformation of their societies, the successful casting off of the burden of traditional backwardness. Such a goal is their only absolute; and within that context they are willing to use any tool which serves their purposes. Beyond such considerations, the leaders of the emergent world are no more, nor less, committed to ideology than any other political leaders; probably less so, for they confront very practical tasks, requiring objective solutions. Modernization, as confronted by men like Castro, or Mao Tse-tung, or Tito, does not appear to be an exercise in ideological absolutism, despite our efforts to so view it, and to ridicule it on these grounds.

The efforts of American Kremlinologists to analyze the Castro revolution in Cuba, for instance, or other "Marxist" and "communist" revolutions, miss the point. "Another exercise in futility . . . has been their efforts to interpret the revolutionary process in Cuba in terms of Marx, Lenin, Stalin, Trotsky, Mao Tse-tung." [32] Such exercises are futile, for despite the influence of all these men on Castro's thinking, ultimately the only criterion by which he will guide his actions is his commitment to Cuba itself. "The socialistic . . . elements in the politics of the intellectuals of underdeveloped countries are secondary to and derivative from their nationalistic preoccupation and aspirations." [33] The same can be said of the communist elements in their politics. In short, the communist or left-wing orientation of some leaders of the emergent world is no proof that they will be impervious to future changes in the conditions of their societies, or that nations which adopt such a leadership are doomed to some kind of ideological absolutism which can never be broken save through the intervention of American military force.

Modernization in the emergent world will produce left-wing authoritarianism not only because the sum total of the conditions of the emergent world dictates an authoritarian transformation, but because such a transformation is defined as a left-wing process. The difference between left-wing and right-wing dictatorship is, by definition, a difference in attitudes toward change. Left-wing authoritarianism mobilizes the society to carry out a revolutionary change, involving the political awakening of the masses and the modernization of the society. By definition, left-wing authoritarianism is authoritarianism dedicated to modernization. Right-wing authoritarianism, on the other hand, is committed to preserving the status quo, its purpose is to *prevent* change. In the emergent world, its purpose is to prevent the kind of dynamic and revolutionary transformation produced by modernization. This difference is succinctly summarized in relation to Russia by Merle Fainsod, who observes in commenting on the work of Sidney Monas on the czarist Third Section: "The object of the Tsarist police was to safeguard the status quo; the aim of the Soviet political police has been to facilitate a reshaping of Soviet society by eliminating all those who bar the way to its realization." [34] The czarist police served a right-wing authoritarianism. The Soviet police functions for a left-wing authoritarianism. The choice, in the emergent world, is not between democracy and dictatorship; such a choice is probably irrelevant. It is between right-wing and left-wing authoritarianism. As between the two, only the dynamic force of left-wing authoritarianism can hope to solve, in the long run, the modernizing problems of the emergent world.

Two historians recently commented in the *American Historical Review*: "The American failure to note distinctions between military fascism and revolutionary Marxism has contributed to a simplistic view of revolutionary and anti-colonial movements in the post-World War II era and has led to the establishment of worldwide alliances and permanent military containment policies in Europe and Asia." [35] The distinction between a right-wing, fascist regime, such as that of Batista, and a left-wing, Marxist regime such as that of Castro is crucial. The fascist regime is committed to preserving the status quo, and to preventing the modernization demanded by national development; the Marxist dictatorship holds out the hope of meaningful change. But does our government fail to distinguish between the two out of ignorance? In fact, does our government fail to make such a distinction? Despite its vocal commitment to democracy, its opposition to authoritarianism in the emergent world is very selective. Our government never intervened militarily to oust Latin American military dictators like Stroessner, or Trujillo, or Batista. It never did anything to end the very oppressive rule of Duvalier in Haiti. It not only has done nothing to pressure the dictatorial governments of Greece or South Africa out of power, but it actively supports them, militarily and financially. The policy of global intervention promoted by our State Department has not been guided by any naive consideration of opposing "dictators." Our government has supported and still supports dictators all over the world. It has clearly seen the difference between military fascism and revolutionary Marxism, and it has decided to oppose revolutionary Marxism, to oppose, in fact, left-wing revolution aimed at the transformation of the emergent societies.

We do not oppose communist regimes because they are authoritarian. We oppose them because despite claims to the contrary, we do not really support the kind of modernizing change which they represent. We oppose them because we are unwilling to make the sacrifices necessary to allow a genuine transformation of the emergent societies; because we are unwilling to accept, or live in, the kind of world that would be produced by the modernizing transformation of non-Western societies. We claim to support a democratic, liberal transformation of the emergent world, after our own model, when, in fact, such a democratic transformation is probably impossible. But we use this pretense to justify an opposition to *any* modernization which imposes sacrifices upon us. We refuse both the material sacrifice required by giving up our economic domination of the emergent world, and the psychological sacrifice needed to accept the potential equality of the emergent societies. We refuse the sacrifice implied in giving up our role of the rich man in the big house looking down benevolently upon a confused and distraught world. We refuse to accept a dynamic, revolutionary transformation of the emergent world which challenges our power, our interests, our prestige, and our self-image.

7

Containing Communism:

A Formula for Frustration

I · *The "Mailed Fist" Policy*

ULTIMATELY, THE MOST COMPELLING REASON WHY THE EMERGENT
nations are likely to turn to communist solutions of the problem of
modernization is the nature and impact of American foreign policy. If communism is seen as an intensification of tendencies inherent in the conditions which all emergent nations face, and if this intensification is indeed related to the severity of the obstacles on the
path to modernization, it is largely in the power of the rich Western
nations, particularly the United States, to determine how many
and how great will be the obstacles encountered by the developing
nations.

United States foreign policy has been motivated, since 1945 at
least, by the desire to affect and determine the nature of the politics
of much of the world, particularly the underdeveloped world; but
the policy of "containing communism," first formulated in 1947,
has produced the exact opposite of what it intended. For that policy, far from easing the path of modernization, has been the greatest single factor enormously complicating and aggravating the
difficulties of the emergent nations seeking modernization. The at-

tempt to contain communism has prompted the United States to intervene in the domestic affairs of nations all over the globe in such a way as to suggest the establishment of a new empire, run by the rich, advanced nations, particularly the United States. This foreign policy has created tremendous pressures on societies seeking to find their own way to development and independence. Our interference becomes a source of concern for nations seeking independent development, not only because it threatens the integrity of these societies, but because our interference, in practice, no matter what our public pronouncements may be, has usually been against the side of genuine, independent development. As we noted in the last chapter, we have consistently opposed left-wing movements in the emergent world, although left-wing movements represent the only possibility for genuine transformation of these societies. Our attempt to coerce the emergent world into the kind of development we are willing to accept has not only failed, but it has made the task of independent development appear so overwhelming that it has become a major factor in producing the kind of revolutionary reaction we call communism.

The United States, of course, has not been alone in this policy of making life difficult for the underdeveloped world. The French in Indochina, in Algeria, in some parts of Africa, the Belgians in the Congo, the Portuguese in Angola and Mozambique, the Dutch in Indonesia, the British in Malaya, have all made their contributions to the creation of that climate of violence and radical polarization which pushes the emergent world toward communism. But whereas these nations have limited their actions to their former colonies, the United States has developed a consistent, *global* policy of intervention; for, in fact, only the United States has the power and the resources to act the role of global policeman. Consequently, the United States has appeared as the symbol of that continued Western domination which prevents the emergent world from achieving its goals.

We have already noted that the leaders of the emergent world are strongly attracted to the Leninist theory of imperialism, in which they play the role of exploited inferiors, and the West plays the role of dominant exploiter. Viewed from that perspective, the Marxist class war has become a war between the rich, white, Western world, and the poor, colored, non-Western world. Communism is one version of such a Marxist-Leninist view of the struggle for development in the emergent world. The degree to which the leaders of the non-Western world act upon such an interpretation depends largely on the actions of the advanced nations; that is, the truth content of this Marxist-Leninist interpretation will depend on whether the Western societies act the role assigned to them in this analysis. If the advanced societies, particularly the United States, play the role of dominant exploiter, intervening in the affairs of the emergent world in such a way as to limit or prevent their freedom of action, to deny the substance of their economic and political independence, the emergent nations will be driven to play the role of a revolutionary class. If the advanced world, particularly the United States, attempts to force its own version of development upon the emergent world, if it resists demands for what may truly be defined as self-determination, then that world will be reinforced in its predisposition to externalize its problems and view the meddling of the strong advanced powers as the chief obstacle to development. Note that the truth content of such an analysis of the problems of the emergent world will depend exclusively on the *actions* of the advanced nations, and not at all upon their words. We cannot combat communism by propaganda, or skillful diplomacy, or clever intelligence agents in the emergent world, because communism is the response of that world to the real conditions which the advanced nations impose upon it by their actions.

The most extreme form of intervention in the emergent world has been military intervention, and the policy of containing communism has meant our willingness, in certain cases, to crush communist revolution by military force, by the use of what Luis Taruc, the Filipino Huk leader, calls the "mailed fist" policy. Despite the consistently optimistic interpretations of the United States military concerning the effectiveness of this mailed fist policy in combating communism, the opposite of these optimistic interpretations appears to be closer to the truth. No single factor seems more decisive in pushing the emergent world into a communist response than the military intervention of the advanced nations, that is, the extreme limit of the policy of containing communism. "The argument the native chooses has been furnished by the European settler, and by an ironic turning of the tables it is the native who now affirms that the colonialist understands nothing but force." [1]

Luis Taruc, in commenting on the "mailed fist" policy of the American-backed Manila government to crush the Filipino communist movement, observes: "the cruel 'mailed fist' policy did not achieve its purpose. It did not put down the rebellion. Instead, it fanned the embers of rebellion and strengthened the peasants' and workers' revolutionary tradition." [2] The same point is made in reference to Algeria by Edmund Behr, who describes French military operations which achieved "little result other than that of alienating the local population through indiscriminate shellings and shootings of suspects." [3] When the Algerian rebellion against the French was launched, in November 1954, the rebels had "less than fifty obsolete shotguns," and numbered "not more than a few hundred." [4] One rebel attack, in 1954, was "ignominiously driven off by a Moslem night watchman armed with a shotgun." [5] Yet, by the end of the war, the Algerian Army of Liberation comprised some fifty thousand well-equipped men, and this tremendous growth was due largely to French military tactics against the peasant population of Algeria, including the use of torture.

The way in which French repressive policy turned the Algerian people into violent revolutionaries is well indicated by W. R. Crocker, a British colonial official, who observed, in 1949: "Algeria . . . is not nationalist but autonomist and would be satisfied with self-government within the French Union." [6] At that time, the Algerians were willing to settle for less than complete independence, and Algerian political leadership had not yet turned to radical national solutions. But even in 1949, Crocker warned: "If the reactionary French settlers get their way they will no doubt in good time create a nationalistic and anti-French movement among the Algerian millions." [7] Not only was the statement a remarkably accurate prophecy, but it throws enormous light on American policies of containing communism, which, in good time, drive the peoples of the emergent world into radical, anti-Western, nationalist revolution.

An article in the French press concerning the conflict in Northern Ireland makes an interesting analogy to Algeria, comparing the role of the Protestants to that of the French supremacist O.A.S., predicting that the policy of suppression will eventually turn the Irish rebels into radical extremists, and indicating that they are already embracing a communist ideology. [8] K. M. Pannikar, an Indian historian, comments: "By a strange process of reasoning, the Europeans have, throughout their relations with Asians, convinced themselves that acts of savagery and inhumanity will increase their prestige in the eyes of Asian people." [9] Our strategy in Vietnam would indicate that we still suffer from the delusion that "acts of savagery and inhumanity" will win the peoples of the emergent world to our side. Such savagery merely convinces the emergent peoples that violence is the only language which will earn the respect of the Westerners, and only force will compel the West to recognize the revolutionary aspirations of the emergent world. The commitment of the Vietnamese people to the communist cause, for instance, has probably grown in direct proportion to the intensity of our military intervention, and our increasing reliance on "acts of savagery and inhumanity." We have just seen, of course, the brutally repressive policy of the Pakistani government in East Pakistan create a revolutionary Bengali movement eventuating in the establishment of Bangla Desh. That state violence and suppression will create counter-violence and revolution would appear to be too obvious to argue were it not for the fact that so much official policy in the Western world continues to be guided by faith in the efficiency of the "mailed fist."

The difficulties of development in the emergent world are not only the result of direct military intervention; indirect forms of intervention, such as the economic blockade of Cuba, for instance, will also increase vastly the difficulties of the emergent societies, and drive them to radical, communist solutions. Critics of Castro in this country argue that he had already demonstrated his anti-Americanism before the United States began putting pressure on him. But the objectionable, communist, "anti-American" aspects of his actions consist, in fact, of the basic goals which any serious modernizing leader will seek to achieve in the emergent world. The purpose of Castro's revolution, as of any modernizing process aimed at genuine self-determination, was to end the dependent relation of Cuba.

In fact, the confiscation and nationalization of foreign properties are but the obverse side of what would be a genuine policy of assistance such as the United States claims to pursue. If we genuinely mean to help the emergent societies achieve their own development, we can do so only by relinquishing our power to dictate the economic lives of the peoples of societies like Cuba. If we had genuinely meant to help Cuba achieve self-determination, we would have adopted a policy aimed at gradually turning over to Castro's government our economic interests in Cuba, and we would have absorbed, out of our own enormous wealth, whatever cost was involved in compensating private American interests. If the French and the English had genuinely wished to see Egypt achieve self-determination, they would have themselves acted to turn over the management and ultimately, the ownership of the Suez Canal to the Egyptians.

In response to the argument that the Cubans and Egyptians had no "right" to these properties, that they did not belong to them, that they were the product of Western economic enterprise, one could of course answer that these economic interests were obtained at the expense of Castro's and Nasser's ancestors at the point of a gun. But one need not make this kind of moral and historical argument; one can simply ask what is meant by our claims that we wish to help the emergent world, if we insist on maintaining our economic possessions in these societies, and our ability to dictate the lives of their people? The white man's burden is no burden if carrying it is not allowed to interfere in any way with the white man's enjoyment of his rights and possessions in the emergent world, if the carrying of that burden compels non-Westerners to remain under the tutelage of the white man. That Castro, Nasser, Allende, and other "anti-Western" leaders have had to resort to confiscation and nationalization of foreign properties is itself an indication of the West's unwillingness to yield its position of domination in the non-Western world, of the unwillingness of Westerners to make sacrifices for the sake of the emergent world.

The morality of the argument is, in any case, irrelevant; for the emergent nations believe that control over their own economies is a *sine qua non* of an independent development. If we refuse to give up our economic empire in the emergent world, we shall be involved in ceaseless interventions to prevent the coming to power of leaders who recognize that the integrity and independent development of their societies depend upon escaping such foreign domination. Our attempts to oppose the development of left-wing revolutions aimed at overthrowing Western domination in the underdeveloped world can only increase the determination of these leaders, and turn them into even more radical, communist, anti-Western paths.

2 · *Guerilla War and the Myth of Counter-Insurgency*

Faced with repeated failures in eradicating communist revolution by military force, many Western leaders have become convinced that the success of left-wing movements is due to their use of a new "secret" weapon, guerilla warfare; that is, we fail to defeat the communists because we fail to use the military means appropriate to the new, diabolically clever weapon of the communists, practiced according to the doctrines of Mao Tse-tung. In fact, these doctrines are badly misunderstood if they are seen as mere technical devices. Guerilla warfare is interpreted by many people in this country as a kind of all-purpose trick which, when understood, can be applied to the successful waging of war in any part of the non-Western world. Its only prerequisite, apparently, is a suitable geographic environment.

But as Chalmers Johnson indicates, "Guerilla warfare is not so much a military technique as it is a political condition." [10] This condition occurs when the military efforts of the revolutionaries in the emergent world receive considerable and active support from the civilian, peasant population; in such conditions, the Western nation is compelled to fight not only the guerilla army, but the entire population. No amount of training and study of guerilla tactics can produce such conditions; if the population of Vietnam is radically sensitized, by our military actions, to despise us, there is no way in which we can "exploit" conditions of unrest in Vietnam to our advantage through the use of guerilla tactics, any more than the Germans in Yugoslavia, or the Japanese in China in World War II, could have "exploited" the social unrest they themselves were creating, and used guerilla tactics to combat their communist opponents. "Terroristic methods are successful in the long run only when the objective for which the terrorists are fighting enjoys popular support." [11]

Mao and other communists have not discovered a secret weapon which enables them to defeat superior power and superior technology. Guerilla warfare reflects today, as it always has, the militant, active opposition of the great majority of the people to the presence of a foreign military invader. Guerilla warfare not only depends on large-scale popular support, it is the expression of that support.

To win a guerilla war, it is necessary to impose our will on an entire population animated by militant hostility. Victory over a guerilla movement is different from victory over a so-called conventional enemy, because the enemy, in a guerilla war, is not only an organized army, but an entire population aroused against the presence of a foreign military occupier. To enforce our will, it becomes necessary to impose total military control over the entire society, as we have done in Vietnam, and as the French tried to do in Algeria. W. R. Crocker understood this point long before the jargon of counter-insurgency techniques had gained wide currency. He indicated that the British could never suppress the Indian nationalist movement in the 1940's, for attempts to suppress it simply increased the virulence of Indian national revolutionaries, until a point was reached where only the ruthless tactics used by the Germans in World War II could succeed. Such a policy, apart from its moral repugnance, would have been too costly for Great Britain, for "it would have required an army of scores of thousands of Englishmen" for the job of "dragooning" the entire population of India.[12]

In commenting on the integration struggle at the University of Mississippi, in 1962, the late Senator Richard Russell remarked: "If it takes that many troops to hold Oxford, then it would take about 17 million men to overcome Cuba." [13] His remarks had a greater import than he realized. For he obviously did not believe it would take that many men to overcome Cuba, and his intention was to demonstrate that something was very much wrong with the policy of a Federal government which required such an excessive deployment of military power to enforce its will on its own people. Senator Russell's appraisal of the degree of white resistance to integration in Mississippi may have been somewhat erroneous. The force and relevance of his argument were not, and it applied much more strikingly than he realized to the kind of military intervention which some people were then arguing we should undertake in Cuba, and which we later launched in Vietnam.

For if it was morally repugnant for the Federal government to seek to impose its will on what Senator Russell believed, rightly or wrongly, to be a wholly recalcitrant population, and if in the face of the popular resistance to integration in Mississippi, the Federal government, in spite of its great military power, was undertaking a futile exercise in "dragooning" the white population of the South, how much more difficult would it be to overcome popular resistance to military intervention in Cuba or Vietnam. The degree of "dragooning" required might be such that Senator Russell's figures would prove to be not facetious at all.

In other words, we have the military resources to impose our will on any of the emergent societies, including communist ones, as the French had the military resources to impose their will on the Algerian people. The Viet Cong do not have the technical means to defeat our superior technology. The reason we have so much difficulty "winning" the war in Vietnam is not because the Viet Cong have developed a new kind of "guerilla" strategy, suited to a jungle environment, which enables them to defeat our superior military resources. The reason is that our task is not winning battles, but "dragooning" the Vietnamese people, and imposing our will on a population militantly aroused against our presence. Such a task requires an enormous deployment of military forces, permanently engaged in a day-to-day police operation aimed at enforcing minimum cooperation from the population. Crocker observes that: "If a colonial power undertakes to suppress a resolute nationalist movement . . . it will be called upon to pay the price, firstly, of a readiness to use force with an energy ranging from ruthlessness to sheer terror, and secondly, of huge expenditures in men and material." [14]

If we are willing to use the kinds of brutal tactics employed by the Nazis, we can, finally, break the back of almost any resistance movement. Such a war inevitably degenerates into a conflict of atrocities, because it is not a war at all; it is a police operation aimed at terrorizing the population into submission. The massacre at My Lai, which does not appear to have been an unusual incident, as well as French atrocities in Algeria, only reflect the reality which is already clearly understood by American fighting men in Southeast Asia; there is no way of distinguishing civilians from military, or friends from foes, because, in fact, the United States is at war against nearly the entire population of Vietnam. Such incidents as My Lai are not "excesses" or unfortunate "tragedies"; they are inherent, and an inescapable part of the process of suppressing large-scale popular resistance. The only way to win a guerilla war is, ultimately, either to terrorize the population into submission, or to threaten its complete annihilation.

All such "victories" as the one we are seeking in Vietnam consist of the creation of garrison states which can only exist through our permanent military presence. The policy of containing communism, therefore, creates the very enemies it intends to contain, and creates its own justification for a policy of establishing a network of American military outposts throughout the world. Not only is the result of such a policy increasingly divergent from its professed aims, but the kinds of military client states we have established as a result represent a liability rather than an asset to our military strength throughout the world.

We fail to "win" such wars, not because we lack the military resources, but because the permanent "dragooning" of large populations in the non-Western world carries costs which, in the long run, Western societies find difficult to pay. For a successful counter-insurgency program to work, we must be prepared to deploy millions of American military men in permanent occupation of increasingly large parts of the globe. Unlike the Germans under Nazism, we are neither willing nor prepared to contemplate the implications of such a policy. Such a policy becomes difficult to implement because of revulsion at home. We refuse to support the kind of military operation necessary for a modern state to impose its will on a weak and backward but recalcitrant people. That is, enough people become aware of the discrepancy between claims of helping the underdeveloped society and the actual process of terrorizing its people into submission to create a severe home-front crisis. Such a state of affairs developed in France over the Algerian War, and in the United States over the Vietnam War. In both cases, atrocities became part of the military strategy, not because the French and the Americans had suddenly become monsters, but because atrocities become inevitable when one is waging war against an entire population.

The hope of fighting communism by turning its guerilla weapons back against itself is doomed to fail, since it is based on the erroneous assumption that guerilla warfare is a tactical trick. The assumption that Mao's victory in China was due to a superior and clever guerilla strategy is untenable. "Otherwise, the success of the communist armies could only be explained by the incompetence of the Japanese and puppet troops for which there is no objective evidence." [15] Yet we persist in believing that our "failure" in Southeast Asia is due to some technical incompetence in our military strategy, or that of our Vietnamese allies.

Revolutionaries will fail to mount a successful guerilla operation only when they fail to obtain the support of the people. The most effective way of assuring that revolutionaries will receive large-scale popular support is a brutal policy of intervention such as we pursue in Vietnam. Containing communism, in short, is the most effective technique yet devised for the spread of communist revolution in the emergent world.

3 · *Law and Order on a Global Scale*

What are our goals in the emergent world? What should be our goals? Richard Barnet has defined the issues in our policy toward the emergent world in a perceptive study, *Intervention and Revolution.* He begins by defining the mentality of what he calls the national security manager; that is, those men who have determined policy in this country since the end of World War II, and who were responsible for the formulation and implementation of the doctrine of containing communism.[16] The very term national security manager suggests the fundamental ideological implications underlying the foreign policy of the United States, which views itself, in Barnet's phrase, as the "Guardian at the Gate." [17] The doctrine of containing communism is based on the assumption that our national interests are dependent upon our ability to maintain international stability, which means, in effect, the international status quo, against forces of revolutionary change, which we view as a threat to world stability and order. The term global policeman would be an appropriate description for the national security manager who sees his task as an international version of the domestic concept of law and order.

Barnet complements his portrait of the national security manager with that of the revolutionary.[18] American leadership views the process of social revolution in the underdeveloped world as a violent and anarchic process threatening a cherished view of an orderly world. The source of this threat is the revolutionary. For Barnet, the real ideological clash in the world since 1946 has been the clash between the view of the world of the national security manager in the United States and that of the revolutionary in the underdeveloped world. These two views, he feels, are ideologically incompatible in a manner which is not true of the conflict between the United States and the Soviet Union, which is essentially a power struggle between major states, involving no irreconcilable conflict of views about world order. "In fact many basic perspectives of Soviet and American leaders have always been remarkably similar." [19] On the other hand, the national security manager and the revolutionary "differ fundamentally even in the way they characterize the issues which divide them." [20]

Clearly, the national security manager and the revolutionary complement each other. The United States is convinced that it must play the role of global policeman in order to prevent the revolutionary from disturbing the peace. "There must be law and order in the world—violence cannot be tolerated." [21] But it is this very kind of police action, in the name of preserving law and order, which is chiefly responsible for the radicalism and militant anti-Western posture of revolutionary leaders. This policy of intervention against revolutionaries has taken on, in the United States, the dimensions of a global crusade, pursued in the name of an international world order dominated by the United States.

Why is the role of global policeman so appealing to so many of us? The willingness of our people to support our foreign policy since the end of World War II, to support the doctrine of containing communism, seems to suggest that it satisfies some image we have developed about ourselves and our role in the world. Lucian Pye, who is no apologist for communism, finds our attitudes toward the emergent world related not so much to rational fears about communism as to personal anxieties concerning authority and control in the human personality.[22] We view the revolution of rising expectations as a process by which the masses of the emergent world are caught in an explosive upheaval which leads them to challenge a structure of authority and order which has profound psychological significance for us, and is related to deep-seated anxieties about the notion of freedom. This irrational fear of forces of destruction in the "uncivilized" emergent world is probably an externalization of doubts and anxieties about violence and the breakdown of law and order in our own society. "One reason why the National-Security Manager has such difficulty in coming to grips with the problem of political violence abroad is that, like most Americans, he has not confronted the issue in his own country." [23]

In fact, our attitudes toward the underdeveloped world are a global projection of our ambiguous attitudes toward domestic authority and freedom, and our obsessive concern with law and order. There is a curious and suggestive parallel between our attitudes toward crime, at the domestic level, and revolution at the international level. Our response, in both cases, is a policy of force, of authoritarian control. At the domestic level we are convinced that "toughness" will solve the problems of criminal and social unrest. We live in daily fear of anarchy, in spite of the fact that our government has such overwhelming police powers that the possibility of these powers breaking down appears negligible. Our fear of anarchy is accompanied by constant warnings against moral decay and the breakdown of the moral fiber of society. Our unwillingness to understand the motives of either individual crime or civil disorder, and our determination to see these phenomena as manifestations of moral decay, suggest that our fear of disorder and anarchy is a moral fear concerning the validity of our over-organized environment. We cannot accept the fact that certain people have rejected social cooperation. Dropping out is the most heinous crime. Our tremendous indignation over the drug problem, our vindictive maligning of so-called "hippies," and our willingness to accept the fantastically distorted and malicious pictures of non-conformist movements presented in the mass media of communications, indicate something more than the rational worry of parents over children, or citizens about the welfare of their society. The criminal penalties to which the individual is exposed if he uses drugs illegally are so unbelievably harsh as to be medieval, when one considers that a drunken driver who commits manslaughter may escape with virtually no penalty. Drug addiction and the hippie scene are related to life styles which are extremely disturbing because, in fact, they question the validity of the internal controls, the rigid disciplines, which middle-class Americans impose upon themselves, and wish to impose, externally, upon others, to prevent them from yielding to impulses of "anarchy" and moral "decay." "The disciplined hate the undisciplined to the point of murder. Thus the working class, disciplined, is a great reservoir of hatred. . . . And the bureaucrats, glad when disorderly men are killed." [24]

That this murderous hatred is related to envy is well illustrated in the recent movie, "Joe," where the violent prejudices, hatreds, and fear of the moral breakdown of society expressed by the main character are obviously signs of a deep resentment that his disciplined, hard-working life has yielded neither joy nor meaning, and his conviction that young people, without making any of the sacrifices of freedom and spontaneity which he has made to maintain moral "law and order" within himself, appear to be enjoying life infinitely more than he has. Middle-class America is constantly on guard against moral threats to the Puritan order in American society, because every middle-class American has to be constantly on guard against moral threats inside himself: threats to a moral system of discipline which he maintains only by a combination of authoritarian control and periodic binges of "sinfulness" and childish stupidity.

In demanding "get tough" policies against crime and disorder, the average middle-class American is probably demanding protection against his own "anarchic" impulses, which he so carefully holds in check. He externalizes his own craving to break from the stifling repression of his authoritarian moral ethic by identifying it absolutely with "evil" and "shiftless" elements in society. He is profoundly anxious about these anarchic tendencies both within the society and within himself; for he has not developed the emotional and psychological means to be free, and to manage his own impulses in an autonomous manner. Convinced that if he were given freedom he would be too immature to manage it wisely, that he would act as, in fact, he does act when he is "out with the boys," he is convinced that everyone else would abuse freedom as much as he would. Blacks, young people, criminals, are an externalization of the forces of disorder and anarchy which the average middle-class American is terrified will find expression in his own repressed and over-organized personality.

Our attitudes toward the underdeveloped world parallel precisely our domestic attitudes. We view the people of the emergent world much as we do the ghetto blacks, the dissatisfied poor, the radical students in our society—as wild, anarchic forces, potentially criminal mentalities, people motivated by exaggerated sensuality, crass materialism, incapable of rational thought, dark, irrational, violent, a kind of smoking pit of hell which can only be covered over and prevented from corrupting the world through the exercise of our superior authority and discipline. We assume that the sources of dissatisfaction of the people of the underdeveloped world are the result of their own shiftlessness, a kind of inherent moral inferiority. We assume that these people, like our own blacks, have natural, inherent tendencies toward violence, criminality, and "anarchy"; that it is these dark forces, in fact, which keep them in their conditions of backwardness. We view our role of global policeman in the same way that we view our responsibility to impose law and order at home, with the great advantage that none of these people are voting citizens of the United States, and therefore we can napalm and bomb them into submission with a ruthlessness which we might hesitate to use at home.

This anxiety concerning the violence of revolutionaries is not incompatible with the philosophy of the white man's burden. In the same way, we simultaneously viewed our own blacks, in the past, as children who needed our superior guidance, and as wild uncontrolled savages who understood only the whip and the scaffold. The spread of Western culture across the non-Western world is a civilizing process, a missionary activity, through which the superior, morally disciplined white peoples save the inferior colored masses from their own depravity, savagery, and lawlessness. This picture of colored peoples is integral to our own image of ourselves as the lawgivers, the bringers of light, the superior power which manages the affairs of these wild children, forcing them, finally, into a civilized pattern of behavior in which they accept our rule, justified by our moral superiority.

There is an obvious parallel between our reactions to social revolution at home and overseas. In both cases, we are anxious to use the power of the United States to restore "order"; that is, we are anxious to contain the eruption of these violent, criminal tendencies which we believe are inherent among people who have not adopted the civilized American way of life. Domestically, we view

174

crime and violence as the expression of an inherent depravity in certain individuals, a kind of evil possession; in the same way, we view the emergence of radical revolutionaries overseas as the machinations of evil men, machinations that, emanating from wherever we happen to locate the center of the international communist conspiracy at any moment, are the equivalent of cataclysms of nature, powerful, but mysterious and unpredictable. Revolution abroad constantly takes us by surprise, shocks us; we cannot believe that so much violence and hatred existed behind those smiling dark faces and shining white teeth. We may recognize that blacks are disadvantaged, but we tend to assume that their condition is their own fault, the product of their own shiftlessness. We may be sympathetic to their dissatisfactions, but we cannot see their conditions as justifying a challenge to the established system.

The psychologist Franz Alexander observes about crime: "Underprivileged members of an organized group who profit least from social cooperation will be the main offenders of peace and order." [25] Social psychology today accepts this fairly obvious conclusion. A policy of coercion against such offenders simply confirms their judgment that the system is organized against them. Ultimately, the attempt to cope with widespread dissatisfaction through coercion leads to the creation of a police state. The moral underpinnings of police state mentality in this society are illustrated by the conviction of many Americans that people who reject the social order have no good reason for doing so—that their dissatisfactions are not justified. Such a moral approach to social disobedience does not allow the individual to determine for himself whether the system is suitable to his needs. Superior moral authority prescribes that it is good for him, and the individual who persists in rejecting the system is guilty of immorality. "In such a well-regulated society, violence is not a phenomenon of politics, but of crime. Those who resort to it . . . are trying to wreck the game." [26]

The doctrine of containing communism combines with our ideological attitudes toward civil unrest and revolutionary disorder

to produce the most potent justification for our role of global policeman, the doctrine of international aggression. The concept of
aggression in international politics is analogous to the concept of
crime in domestic politics. Both are based on the assumption that a
system of order and authority exists which is morally justified and
accepted voluntarily by the majority of people. More important
than its popular acceptance is the fact that this system of authority
guarantees peace, tranquillity, and happiness for all people. To
tamper with the established order, at the domestic or at the international level, is to imperil the safety of all the members of society.
Our role as global policeman gives us the right to punish aggression, an international crime which must be "deterred," in the same
way that we use domestic police powers and the threat of punish-
ment to "deter" domestic criminals. The doctrine of aggression is
based on the assumption that international conflicts are caused by
"unruly," anarchic, evil states, who refuse to accept the rule of law
and order, and attempt selfishly to promote their own ends by
criminal acts. This doctrine is of limited application. In the same
way that the stability of the domestic system holds no virtue for
those who believe that it works against them, the stability of the international system holds no virtue for those societies who believe
that the world of international politics is organized against their interests.

The international system is heavily weighted against the underdeveloped, that is, the underprivileged societies. Not too surprisingly, they see little reason to lend their support to maintaining
such a system, and attempts to preserve the international status quo
do not appear to them as exercises in preserving law and order. Exhortations on the importance of stability and the end of revolutionary violence fall on deaf ears among the Palestinian refugees, the
blacks of Rhodesia, the peasants of Mexico or Vietnam, or the in-
habitants of Brazil's innumerable shanty-towns; among any people,
in short, for whom the established order means inferiority, poverty,
and lack of freedom. Our attitude toward revolutionary commu-

nism is identical to our attitude toward crime. Communism is the expression of a kind of metaphysical evil, and can only be extirpated by force. Our attempt to cope with communism through force produces an international police system, based on our rule as global policeman, analogous to the police state we create at home in coping with civil disobedience.

The concept of aggression is based on the assumption that the international status quo can be frozen at a particular moment in time. Such a freezing of the international status quo, however, can have no moral justification; for there is no reason to assume that the arrangement of international relations, the distribution of power, of resources, the functioning of the system, is necessarily perfect at any particular point in time. Nor is the objection valid that if the international system is not "fair" to certain societies, change should only come through peaceful means, and with the mutual agreement of all parties concerned. For the powerful and wealthy nations will not consent to any change in the international status quo which involves loss of any part of their power, wealth, or prestige, unless the cost of preventing such change becomes so great that they conclude it is not worth paying. This unwillingness to pay the cost of empire, among the European nations, was due partly to their excessive weaknesses and economic liabilities following World War II; but in many cases, the only way the powerful and wealthy nations can be persuaded that they are not prepared to pay the price for maintaining the international status quo is to make that price very high through the threat of revolutionary violence. Procedures of peaceful change can certainly be accepted as virtuous in international relations. But in fact, wealthy and powerful nations which would be adversely affected by such change will tend to resist it; and neither the League of Nations nor the United Nations has demonstrated any ability to compel major powers, least of all the United States, to make voluntary sacrifices of their positions.

Whether a reorganization of global political conditions, including the domestic reorganization of the emergent societies, can occur peacefully, without "aggression," is wholly dependent upon the advanced nations, particularly the United States. But "the National-Security Manager does not grasp or will not admit that there are societies . . . where the channels of 'peaceful change' have totally broken down or never existed." [27] As a result, he condemns all forms of revolutionary violence in the emergent world as unjustified and morally reprehensible. His self-righteousness appears particularly hypocritical when one notes that it is frequently our intervention, as in Vietnam, which is chiefly responsible for breaking down the channels of peaceful change. Douglas Pike asserts that in fighting communist revolution in Vietnam and elsewhere we are trying to help "nations develop along orderly, constructive lines." [28] It would be hard to imagine a less orderly or constructive process of development than what we have imposed on Vietnam.

The concept of "aggression," and the notion that attempts to change the current distribution of power, territory, and resources are "criminal" actions, do not constitute a moral approach to international politics; they represent an attempt to maintain permanently a current international arrangement which greatly favors the United States. Unless we are willing to yield our sovereignty and allow some higher power, such as the United Nations, or a world government, to determine on the fairness of the distribution of wealth and power among the societies of the world, we cannot justly claim that our determination to maintain global law and order is an expression of moral dedication.

4 · *The "Communist Conspiracy"*

The chief way in which we convince ourselves that we must oppose communism in the emergent world is by claiming that it is not, and cannot be, the legitimate expression of the political demands of any people; that it can never be more than an expedient political movement, concerned solely with selfish power. This rejection of communism is usually associated with the even more dubious claim that communism is wholly the product of a sinister, international conspiracy. Whether we see the center of this conspiracy in the Kremlin, or Peking, or existing outside and beyond any particular state, the conspiracy theory, as we have suggested earlier, can yield no possible insight into the mechanics of communism in the emergent world.

The cynicism and insincerity of communist leaders is taken for granted in the West, and used as justification for the belief that a communist movement can never express the legitimate grievances of people in a society; that its success is always due to an unexplained skill that communists possess in managing conspiracies. This refusal to view communism as a legitimate expression of the political life of a society, the assumption that it is "unnatural," and motivated purely by cynical expediency, produces some peculiar twists of interpretation. Since we refuse to grant the legitimacy of communism, it becomes possible to interpret any attempt by the communists to win power as evidence of their dishonesty and insincerity. Lucian Pye, for instance, reviews the various strategies of the Malayan Communist Party in seeking to win control of Malaya, and points to these activities as evidence of the fact that the communists were selfishly concerned with the extension of their own power.[29] The same kind of argument is used by anti-communist writers about Vietnam, where every instance of communist attempts to gain political power is used as evidence of their selfish and cynical expediency, while the attempt of the Mao regime to strengthen its position in world affairs is taken as conclusive evidence of the immoral and cynical aggressiveness of Chinese Communism.

Yet the attempt of other political forces or individuals to gain power for themselves and for the political movement they represent is not viewed as evidence that they are cynical, or do not express a legitimate political interest. Why was the attempt of Ho Chi Minh to gain political control of Vietnam any more expedient, cynical, or illegitimate than the attempt of Richard Nixon to gain political control of the United States? We claim that our rejection of communism stems from its willingness to use violence, or from its authoritarian methods; but certainly the history of the world, including the United States, has been punctuated by political violence, and we have never held the view that every political movement which has turned to violence is incapable of expressing a legitimate political interest. Nor have we ever acted as if authoritarian methods were an insuperable obstacle to our support and active friendship. In fact, not only have we not hesitated to grant support to many authoritarian political movements which have come to power through violence, but we enthusiastically used our own military power to establish the Lon Nol government in Cambodia through violent means.

The point is not that Communist Parties are made up of selfless, dedicated, virtuous persons, whose only concern is the welfare of the people. The point, rather, is that the success or failure of communism, like the success or failure of any political movement, has to be related to the substance of what it is doing, the appropriateness of its actions, its ability to cope with and solve the problems of its society. Communism, like any other political movement, is itself the expression of an attempt to confront the problems of a society. The fact that one may disagree with the communist response or the communist solution to the problems of society does not invalidate communism as a legitimate expression of that society's political configuration.

The attempt to "explain" communist success exclusively in terms of propaganda skills and conspiratorial techniques finally plunges many anti-communist observers into the ultimate non sequitur of political analysis, the conspiracy theory. The trouble with any conspiracy theory is that it fails to explain the objective reasons for events; partly because it directs attention away from real conditions and real grievances, partly because it is an all-purpose explanation, which can be related to any circumstances.

Conspiracy theories, by their very nature, begin with false assumptions. Not that people, including communists, do not plot, and conspire, and act in devious and indirect ways to achieve their ends, but conspiracy theories assume that such actions are unrelated to real grievances, real needs, or real satisfactions. They assume that people act, not in response to genuine, felt needs, in rational response to objective problems, leading them to pursue certain kinds of political action to satisfy these needs and grievances, or to achieve goals of their own, but that they are passive puppets of master manipulators, who "exploit" them, and either "use" real grievances or, in most cases, simply fabricate grievances out of thin air, make trouble, and, by a mysterious and never explained process, gain unlimited control over people. Conspiracy theories to "explain" student unrest on our campuses, for instance, are totally irrelevant, not in the sense that students do not conspire together to achieve their ends, not in the sense that individual leaders are not motivated by selfish interests, not in the sense that communists and other militant groups are not active among student movements, but in the sense that none of these factors "explains" student unrest. Student unrest would exist whether or not such "conspiratorial" activity took place; it is not *caused* by "agitators" and conspirators. The opposite is true. The objective cause of student unrest produces the conspiratorial activity, which is designed to satisfy the grievances which cause the unrest. The conspiracy theory assumes that people are a completely passive entity, with no will, no interests, no problems, no grievances, no goals of their own until "agitators" create these grievances for them, that their actions are determined wholly by "conspirators" and "plotters" who manipulate them at will.

The bankruptcy of such an explanation becomes obvious when it is related to communism. Why does this complete passivity, this utter vulnerability to manipulation, lend itself only to "exploitation" by communists? If people are complete puppets, at the mercy of conspirators, it is hard to see why they are not equally vulnerable to "exploitation" by anti-communist conspirators. In fact, as we noted earlier, many anti-communists have, through the techniques of counter-insurgency, and through such organizations as the C.I.A., sought to play the role usually assigned to "communist plotters." Not surprisingly, this mechanical approach to politics, in which political events are determined by the machinations of spies and agents, finds its only success in the imaginary world of movie and television drama.

The conspiracy theory is particularly appealing to American anti-communists. The national security manager "casts his adversary, the Revolutionary . . . in the inevitable role of foreign agent." [30] The success of communism is explained by the machinations of an *international* conspiracy, related to the strategy of the Cold War. Our hostility to communism in the emergent world is part of a larger campaign we are waging against a world-wide international movement which threatens our freedom and security. It is difficult to see how anyone today could persist in interpreting the various communist revolutions of the emergent world as part of an international conspiracy. Surely, no one can believe that the development of communism in China, or Cuba, or Vietnam has been the result of decisions made in Moscow. These societies are not satellites of the Soviet Union, or of each other. They were not taken over by communists as a result of moves conceived, planned, and supervised in Moscow, and they are not subject to the dictates of Moscow, except to the extent that the demands of the international situation force every state, at all times, to be restricted in what it can do by the pressures created by other states. The Soviet Union does maintain satellite control over a number of eastern European countries; the status of these countries is in no way comparable to the status of communist states which are ruled by independent communist parties. The communist and Marxist movements of the emergent world all have indigenous roots in the conditions of their own societies. Something of the kind would have occurred if the Soviet Union had never existed. They are not the products of machinations by men in the Kremlin.

It is the sense of being engaged in a struggle against a common enemy which gives an international dimension to the national struggles of the emergent world, where the United States is viewed, unfortunately and tragically, as "the major obstacle to the revolution of rising expectations." [31] Revolutionary war provides a bond of comradeship between the leaders of modernizing movements all over the emergent world. Not only are they engaged in similar enterprises, but they are facing a common enemy, the superior forces of the Western world, and all are compelled to overcome the same problem of backwardness in the face of the technologically superior world of their enemies. Inevitably, the leaders of these various revolutionary movements look to each other for psychological support, even when their resources are too meager to provide much material support. They look upon Communist China as the great model and inspiration because it appears to be conducting its revolutionary conflict to a successful conclusion. Undoubtedly, the knowledge that other poor and ill-equipped emergent societies are facing the same momentous struggle provides an inspiration, and helps the leaders of the emergent world to overcome the sense of inferiority which is built into the very conditions of their struggle. Luis Taruc makes this point in these words: "We were, of course, influenced by the long struggle of the Chinese Communist guerillas. . . . And the Communist victory in China had inspired us and influenced our policies." [32] The fact that Taruc looked to Communist China for inspiration, that Francisco Juliao in Brazil, looks to both Cuba and China for inspiration, does not indicate that the actions of the Huks, or the Chinese Communists, or the Brazilian peasants were determined, controlled, and guided by the center of some international conspiracy.

By attacking communist and revolutionary movements all over the world, we increase this sense of kinship and comradeship among these revolutionaries; we create, in fact, a kind of international revolutionary movement, motivated by a common desire to break American domination in the emergent world. In a sense, we *create*, by our hostility, the "communist conspiracy" we seek to contain all over the world.

Our fear of this "communist conspiracy" is rooted, apparently, in the fear we developed toward the military might of the Soviet Union as a superpower in the Cold War struggle. The strategy of the Cold War demands that we fight communist regimes all over the world, because such regimes side with the Soviet Union in its great-power rivalry with the United States. The tendency of revolutionary, communist regimes to gravitate to the Soviet Union, however, is in no sense the result of the fact that they have been "won over" by the Soviet Union, that they have an ideological commitment to the Soviet regime. The tendency of the revolutionary leaders of the emergent world to side with the Soviet Union is itself largely the product of the attitudes of the West, and a reaction to the hostility of the United States.

The policy of containing communism is based on a considerable misreading of the issues in the emergent world as they appear from the perspective of the underdeveloped nations themselves. For the peoples of Latin America, for instance, "the basic struggle in the post-war world has appeared to be a struggle not so much between communism and capitalism or between the Soviet Union and the United States as between those who desire and those who do not desire to advance their social and economic welfare." [33] We have done more than misread the meaning of this struggle; we have arrogantly assumed that the struggle would not present itself to the emergent nations in relation to their own needs and desires, but in relation to *our* needs and desires. We have arrogantly assumed that the emergent nations were engaged in a struggle in which the chief criterion would be not what would serve their interests, but what would serve *our* interests. We have justified this chauvinism by the formula that what helps the United States helps the so-called free

184

world, and thereby helps everybody, a curious parallel to the Soviet claim that whatever helps the Soviet Union helps the working peoples of the world. But as Julius Nyerere indicates about the people of Tanzania, when they received assistance from Communist China during the great federation crisis of 1964: "What did they know or care about the Cold War? They thought there were good people who were helping them and bad people who were not." [34]

The emergent nations turn to Soviet help because it is frequently their only available means of combating United States power; and the Soviet Union is available for such help partly because of its own conflict with the United States, partly because it is outside the United States system of international economics, and therefore immune to the kinds of pressure we bring to bear on other societies. Cuba, for instance, could turn to Soviet aid because the Soviet Union was free to ignore United States pressures to support the economic blockade on Cuba, pressures which were more successful with the Latin American, and some of the European nations. "This global rivalry provided Castro with alternatives denied previous rulers of Cuba, he was able to brush aside American objections to his program by turning instead to the Soviet Union for aid." [35] The willingness of such revolutionaries to seek help from the Soviet Union does not reflect the existence of an international communist conspiracy. It reflects their desperate need to counterbalance the tremendous might of the United States. The same point can be illustrated from the French colonial wars in Indochina and Algeria. The rebels sought outside help from such major powers as China and the Soviet Union as a counterweight to the heavy aid which France could obtain from the United States; "the fact that the enemy was a major Western power, and used N.A.T.O. weapons, led the F.L.N. to draw close to China and Russia." [36] An Irish Catholic rebel in Belfast commented: "All aid is welcome. Even from the communists." [37] His willingness to receive communist aid has nothing to do with attitudes toward the Cold War, and everything to do with his own revolutionary struggle against Eng-

lish domination. Wherever Western powers have opposed revolutionary national movements in the emergent world, this opposition
has not only increased the anti-Western bias of these national
movements, but it has compelled them to seek outside aid. And in
the context of the Cold War, such aid has been available from the
Soviet Union.

If the new nations seek Soviet aid to combat Western domination, the reverse is not very likely. Not because the Soviet Union is
a more virtuous nation than the United States, not because the Soviet Union is less willing to pursue imperial designs of conquest, but
because it is the United States which has the power and resources
to intervene globally in the domestic affairs of the emergent world.
The United States has the power and the will to play the role of
global policeman in a way which is beyond the capabilities of the
Soviet Union. The United States arrogates to itself the right to control the fortunes of the emergent world, and on the grounds that it
is containing communism, it has built a military-economic empire
all over the world. Soviet imperialism, on the other hand, was restricted for a long time to eastern Europe, partly because of limited
resources, partly, perhaps, because Soviet leadership has been less
animated by fantasies of global omnipotence than our own leadership.

Further, the kind of foreign domination to which the emergent
societies are likely to be most sensitive, and which will be viewed as
more menacing than any other, is domination by advanced nations
in general, and the United States in particular—not because the
West, behind a mask of liberal benevolence, is "really" more evil
than the Soviet Union, but because historical circumstances have
placed the Western world squarely athwart the path to modernization and independence of the emergent world, while the Soviet
Union does not appear as an obstacle to that development. The
domination which the emergent world most fears is a domination
which, historically, has emanated, logically enough, from the advanced nations, not from backward Russia.

From the perspective of the emergent world, the absence of the Soviet Union from the ranks of those powers which have traditionally opposed their development represents a diplomatic windfall, an opportunity to obtain assistance from a major power in their struggle against former colonial masters. The emergent nations find it easy to exploit Cold War rivalry and enlist Soviet aid against the American giant. In fact, the international solidarity between the emergent nations and the Soviet Union stems from the fact that they seek the same diplomatic goal: the reduction of United States power in the world. This anti-American attitude, however, is not caused by the fact that the emergent nations have been "captured" ideologically by Soviet communism. The hostility of the emergent world toward the United States is the result of objective conditions, including the policies of the American government. It is, in a sense, a coincidence that the emergent nations, seeking the path to national self-fulfillment and development, are confronted by the same enemy as the Soviet Union, seeking its own path of superpower status and political influence. In this case, however, it is the tail that wags the dog. Instead of the Soviet Union using the emergent nations to promote something called world communism, these nations use the hostility of the Cold War to exert diplomatic leverage against the United States.

The goal of the emergent nations is neither the status of a Soviet satellite nor that of a Western "ally," but genuine independence and self-determination. It is not so much that the emergent nations want to find a "third" path, but that they want to achieve their own revolution, and if it is a communist revolution, it will be a *national* communist revolution, to satisfy their *national* needs, not to serve the interests, economic or political, of either superpower.

5 · *The "Dualism" of Soviet Policy*

Our determination to interpret the revolutions of the emergent world in the context of the Cold War is related to our conviction that the Soviet Union is not a "normal" state, that its policies cannot be interpreted in terms of traditional, conventional international politics, that it is not motivated by the "normal" pursuit of national interest, but by purely ideological considerations that transcend national politics: by the drive to spread communism. A full discussion of this issue is beyond the scope of this essay; but it requires a brief comment.

The inevitably national basis of communism in the modern world was long obscured by the existence of a so-called international Communist movement, embodied in the Third, or Communist, International. That organization, as well as its successor, the Cominform, no longer exists. The point, however, is not that Communism has gradually lost its international character, as a result of such phenomena as polycentrism, or the Sino-Soviet split. For, in fact, the international Communist movement was never an international movement in the same sense, for instance, that the Second International had been; from the beginning, it was associated with the Soviet government, and existed to serve Soviet state interests. The concept of polycentrism, of "national" Communist movements, misses the point, for it is based on the assumption that Communism, somehow, exists outside the framework of national states; that the development of separate Communist movements in the world was a "national" challenge to the international character of the Communist movement. But "national Communism is not new at all and was not originated by Tito. National Communism was invented by . . . the Soviet Union itself." [38]

The notion that the Soviet Union is a "peculiar" state leads to the conclusion that the rulers of the Kremlin are guided, in their actions, not only by conventional factors of national interest, but, in addition, by ideological considerations; they seek to promote not only the *national* interests of Russia, or the Soviet Union, but the *international* interests of Communism; their second motivation is purely ideological, and presumably takes precedence over the first. But in fact, as the Soviet leaders themselves recognize, the international demands of the ideological crusade to promote Communism, and the national demands of the power politics interests of the Soviet Union, are identical. Whatever serves the interest of the Soviet Union is assumed to serve the interest of international Communism. It is impossible to point to any instance when the Soviet Union subordinated its *national* interests to the *international* interests of Communism. In fact, the distinction between the two does not exist in the minds of the Soviet leadership. Consequently, the attempt to create an extra dimension to Soviet foreign policy, by adducing the existence of an ideological factor not found in other "normal" states, and existing over and above conventional political interests, seems to serve no purpose. In fact, all other states are equally motivated by ideological factors, which have no more nor less relevance to the mechanics of their foreign policy than they do in the Soviet Union. All other states, including the United States, have a moral dimension to their foreign policy, which justifies the pursuit of national interest. Each nation convinces itself that the promotion of its own national interest is not only practically necessary for the security of its people and the state apparatus which serves them, but is morally virtuous because the pursuit of its national interest serves to promote the moral, ideological content of its way of life. Such a moral, ideological dimension to foreign policy, however, is not of much relevance in explaining the mechanics of international affairs, since every state makes the same identification as the Soviet Union does between its national interests, viewed in conventional terms, and the moral imperatives of its way of life, the "ideology" identified with that national interest.

Kurt London attempts to differentiate between nationalism and communism by asserting that nationalism is "different" in a communist country because "Soviet 'patriotism' combines attachment to the motherland with dedication to the system under which it lives." [39] Such a dedication to the "system" of one's motherland, however, is one very important way in which all people define their national identity, and it would be hard to argue that Americans define their patriotism with any less fervent attachment to the system under which they live than do the citizens of the Soviet Union. The clearest summary of the argument that Soviet foreign policy is most conveniently explained by reference to traditional concepts of national interest is found in an essay by Samuel Sharp, "National Interest: Key to Soviet Politics," in which the author concludes: "When the entire record of Soviet success and failure is summed up, the achievements are clearly attributable to Soviet power and diplomacy with no credit due to the International Communist movement." [40] All Soviet foreign policy actions can be related to conventional notions of national interest; and the introduction of an ideological factor provides no useful additional insight into the mechanics of Soviet policies. The observer who seeks the key to Soviet behavior in national interest "is not likely to violate the 'law of parsimony' by unnecessarily piling up hypotheses which are unprovable and which in any case simply confuse the issue." [41]

The use of the term "national" interest is perhaps unfortunate and misleading in this context, and the point might become clearer if we substituted the term state interest, and spoke of the *state interests* of governments; the criteria which guide Soviet policy would be more accurately defined by the expression *raison d'état.* The phrase "national interest" suggests that the behavior of Soviet leaders, or that of any other political rulers, is determined by their personal, subjective feelings about nationalism as an emotion, or an effective idea. The so-called "national" behavior of the Soviet Union, like that of any "normal" political state, is not determined by the feelings of its political leaders about the *idea* of nationalism, it is determined by the *institutional* framework of the modern state system. Regardless of the ideological preferences of the Soviet leaders, they are compelled to work within the framework of the state system. One need not question the sincerity of their commitment to something they call Communism; this commitment, however, does not, and *cannot,* alter the institutional structure of the state system within which they function.

The Soviet leaders *must* work for the interests of the Soviet state, because that state is the instrument, the *only* instrument, for the implementation of their ideological system. The only way the Soviet Union can promote its "ideology" is to promote the interests of the Soviet state; and when the Soviet leaders assert that whatever serves the interests of the Soviet Union serves the interests of Communism, they are pointing to an identity between ideology and the institutional structure of the state which is found in all nations. Even if the Soviet leaders are possessed with a conviction that Communism represents a superior way of life, the promotion of that way of life can only mean, in practice, the extension of traditional Soviet state interests. The fact that Soviet leaders believe that in promoting Soviet state interests they are promoting what they call Communism does not really add to our understanding of Soviet behavior, which would be precisely the same, and could be explained by the same analysis of Soviet "national" interests, if the Soviet Union were peddling a different brand of ideology.

Stalin's conviction that foreign Communist Parties which he could not control were of no use to him was not the expression of personal megalomania. It was a recognition of the elementary facts of political life. The spread of what emergent nations call communism will not serve the interests of *Soviet* Communism, if these communist movements do not represent an extension of Soviet power. The Soviet Union is *only* concerned with the extension of Soviet power, even to the extent that its leaders are guided by ideological considerations, for the Communist ideology which they serve is the ideological content of the *Soviet* political state. The triumph of an independent communist movement, as in China, represents in no sense a "victory" for the Soviet Union in its Cold War conflict with the United States. For an independent communist state will be guided by considerations of its own state interests, which *it* will view as identical with *its* definition of communism.

The point might be settled once and for all with an analogy from computer science. The late British mathematician Alan Turing devised a method, called after him the Turing game, to test whether, in fact, the behavior of computers is different, in any fundamental sense, from what we call "human" thinking. The basic principle of the Turing game is to answer this question: "Are the responses to questions made by a given computing machine indistinguishable from the responses to the same questions made by a given person?" [42] To the extent that the questioner cannot determine which answers come from a computer and which ones come from a human being, it is assumed that the processes of problem solving of the computer are identical to those of a real person. The actual play of the Turing game is somewhat more sophisticated, but for purposes of this argument, understanding the basic principle is all that is required.

I contend that if one could devise a Turing game for the diplomatic behavior of the Soviet Union, one would find that there would be no way of distinguishing the processes of political behavior of Soviet leaders from those of a "normal" state. If one were to take the history of Soviet foreign policy since 1917, and that of any other "normal" state during the same time period; if one could then feed these two histories to an analyst unacquainted with the facts of world history since 1917, and therefore incapable of recognizing the diplomatic record of either state, I contend that there would be no way for such an analyst to determine which course of action represented the behavior of a "normal" state, and which one represented the behavior of that "peculiar" ideological state, the Soviet Union.

Lacking the capability of constructing such a Turing game, we can approximate its methods. Kurt London believes that Soviet foreign policy cannot be understood in conventional terms, that it partakes of a "dual" nature, related to its ideological dimensions.[43] One can take London's essay, and for every point in his analysis it is possible to construct a parallel and completely satisfactory explanation of Soviet behavior by relating it to conventional state interests; conversely, one can take London's analysis and ask, at every point, what would the Soviet government have done if it had been a "normal" state pursuing conventional state interests? In every case, one's answer will be the same as that reached by London, who is assuming that Soviet behavior is guided by unconventional, "ideological" factors.

It is impossible to distinguish the behavior of a "normal" state from that of an ideological state because the institutional framework of the modern state system compels political rulers to completely identify the ideological content of their political system with the conventional interests of that state. *Raison d'état* becomes identical with ideological commitment because of the nature of the political state system in the modern world; *raison d'état*, therefore, remains an adequate explanation for the behavior of political states, and the attempt to equate an international, world Communist movement with Soviet political interests adds a confusing hypothesis which does not serve to explain Soviet political behavior, and which in no way helps us understand the revolutionary ferment in the emergent world.

6 · *"An Open Door for Revolution"* [44]

The policy of containing communism is, in effect, the perfect example of the self-fulfilling prophecy. By assuming that revolutionaries who wish to establish independent modernization, free from Western domination, are communist enemies of the United States, and by treating them as such, we turn such revolutionaries into anti-Western communists. But must we oppose radical revolution everywhere? Can we not envisage a future world, capable of realization, which will serve our interests better than a world in which the United States has become a garrison state, an island of power and wealth in a sea of resentful and bitterly hostile people? If we are concerned primarily with ourselves, will the interest of our own people, of our traditional forms of representative government, be well served if we become, like ancient Sparta, a military totalitarianism, eternally prepared to defend itself against a growing horde of enemies, enemies whom we have ourselves created through our own policies? Can we not envisage a world in which our interests are served in spite of the fact that we do not control every corner of it?

If the powerful Western world holds the trump card in determining the conditions under which the emergent world will confront modernization, can we not, instead of making the task difficult, make it easy? Can we not use our power and wealth to *support* revolutionary change in the emergent world, and smooth the path of modernizing transformation? It is a measure of the rigidity of our thinking, of the extent to which it has become locked into ideological patterns, that few of us can even entertain the possibility of *supporting* Marxist, leftist, or communist movements in the world.

And yet such a policy can in no way be demonstrated to be harmful to the national interests of this country. Our objections to communist or Marxist movements in the emergent world can only be justified on two counts: that left-wing regimes in general, and communist ones in particular, are harmful to the peoples of the emergent world, that we oppose them on idealistic grounds, out of humanitarian concern for the peoples of the emergent nations; or that communists and Marxists are inherently our enemies, members of an international conspiracy committed to destroy us, and to destroy freedom and democracy throughout the world, that we oppose such revolutionaries because they pose a threat to our own survival and security, and to the security of the so-called "free" world. The second claim is obviously the one with the greatest weight and influence in both our national consciousness and the thinking of our political leaders. Neither claim, however, is borne out by an honest examination of revolutionary conditions in the emergent world.

If our concerns are humanitarian, we must note that our opposition to revolutionary change in the emergent world not only reinforces the appeal of communism, but enormously increases the cost of modernization, hence the stringency and discipline of communist authority. It is, in fact, the increased cost and difficulties encountered by the emergent nations which make communist discipline acceptable. A policy of helping the emergent peoples achieve radical transformation, a policy of assisting communist, Marxist, and other revolutionary regimes achieve their goals would certainly greatly reduce the costs of modernization, and reduce the discipline and harshness of communist rule. The communist transformation of their societies may not be the ideal experience for the people of the emergent world, but if we are genuinely concerned with the pain of revolutionary transformation for the emergent nations, we can ease that pain most readily by supporting the process of transformation, so that it will require less discipline, less sacrifice, less human cost.

Even less convincing is the argument that we must fight communism in the underdeveloped world because it is a force dedicated to our own destruction, or because it threatens to engulf the "free" world; that we must resist communism to protect the free world from totalitarianism. Communism in the emergent world is a threat neither to ourselves, to our own security, nor to the freedom of the liberal societies of the West. Communism in particular, and left-wing revolution in general, is a response, in the emergent world, to its own problems and circumstances. Ideologically, it is irrelevant to the conditions of an advanced society such as the United States. The concept of freedom which we claim to defend is one which is restricted to advanced societies. None of these societies is likely to be contaminated by the ideological appeal of communism, a system for the rapid modernization of backward societies. The techniques of modernization in China, for instance, can have no possible relevance in France or Italy. In such countries official Communist Parties express a doctrine substantially different from what is being promoted in the emergent world. Our belief that communism in the emergent world, as a system, as a doctrine, represents a mortal ideological threat to ourselves, and to free nations in general, can rest only on a remarkable lack of confidence in our own institutions and the validity of our system.

If communist movements in the emergent world are our enemies, it is because we have made them so, by our actions and by our hostility. The notion that communist regimes are automatically and inescapably our enemies is based on a new and remarkable view of international diplomacy, that political states have a kind of metaphysical reality which determines their behavior, *a priori,* and for all times—that their behavior is not affected by the actions of other states. It is true that most communist states are our enemies in the world. It is equally true that we have *made* them our enemies. With a different policy, we could have considerably reduced the hostility which all revolutionaries in the emergent world tend to feel toward the West. Unless we assume that our actions in the international arena will have no effect in determining the policies of other states—a conclusion strangely at variance with the assumptions of omnipotence on which the *realpolitik* of our national security managers is based.

It is true, of course, that the leaders of the emergent world will have an inherent hostility toward the West. But since that hostility is the result of past actions by the Western societies, it is not beyond our power to mitigate that hostility by pursuing a different course of action in the future. We are not faced with an *inevitable* and inescapable hostility from the underdeveloped countries of the world, unless we are unwilling to make the sacrifices, not in our own freedom, but in our relative wealth and power, and in the image of ourselves as the benevolent supermen of the world, which are necessary in order for the emergent world to achieve its goals. We can act in such a way as to turn the revolutionary leaders of the emergent world into our enemies by refusing to grant the legitimacy of their demands, by refusing any sacrifices for the accommodation of their aspiring nationalism, by asserting that any attempt to reduce our power and influence in their societies is produced by irrational hatred of the United States.

Or we can facilitate the task of modernization in the emergent world by *assisting* revolutionaries in their goal of dismantling the traditional structure of their societies, and by assisting them with capital and technical aid, accepting the fact that these people can only use such aid for genuine transformation if it is offered with no strings attached, if it is offered for them to use for the achievement of *their* goals, reached in *their* ways. We must further accept that a primary goal of all change in the emergent world is the severance of the special privileged relations which obtain between the powerful West and the impoverished emergent world.

A policy of "open door for revolution," including support of communist movements, would serve our national interest in several ways. It would insure, in the long run, the friendship of all these new nations which may, if they succeed, as China probably will, eventually become modern powers in the world. The fact that we had helped, with our deeds, the leaders of the emergent world in the solution of their problems would place that friendship on the most firm basis. Such a friendship would be infinitely more reliable than the friendship produced by the exercise of international blackmail, or by threats of economic pressure, or the support of military dictators bought by American money, whose friendship and support, like that of Thieu in Vietnam, is as much of a liability as an asset because it depends on the permanent alienation and hostility of their own people.

Such a policy of open door for revolution would free us from the oppressive need of maintaining an ever increasing military establishment abroad for the purpose of forcing the emergent societies to accept our tutelage. The removal of such an establishment would certainly ease tensions, both domestic and international. It would ease the domestic tensions created by the reluctance of our young people to serve in the maintenance of this military empire throughout the world; it would ease the international tensions created by our constant intervention in the domestic affairs of other countries. Every time we intervene to suppress revolution in the emergent world, we create a point of international tension. Each domestic crisis in the emergent world is then transformed into a Cold War crisis. Finally, a policy of open door to revolution, by facilitating the process of modernization, would create the possibility of confronting, in a realistic way, the problem of international stability, by removing one of the chief causes of instability, and by seeking an international order based to some degree on international consensus, rather than one imposed by superior American power.

8

Prospects for the Future

I · *The Future of American Foreign Policy*

RECENT CHANGES IN UNITED STATES FOREIGN POLICY, IN-cluding particularly the withdrawal of our forces from Vietnam and our gradual approaches to Communist China, combined with an apparent abatement of radical, left-wing political leadership in the emergent world, might incline some observers to conclude that the international scene is neither as polarized nor as fraught with revolutionary potential as this essay suggests; that the United States is showing signs of changing fundamental attitudes, developing greater understanding and tolerance; and that the problems of the emergent world will be solved within the kind of framework which official United States policy has been willing to support in the past. A closer examination of these developments, however, fails to warrant such a conclusion.

Although the United States is withdrawing its troops from Vietnam, this withdrawal does not seem to be predicated upon our having learned anything useful from the Indochinese debacle. In fact, one might much more plausibly conclude that our government has learned nothing from Vietnam, that it has failed completely to alter its fundamental interpretation of the emergent world and of American security needs in that world, and that the majority of the American people have learned either no lessons or, even worse, the wrong lessons from the Vietnam fiasco. What we think we have learned from Vietnam is that we used the wrong means to achieve our ends; that the intensity of the communist threat was not as great as we might once have believed; that sending troops to fight in a land war in Asia was an erroneous strategy; that we have failed to understand how to cope with Asians; that we need to understand the tactics of guerilla strategy. Such lessons are worse than no lessons; for they are not only the wrong lessons, but they keep alive the fundamental error of our foreign policy posture in the emergent world. It has not been our means which have been at fault in Vietnam, but our goals. They have been wrong, from the very beginning, because they were based on a misreading of the nature of revolution in the emergent world, a misconception of the nature of our interests in that world, and a completely unrealistic notion of the kind of solution we might develop. Vietnam was a mistake, and is still a mistake, because we are fighting the wrong enemy, for the wrong reasons, and in the quest of insane goals. It was a mistake because it was based on the assumption that our goal in Vietnam should be the containment of communism. There is little evidence that either our government or our people have given up this fundamental assumption. As long as our foreign policy is based on containing communism, it will continue to be disaster, for ourselves as well as for the rest of the world.

The present policies of our government represent no change in our goals in Vietnam, merely a change of means. Because the American people are no longer willing to pay the price of thousands of American lives for the "pacification" of Vietnam, our government is seeking to achieve this "pacification" by other means. Its goal remains the shoring up of a worthless, bankrupt Saigon regime, and it still views a communist take-over in Vietnam as a "defeat" for the United States. And although the American people have decided that they are no longer willing to make the sacrifices demanded of them in the past to "save" Vietnam from communism, there is little indication that they disapprove of such a goal. Our revulsion seems to be a specific revulsion, caused by our conviction that we have done all we can to "help" the Vietnamese people; that our government misled us into believing that these people, with our help, could resist communist "aggression"; whereas the Vietnamese have demonstrated that they are not worth our sacrifices. None of this interpretation implies any questioning of our basic goals in Vietnam. We have become disgusted with the Vietnam War, and by the colossal deception practiced by our government in waging that war. There is little evidence that we have become disgusted with the fundamental anti-communism of our foreign policy.

It is true that the revulsion against Vietnam has had echoes beyond that specific war. But these echoes have as yet suggested little positive reorientation in the thinking of the American people. On the contrary, the revulsion against Vietnam has produced a negative reaction against all American involvements abroad. Although it is true that anything which would reduce our tendency to mount military interventions abroad is to the good and should be encouraged, such a tendency will not have a lasting or positive effect if it expresses a simple negative and isolationist mood. For there is no such thing as an isolationist American policy. Our power is too great, and our interests too far-reaching. Everything we do or fail to do will have an enormous impact on the rest of the world. The so-called isolationism implicit in the revulsion against the war consists partly of an unrealistic refusal to acknowledge the nature of our impact on the world, a naive belief that all we have to do is "withdraw," and the problems of foreign policy will go away. Such an isolation does not represent any genuine rethinking of our foreign policy. It consists of rejecting any policy that resembles Vietnam, simply because of its traumatic associations, not out of any understanding of what was wrong with our Vietnam policy, or any genuine desire to discover what was wrong. Such isolationism feeds a know-nothing attitude toward foreign policy which could have dangerous implications.

In fact, the revulsion against the Vietnam War, if it is not accompanied by any real understanding of what was wrong with the war in the first place, could have very adverse effects on both our domestic and foreign policies. For this withdrawal is going to be viewed, and eventually condemned, as a defeat. Once the futility of Vietnamization becomes apparent, if we continue to accept that the fundamental goal of our policy is the containment of communism, the whole Vietnam episode will be viewed as a major defeat, much as the Communist victory in China came to be interpreted, in the light of our assumptions, as a "defeat" for the United States. A conviction on the part of large numbers of Americans that we suffered a major defeat in Southeast Asia will not only bring out in full cry the demagoguery of "betrayal" which accompanied the China episode in the 1950's, but it will create a panic that we are once again "losing" the global contest against communism. Not only will all the follies and insanities of containing communism be revived, but such policies will now be implemented in an increasingly rigid manner, in consequence of the belief that we are in "retreat," and must restore the balance against the communists.

Much of the same argument applies to the so-called change in our China policy. Such a change, although certainly to be desired, will be of little moment if it is not accompanied by a genuine reappraisal of our attitude toward the problem of communism, and a genuine effort to discover the sources of the failure of our China policy in the past. The change in our China policy does not reflect any such fundamental reorientation, nor is it based to any degree on acknowledging that our past hostility to the regime of Mao Tse-tung was unnecessary and unprofitable. Rather, it is based on the continued conviction that our chief goal is the containment of communism, but that the methods used in the past, blockade, non-recognition, international ostracism, were crude and ineffective. There are few signs that our establishment believes that the Chinese Communist regime is not, in the long run, an enemy. The détente with China is a tactical concession, a recognition that the previous strategy had failed. It is not a conversion to the belief that Communist China need not be an enemy. As a result, the rapprochement with China contains two potentially dangerous implications. It is based on the continued illusion that if China is to cease, eventually, to be an enemy of the United States, this "conversion" will be the result of our firm opposition to communist expansion. In other words, it is based on the very dangerous illusion that China's hostility toward us proceeds from the "evil" nature of communism, an evil which can only yield to our moral and military pressures. Actually, of course, China's hostility toward the West has deep historical roots. Secondly, the rapprochement with China will be viewed as a concession wrung from us by the enemy. It will be viewed, therefore, like the settlement in Vietnam, as a further defeat, a further retreat. It must so be interpreted, sooner or later, in spite of the current euphoria, if we continue to believe that the containment of communism is vital to our interests and security. In fact, it is becoming increasingly doubtful whether the Nixon China policy is as "new" as it first appeared to be. The fiasco surrounding the battle for China's seat in the United Nations suggests that the "new" line on China was primarily a public relations play, typical of the shallow, hucksterite thinking which marks this administration, tossed off in the pursuit of immediate, short-run, domestic political gains, but accompanied neither by any attempt to rethink the basic premises of our foreign policy nor even by any consideration of the immediate consequences of this "new" line in Asia. There are few signs, at least to this writer, that the current administration has in any way moved away from the rigid, unrealistic, and disastrous anti-communism which has governed our foreign policy for the last twenty-five years.

The most hopeful reorientation in American foreign policy has been the evident desire of our legislators to review and rethink the foreign aid program. The real, if unacknowledged, goal of foreign aid has been in many ways the very opposite of what its name suggests, since foreign aid has been used primarily as a means of maintaining America's informal overseas economic empire. Hence, its reform is not only to the good, but reflects a willingness to move away from rigid adherence to earlier commitments. But the curtailment of foreign aid also rests on more questionable assumptions. Certainly the decision, subsequently revoked, to abolish foreign aid completely, in response to the expulsion of Nationalist China from the United Nations, expressed all the worst American fantasies about global omnipotence, and the petulant desire to "punish" the emergent world for rejecting American paternalism. In other words, second thoughts about foreign aid reflect to some degree a mood of pique, of disgust with non-Western nations, rather than an intelligent reappraisal of the problems of the emergent world. And despite the desire to genuinely reform the foreign aid program, we continue to provide various forms of military and security assistance to reactionary regimes in many parts of the world. Most importantly, we continue to provide enormous military aid to the worthless Thieu regime in Saigon.

Nor can the failure of radical, left-wing communist revolution to sweep the underdeveloped world in recent years be taken as evidence that the basic argument of this essay is faulty, and that United States foreign policy, in spite of occasional mistakes, is fundamentally sound. For there is no evidence that those societies which have as yet avoided some of the revolutionary responses discussed in this essay have discovered solutions to their problems within the framework of a conservative, traditional order, and without challenging the hegemony of the United States. Given the nature of modernization, our claim that we are looking for a democratic model of development is impossible of fulfillment. Until and unless we can demonstrate that genuine modernization and autonomous development can take place without the kinds of radicalism suggested in this essay, and without the basic changes in American policy urged here, we cannot argue that the expectation of such radical response is unfounded.

It may be too soon for radical revolution to have matured in all parts of the emergent world; but there is no evidence that the factors which will produce such radical revolution, which we have been examining in this essay, are being eliminated, and plenty of evidence that the scenario of China, Algeria, or Cuba is likely to be repeated eventually in such places as Brazil, Bolivia, the Middle East, Southeast Asia, and parts of Africa. It may, of course, prove possible for us to assert a national interest based on the suppression of revolution and communism in the emergent world. Such an eventuality appears doubtful, for our success in institutionalizing a permanent empire to suppress communist revolution in the emergent world depends on the cooperation of the Soviet Union. Although there have been hints from time to time that the two nuclear giants are tempted to bury the hatchet, divide the world, and support each other in a policy of international, conservative authoritarianism, there are too many historical and traditional factors, too many years of suspicion and hostility, too many fears generated by nuclear weapons, standing in the way of a genuine reconciliation between the two superpowers. In addition, sooner or later such a global empire would have to include, as a full-fledged partner, Communist China, and eventually Japan and western Europe. As long as the Soviet Union and China are available to provide some form of aid and encouragement to radical revolution in the emergent world, and as long as they remain convinced that their hostility to the United States warrants supporting such challenges to American supremacy, it will be difficult, if not impossible, to achieve the goals of the national security managers, and to permanently suppress communist revolution in the emergent world.

But even if the national security managers succeed, even if they manage to create a global empire dedicated to the permanent subjugation of the emergent world, even if they fight enough Vietnams, and with sufficient ruthlessness, that instead of increasing revolutionary radicalism, such "police actions" succeed in terrorizing and crushing the emergent peoples into a more or less permanent acceptance of American domination—even if the national security managers can make their definition of the national interest work, it would still be possible to argue against the policy of containing communism, and to demonstrate that its costs are too great, not only for the emergent peoples, but for us. For the only way we can maintain our national interest without yielding to the demands of revolutionaries in the emergent world is through the continued and increasing militarization of our society, by turning our society into an armed camp. Such a militarization will accelerate current internal crises and disorders in our society, as our young people increasingly refuse to support a foreign policy based on waging the kind of war we have been waging in Vietnam, and as resources urgently needed for domestic rehabilitation are squandered on weaponry. Although communism in the emergent world has little relevance for a society such as ours, a bond becomes established between those Americans who reject our foreign policy and the victims of that policy in the emergent world. Such a bond, based on sympathetic suffering, rather than on any ideological identity, is what is being expressed by those demonstrators who carry Viet Cong flags. Such sympathies do not indicate that our young people are becoming "communists," but that they are increasingly alienated from a foreign policy which victimizes the people of the emergent world, and from a society which permits, in fact encourages, such atrocities. The internal crises produced by this alienation can only aggravate the climate of confrontation, which will then, by a reciprocal process, feed the militarization of our society.

In addition, the success of the policy of the national security managers depends on maintaining a very high risk of nuclear conflict with the Soviet Union, which cannot accept passively the establishment of a global American empire. Finally, such a policy can only succeed at the expense of the continued misery of the peoples of the emergent world. Awareness of that misery must work constantly at cross purposes, as it already does today, with all those sincere professions of humanitarianism which emanate from our people. It will be increasingly difficult, with time, for our people to simultaneously support programs to alleviate the misery of the emergent peoples of the world, and a foreign policy which is the chief factor in maintaining that misery.

In short, the policy of containing communism, even if it can be made to work by sheer brutality, can only create conditions in our society, on the international scene, and in the emergent world, which I would view with enormous distaste, and which I am confident would be equally repugnant to most Americans.

2 · *Communism and Power Politics*

But can we support an "open door for revolution," if that revolution involves the creation of totalitarian communist states? Can we reconcile our humanitarian concerns for non-Western peoples with the imposition of such authoritarian systems? In short, can we hope that the peoples of the emergent world will be able to throw off the discipline of communism if their transformation succeeds? Will they be able to resist further exploitation and authoritarian control if, in the process of their development, they are fettered securely with the chains of a collective totalitarianism? If communism is to be redefined as instrumental rather than terminal, if it is a process of modernization, rather than its end product, will not the nature of that end product be influenced by the means used to reach it? The point, as Aldous Huxley used to remind us, is not whether the end justifies the means, but that the means determine the end. The experience of the Soviet Union gives no clear answer, or at best, a depressing answer. But so does, in a different way, the experience of the United States, and that of most other Western societies. The challenge of modern authoritarianism is not limited to any particular communist expression. The dilemma of the emergent world is part of a crisis of values related to modernization, to a loss of individuality in modern societies which stands in contradiction to the liberating hopes of development, and of which communism is only one, if an extreme, variation.

Modernization has failed to liberate man, and the liberal promise has not been fulfilled; our disillusionment with the modern world is expressed in our disillusionment with progress. The problem of freedom and authority, of freedom and order, is a basic one in all modern societies, and the ability of the emergent nations to achieve genuine freedom has less to do with any specific communist experience they may confront than with the ability of modern societies in general to transcend the authoritarian tendencies of civilized organization. If the emergent societies are threatened by totalitarianism, it is not so much that they have been "captured" by totalitarian communists as that modernization itself, although it has increased, in some ways, the area of freedom, has done so at the price of new disciplines which make every modern society, including the United States, vulnerable to a collective authoritarianism which culminates at the extreme limit in totalitarianism, a political phenomenon peculiar to the modern world, and unknown in traditional societies.

The problem of totalitarianism is the problem of all modern societies, the expression of a pathological condition in modern civilization itself, in no sense restricted to communist states. If communist totalitarianism is considerably more rigid and pervasive in the Soviet Union today than similar coercive tendencies in many Western countries, if the United States, with all of its tendencies toward gigantic corporate control, is still considerably freer and more open than the Soviet Union, the difference is the result of different historical circumstances, rather than of "ideological" differences between communism and capitalism. They are differences resulting from the different routes the two societies pursued in achieving modernization. As this essay has sought to demonstrate, the circumstances under which the United States modernized were uniquely favorable, and considerably mitigated the authoritarianism inherent in modernization. A glance at our current political scene should quickly convince us that the capitalistic nature of our society in no way protects us from totalitarian pressures, totalitarian mentalities, or the appeal of totalitarian slogans.

The great force for modernization in the West, as we suggested earlier, was power politics. The European nations modernized because failure to achieve this kind of development meant vulnerability to manipulation and exploitation by better organized, more developed, hence more powerful nations. This factor is now the basic motivation behind modernization in the emergent world. Consequently, modernization in that world cannot be limited to a fight against absolute poverty, for the solution of that problem, or any other problem, the very survival, in fact, of the society as an independent unit depends on the creation of states which are no longer vulnerable to exploitation by their more powerful colleagues. It is that stress on the demands of power politics which creates the conditions for political authoritarianism in the emergent world, as it has created pressures for similar authoritarianism in the West. There is no doubt that the health, welfare, and happiness of the peoples of Africa, Asia, and Latin America would be better served by a global, non-political program of economic aid, growth, and development, of education, health care, and nutrition that was not tied to the necessities of big power political competition. If all the peoples of the world cooperated in a joint effort to aid those less fortunate than themselves, without consideration of political motives, or the demands of the Cold War, the interests of the peoples of the emergent world would be served much more effectively than they are today. Unfortunately, such a non-political approach to modernization is not possible; or at least, it cannot be up to the emergent societies themselves to make it possible.

The stress on modernization for purposes of political power is not the result of "evil" communist influences. It is the result of the existing political organization of the developed states. If the game of power politics is debilitating to the efforts of the emergent world to liberate itself, it is the advanced, civilized world which imposes this global pattern of war and competition. If the present system of international politics is to be reformed, and its destructive pressures alleviated, the emergent nations are in no position to take the initiative in instituting such a change. If the pattern of power politics is to be broken, the advanced nations which created this pattern have the initial responsibility for doing so.

If any single factor would reduce the pressures for totalitarianism, both in the Soviet Union and in the United States, it would be a reduction of international tensions, of the fears and insecurities created by the Cold War. We need hardly remind ourselves that war has everywhere been the single most important factor in producing totalitarianism. Although not all observers agree on whether a reduction of international tensions would encourage a domestic liberalization of the Soviet regime, the factors inhibiting such a liberalization are certainly related to the status of the Soviet Union as a superpower. We noted earlier that the modernization of such states as Sweden or Denmark has not produced the pressures for collective authoritarianism found in a country like Russia. The difference would appear to be related to the demands of power politics. In Russia, what Von Laue calls the gap between resources and ambitions was a much more pressing problem than in Denmark, because of the status of Russia as a major power. If modernization is related to power it might be reasonable to assume that many of the emergent nations could escape the worst pressures of collective authoritarianism, that their communism might become much more liberal if they remained outside the mainstream of international power politics, and outside the pattern of Cold War competition. On the other hand, the attempt of the advanced West to maintain domination over the emergent world creates, for these nations, great demands for political, economic, and military power to resist such domination. And the doctrine of containing communism, through which we justify this informal Western empire, is the chief way in which the Cold War is exported into the emergent world. Free of excessive concerns for power and security, the emergent world could confront modernization more rationally, and relate it more to the needs of people, and less to the power demands of the state. The attempt of China to achieve status as a major power gives an urgency to her modernization which makes such extreme forcing methods as communism much more attractive than among less ambitious states. On the other hand, the political ambitions of China are related not only to her traditional status as the major power in Asia, but to the fierce pressures of the United States to prevent China from recovering that traditional position.

The argument that the emergent societies do not need modernization, that modern civilization will not bring happiness to these peoples, that they are better off within their own traditional world, is at best irrelevant, at worst insufferably patronizing. Conservatives who look back nostalgically on the good old days when a white man could enjoy a good life, prompt service, and the charm of "unspoiled" traditional folkways in "the colonies," when he could sample the fine delicacies of Chinese cuisine in Shanghai, stroll unchallenged through the beautiful streets of Saigon, enjoy the plush night life of Havana, sit in the sun and be served by the quaint, childlike people of the West Indies—such people would under no circumstances accept within their own societies the backwardness which made these lands such fine tourist attractions. It is disingenuous in the extreme for the advanced nations, while clinging to the accoutrements of power, to decry the attempts of the emergent peoples to emulate them.

Modernization may be a cure worse, in many ways, than the disease of backwardness, but it is one that we ourselves have embraced enthusiastically; and it is not for us, who have forsaken the powerlessness of backwardness, to criticize the attempts of emergent peoples to break similar shackles, and to tell them that they are really happier in their condition, when one aspect of that condition is to place them in a subservient relation to us. It would be hypo-

critical, as well as futile, at this point, to tell the Vietnamese people
that they should stay away from the strong liquor of modernization,
when their failure to drink that heady brew has turned their home-
land into an inferno in which they do not have the means, or the
power, to eject the intruders who are destroying their country.

3 · *The Liberation of Modernization*

The greatest liberation of modernization has been to break the
grip of traditional ideology over the minds of people. Modernization in the emergent world is a liberating force, even at the cost of
communism, to the extent that it transforms the social environment, and the people within it, in such a way that they are no longer vulnerable to the exploitation of traditional elites. The great
gap between the developed and the underdeveloped world made
the peoples of Asia, Africa, and Latin America particularly vulnerable not only to the exploitation of their own ruling classes but to
the much more intensive exploitation of Western peoples. Although
communism substitutes for the role of traditional elites that of party
functionaries and professional bureaucrats, its net impact will be
liberating in one fundamental respect. For the end result of communist authoritarianism will be to create a modern, developed society, the members of which will no longer be manipulable in the
same way. Their vulnerability to manipulation was the expression
of the backward conditions of their societies. Particularly, they will
be resistant to the kind of manipulation and exploitation to which
their backwardness has subjected them in relation to colonial powers, and the advanced world of the West.

For the peoples of the emergent world, communism is a liberating force to the extent that it opens the door to the possibility of
progress. No matter how harsh and painful, it holds out the possibility of a better life, simply because it is destroying the traditional
order, and moving the society toward a modernization which may

end their perennial weakness. Communism is a liberating force to the extent that it is an instrument for ending the traditional powerlessness of emergent societies.

Despite all the disciplines of modernization and civilization, these processes eventually create a population which is aware, intellectually, of the possibility of a better world. It is this intellectual awakening, in fact, which creates so many of the internal tensions and frictions in our highly disciplined societies. For the citizens of modern states are no longer willing to accept that whatever is, is right. Modernization and development mean, inevitably, the modernization and development of people themselves. And the transformation of people which accompanies modernization changes people in such a way that they can no longer be put back into the sleep of traditional stagnation. The motivations of individual communist leaders, therefore, the sincerity of their desire to work for the good of their own people, may be partly irrelevant, for their concern for political power is the guarantee that they will work for the modernization of their own people. Communist revolution in the emergent world will of necessity create modern people who will share with their contemporaries in the West, regardless of the intensity of communist authoritarianism, an intellectual awakening in which they will no longer be satisfied with traditional apathy.

Whether the dilemma of freedom and authority can be resolved, whether the limitations of civilization can be transcended, and whether civilization can be made into an instrument for the authentic liberation of man is a global problem which we must all confront together, and which will not be solved if we restrict ourselves to combating its communist expression, or if we convince ourselves that communism itself is the only obstacle to the realization of the liberating potentials of modern civilization. "Today, all of the peoples of the world are participants in a universal civilization characterized by ever-rising aspirations for material and intellectual satisfactions." [1]

The real conflict in the world today, the real conflict in our own society, the problem we seek to externalize by blaming communists for all our difficulties, is the conflict between the authoritarian and the liberating implications of modernization. In this struggle, the real issue is between those who would preserve the status quo domestically, as well as internationally, and the forces working for a liberating change in the bureaucratic authoritarianism of modern society. In this struggle the forces of law and order and bureaucratic repression are on the same side of the ideological fence, whether they are the agents of a gigantic Federal bureaucracy in Washington, D.C., or the agents of the Communist Party in the Soviet Union. In both cases, they are most accurately defined, ideologically, as conservatives. For conservatism is based essentially on the notion that modern democracy is a failure, and the liberalism implied in modernization is a sham, not because liberalism and democracy have been betrayed, but because people, in fact, are limited, incapable of freedom, and require the authority of their "betters" as expressed in the workings of the "benevolent" therapeutic state. The Communist Party of the Soviet Union is today a typical conservative institution, and wherever the Soviet Union has maintained control and influence over foreign Communist Parties, these parties tend to be equally reactionary. Our own conservatives share many of the ideological assumptions of the Soviet leaders. They fear anarchy; they distrust individuality; they are convinced that permissiveness (a code word for freedom) threatens the established order; they emphasize obedience, respect, authority; they are suspicious of expressions of individual creativity, which are viewed as symptoms of moral decay. Their view of a perfectly ordered world is very similar to the one entertained by Soviet leaders; it is one marked by order, discipline, regimentation, and a great fear of the "mob." Conversely, radical revolutionaries share the same ideological assumptions all over the world, whether they live in a democracy like the United States, or a communist dictatorship like the Soviet Union.

In this struggle to achieve the genuine liberation which modern civilization promises, communism and the philosophy of Marxism, in and of themselves, do not represent an ideological obstacle to such a liberation. There is nothing in Marxist ideology, or in the practice of communist states, to suggest that communism is inherently, because of its ideological presuppositions, incapable of overcoming the totalitarian organization which it has developed in response to the needs of development, or any less capable of moving toward an open society, than any other system.

The libertarian aspects of Marxism, like those of so many other liberal philosophies, were distorted in many places by the pressures of modernization. Marxism became a victim, like liberalism itself, of modern totalitarianism. In the Soviet Union, Marxism has become a fanatical, doctrinaire religion, a fact explained by the nature of the Soviet system, but in no way dependent on the character or content of Marxist ideology.

Recent events in Czechoslovakia, as well as in Yugoslavia, seem to demonstrate that it is entirely possible for a Communist Party to move in the direction of democracy and a more open society, given the right circumstances; and one factor that will produce this liberalization is the felt need for greater popular commitment if modernization and stability are to be achieved. Both the Czech and Yugoslav Communists returned to earlier, Marxist, pre-Soviet definitions of communism which, in the case of Czechoslovakia, might well have pushed its Communist Party closer to what has come to be called in the West social democracy. "The successful evolution of a unique, communist-ruled democracy in which freedom and dissent are institutionalized even more securely than they are in Yugoslavia . . . should not be excluded from the range of possible alternatives." [2]

The liberal experiment in Czechoslovakia was originated and instituted by the Czech Communists themselves. They were defeated by Soviet intervention, an intervention dictated by the needs of power politics. Soviet leaders became convinced that their own security needs made it imperative that Czechoslovakia continue under Soviet domination. In short, Soviet intervention in Czecho-slovakia paralleled, in its motivations and view of the world, United States intervention in Vietnam. The fact that Communist Parties have been the victims of both interventions should raise doubts in the minds of those Americans who are convinced that the ideological struggle between communism and the "free world" explains the pattern of international politics.

4 · *A Redefinition of American Interests in the Emergent World*

This essay began with a challenge to certain assumptions underlying American policy in the emergent world, and I have sought to demonstrate the validity of that challenge by re-examining and redefining the nature of the revolution of the emergent world. I have argued that the fight against communism in the emergent world is based on false assumptions which cannot justify our present policies. In the process, however, we have uncovered a deeper layer, as it were, a more fundamental basis for our policies. We are not really fighting communism to defend our freedoms from the presumed ideological threat of an international conspiracy; we are defending our enormous wealth and power from the challenge posed by the revolutionary transformation of the emergent nations. And we fight communism because it is the central expression of that revolution. By redefining in this way our struggle to contain communism, we also redefine with sharper clarity the issues facing us in the emergent world. Our choice is a simple one. Either we prevent the development of emerging societies, stifle their revolutionary challenge, force them into modes which threaten neither our power nor our wealth, or we learn to live with them. The fight against the revolutionary transformation of the emergent world, which is the real meaning of the containment of communism, will be, in the long run, counter-productive, aggravating the severity of the communist response, increasing hostility between ourselves and the emergent nations, exporting the Cold War to the emergent world, poisoning international relations, forcing us into the uncomfortable role of policeman of the world, and converting us, in the process, into a police state.

This essay has suggested, as an alternative, that we learn to live with the revolution of the emergent world; moreover, that the best way to live with that revolution is to support it, to promote it vigorously, to offer, in fact, an "open door to revolution." Learning how to live with the emergent world, how to *help* the emergent world achieve its goals, requires, however, a profound reorientation of our policies. We must be prepared to grant a generous amount of capital and technical resources, of which we possess considerable surpluses, without the usual strings attached; that is, not in return for the kinds of military and economic concession through which we maintain abroad that informal American empire, the continued existence of which defeats the purpose of a genuine program of foreign aid. Aid must be granted, not with an eye to American business opportunities, or strategic military interests, but with the intention of genuinely facilitating growth and independent development. Even more important, we must be prepared to give up many of our economic advantages in the emergent world, ceding positions of economic power which provide generous returns for American business. We must be prepared to alter the terms of international trade in such a way as to give up the enormous advantages granted the advanced world by the structure of the international economy. We must sacrifice, in short, our willingness to exploit the weakness of the emergent world for our own economic advantage.

If our goal is to *assist* the emergent world, we must accept communist or socialist regimes, giving up the paranoiac notion that the actions of the emergent nations can be meaningfully explained as the expression of a popularity contest about the United States. The motives of the emergent nations are explained only in reference to their own national goals, and their attitudes toward the United States are no more than a response to what we do about their struggle for development.

We must help the emergent nations achieve what *they* want to achieve, in response to their own felt needs, giving up the comforting illusions of the white man's burden, that we have a paternalistic responsibility to impose our enlightened tutelage over them. Such a policy should not be interpreted, however, as indiscriminate support for *all* political forces in the emergent world. Our criterion for evaluating these forces can be defined very simply. We should support all groups demonstrating their willingness and ability to promote modernization, while we should oppose all groups actively engaged in resisting this revolutionary transformation. There are so many ways in which we can help development in the emergent world, particularly through the exercise of our enormous economic power, that we need not engage in direct military interventions to promote revolution. The forces fighting for change in the emergent world will have little difficulty gaining the upper hand once we cease shoring up reactionary regimes. In summary, we must do everything possible to facilitate the transition of the emergent world into the contemporary world, and be prepared to accommodate our own position and interests to the existence of these new nations.

A question remains, however: why should the United States submit to such an agonizing reorientation of its traditional policies toward the emergent world, if this reorientation entails the voluntary surrender of so many of its interests? Why should we be prepared to make this kind of sacrifice for the emergent world? It would be possible, of course, to put the answer on humanitarian grounds, to suggest that such a course of action would result in a *genuine* improvement in the traditional conditions of poverty, hunger, ignorance, and disease in the emergent world. It would be possible, in short, to appeal to American generosity, benevolence, and compassion, reminding ourselves in passing that the reforms suggested in this essay require only minimal sacrifices in our enormous wealth and power. Pleas for a reorientation of our policy in the emergent world usually rest on such grounds, and they are both valid and compelling.

An equally plausible and meaningful case can be made for the open door to revolution on the grounds of enlightened self-interest. That case, in fact, has been made throughout this essay. But in order to understand why the surrender of some of our power and advantages in the emergent world can be related to enlightened self-interest, it is necessary for us to redefine traditional concepts of the national interest. For despite inflated claims at the end of both World Wars that the United States was ushering in a new era of international relations, rejecting the outmoded techniques of European power politics, our foreign policy has consistently displayed the same narrow, petty, and short-sightedly selfish definition of national interest which so frequently brought disaster to the European powers in the past. Our current definition of national interest identifies that interest with all the economic advantages, all the weapons of political domination, all the ingredients of power which we enjoy all over the world, and promoting the national interest is defined as increasing these advantages, enlarging our power, spreading the area of our domination. Such a definition, of course, has been traditional in Western power politics.

The weakness of this tradition is that it defines our interests *at the expense of others.* It assumes an unlimited struggle in the world of power politics in which national interest is measured by comparative advantages *against* other players in the game. The history of the modern world should have demonstrated the sterility of such a concept. The only meaningful definition of national interest is one which accommodates the existence and viability of *other* states. Not out of some kind of fuzzy idealism, or "globaloney," but out of a hard-headed recognition that peaceful co-existence is not an exhortation to brotherly love but a necessary precondition to survival in the modern world. A definition of *national* interest, in short, depends on a definition of an *international* world order which not only allows for the existence of a multiplicity of states, but recognizes that the safety and survival of each member depends on the stability of the entire system.

A successful international order requires the United States to compromise its dominant positions in order to live with the rest of the world. The alternative is written clearly in the history of the twentieth century. Major powers either learn how to live with the rest of the world, accommodating their interests to those of others, or they live in perpetual conflict *against* the world. Germany remains a sobering reminder of the fate of a major power which chose the second alternative. A definition of national interest based on the accumulation of advantages over other states, and the extension of power in relation to the rest of the world, far from being a shrewd exercise in *realpolitik,* has quite regularly brought disaster to its practitioners, from Louis XIV to Wilhelm II, from Napoleon to Hitler. Not only is such a definition of national interest disastrous at the international level, but its domestic impact is equally repugnant, as was suggested earlier in this chapter. For if one defines the national interest chauvinistically, *against* the rest of the world, then one is eventually driven to what the Italians call *sacro egoismo,* a conviction that one's interests have a *moral right* to take precedence over those of others. National interests become moral imperatives, pursued for purposes of national grandeur, or for the satisfaction of boasting that one's nation is number one. Nazi Germany is once more a frightening example of what happens to a society which becomes convinced that its national interests are moral imperatives which justify the use of any means for their fulfillment. Analogous outbursts of savage chauvinism in our own society in the last twenty-five years indicate that a society which refuses to see its own interests as part of a larger international order must sooner or later, in the constant struggle to assert itself against the rest of the world, move toward that complete and completely disciplined mobilization and militarization which we call totalitarianism.

Our present determination to stifle the revolution of the emergent world is a case in point. Ultimately, we have no assurance that we can prevent development indefinitely, that we can permanently prevent the emergent world from playing the role it seeks to play in the international system. By defining our interests narrowly, by viewing the successful development of the emergent nations as injurious to our interests because it entails losing some of our power and some of our economic advantages, we duplicate the conditions of Soviet and Chinese development; that is, we insure that once any part of the emergent world does succeed in breaking the shackles of backwardness, its development experience will condition it to profound hostility toward the United States, and a determination to assert its own interests at our expense. Because if we define our interests as comparative advantages over other players in the game, if we define our interests *against* the rest of the world, the rest of the world must define *its* interests against *us,* and must interpret the promotion of its own interests as an unlimited struggle against our power.

Defining a viable international order which accommodates the emergent nations is not, of course, an easy task. It need not be viewed rigidly, as defining some perfectly ordered status quo, and its definition requires constant readjustment. It is possible, however, to define with considerable precision the key to such a successful international order. The goal of American foreign policy ceases to focus on the promotion of *American* advantages at the expense of the rest of the world; it becomes, instead, committed to the dynamic equilibrium of the whole system. If we are committed to constructing a viable international order, the open door to revolution appears the only means of accommodating the interests of the emergent world to such a system. It appears to be the only means of coping with the revolution of the emergent world which guarantees the ultimate stability of the system and our own security within it.

It is true that the redefinition of national interest outlined above applies equally to the Soviet Union. But our ability to influence Soviet policy directly is necessarily limited. We must concentrate on what *we* can do, hoping that our willingness to give up an unrealistic "hard" line will change the international scene in ways that will allow the Soviet Union to give up its own narrowly chauvinistic definition of national interest. On the other hand, because of our paramount power, our responsibility to the creation of a world order is primary. Weak states, such as the emerging nations, *must* struggle to express their own interests unilaterally. They do not have the power or the resources to affect the structure of the international system. Their own existence within that system appears precarious, and they are engaged in a constant struggle for survival. They do not see that survival as necessarily dependent on an international order which has assigned them to a position of weakness and poverty. In fact, a successful international order would be one to which the emergent nations could commit themselves, which they no longer viewed as a status quo stacked against them. Responsibility for creating such a system rests upon the major powers, not only because of their power, but because they have much more to lose as a result of major international cataclysms.

Ultimately, of course, the success of all aspects of our foreign policy will depend on the reduction and eventual elimination of Cold War tensions. Only in this way can we provide an international framework for a genuinely successful development of the emergent world. But the open door to revolution would itself be the most fruitful way of reducing world tensions, therefore of reducing the areas of possible friction between ourselves and the Soviet Union. Most important, it would prevent a new and tragic Cold War from developing between ourselves and the emergent world.

Biographical Note

THE LITERATURE CONCERNING THE PROBLEMS OF THE EMERGENT WORLD, and communism in the emergent world, is enormous, and this bibliography makes no attempt at a comprehensive listing. It is not only a selected bibliography, but its selectivity is related specifically to the argument of this essay.

The bibliography is divided into two parts: A general bibliography including works relevant to the entire theme of this essay, and a more specialized bibliography. The general bibliography is divided into two sections: works dealing with the whole range of problems of the emergent world, and a series of specific studies, concerned with particular areas. The specialized bibliography is divided into topics which parallel the chapter organization of this book.

I. GENERAL BIBLIOGRAPHY

A. One of the basic works on the politics of development, a kind of pioneering effort in defining problems and issues, is Gabriel A. Almond and James S. Coleman (eds.), *The Politics of the Developing Areas,* Princeton University Press, Princeton, N.J., 1960. Also valuable is the earlier work of Gabriel Almond, *The Appeals of Communism,* Princeton University Press, Princeton, N.J., 1954. One of the great studies of the emergent world is the massive work of Gunnar Myrdal, *Asian Drama,* Twentieth Century Fund, New York, 1968, which limits itself to Asia, but provides a thorough and detailed analysis of the empirical evidence for that continent. A comparable, earlier study, concentrating on Africa, is Rupert Emerson, *From Empire to Nation,* Beacon Press, Boston, 1960. Another good general introduction, focusing on problems and possible solutions, is Barbara Ward, *The Rich Nations and the Poor Nations,* W. W. Norton & Co., New York, 1962. A particularly good theoretical work, reflecting the new techniques in political science research, is David Apter, *Some Conceptual Approaches to the Study of Modernization,* Prentice-Hall, Englewood Cliffs, N.J., 1968.

B. On Africa: James S. Coleman and Carl G. Rosberg (eds.), *Political Parties and National Integration in Tropical Africa,* University of California Press, Berkeley, Cal., 1966, a basic work with a wealth of empirical information concerning the struggle to create autonomous political states and viable modern societies in Africa. Particularly valuable are Immanuel Wallerstein, *Africa, the Politics of Independence,* Vintage Books, New York, 1961, and Immanuel Wallerstein, *Africa: The Politics of Unity,* Random House, New York, 1967; these two works are among the best introductions to the study of emerging Africa. A more recent study, by a former reporter for the *Washington Post* with a close personal acquaintance with African societies, is Russell Warren Howe, *The African Revolution,* New African Library, Croydon, England, 1969.

On China: A good general introduction is O. Edmund Clubb, Jr., *Twentieth Century China,* Columbia University Press, New York, 1964. Clubb, whose father was in the American diplomatic service in China, was born in Peking, and possesses not only an intimate knowledge of China, but a sympathetic understanding of its problems. K. S. Karol, *China,* translated from the French by Tom Baistow, Hill and Wang, New York, 1967, is particularly valuable because of the background of its author. Karol, who was born in Poland, lived for many years in the Soviet Union, and was a member of the Communist Party; after World War II, he broke with Soviet Communism and moved to France, where he now works as a journalist. This book is an account of a long journey undertaken by Karol to China in 1965, at the invitation of Chou En-lai. Karol, despite his political background, sees the communist experiment as a very hopeful possibility. Barbara Tuchman, *Stilwell and the American Experience in China, 1911–1945,* Macmillan, New York, 1970, traces the history of America's response to the revolutionary crisis of China in the twentieth century, as seen through the career of General Joseph Stilwell. Although it is not Mrs. Tuchman's intention to provide an apology for Chinese Communism, her account illustrates the *functional* reasons for the victory of Mao Tse-tung over Chiang Kai-shek.

On Vietnam: The best work is Bernard Fall, *The Two Vietnams,* Praeger, New York, 1967, by the late French journalist, who became a victim of the war, the tragedy of which he sought to explain and publicize. Robert

Shaplen, *The Lost Revolution,* Harper & Row, New York, 1965, is a fine study which, because of the excellence of the reporting, illustrates clearly the weaknesses of anti-communist interpretations of the emergent world and of the anti-communist orientation of our foreign policy.

On Latin America: Gerald Clark, *The Coming Explosion in Latin America,* David McKay, Inc., New York, 1962, an excellent study of the problems of Latin America, which challenges our preoccupation with an anti-communist strategy in the emergent world. Ramon Ruiz, *Cuba,* University of Massachusetts Press, Amherst, Mass., 1968, one of the best historical surveys of Cuba, which provides necessary background material to an understanding of the nature of the Castro revolution.

II. Specialized Bibliography

1. *Communism: The Revolution of Modernization*

T. H. Von Laue, *Why Lenin? Why Stalin?,* J. B. Lippincott Co., Philadelphia, 1964, is the basic work, the first completely successful attempt to analyze the communist experience in Russia as a revolution of modernization. T. H. Von Laue, *Sergei Witte and the Industrialization of Russia,* Columbia University Press, New York, 1963, analyzes the attempts of czarist Russia, shortly before World War I, to confront the problem of modernization. Sergei Witte was a czarist bureaucrat who saw the problems of Russia in a way not substantially different from that of the communists under Stalin, despite the fact that Witte was a "conservative." See also Bernard Kiernan, "The Nature of Communism in the Emergent World," *Yale Review,* Spring 1970, vol. 59, no. 3. Cyril E. Black, *The Dynamics of Modernization,* Harper & Row, New York, 1966, is one of the great studies of the problems of modernization, presenting an analytical framework different from the one in this essay. C. E. Black, "Revolution, Modernization, and Communism," in C. E. Black and T. P. Thornton (eds.), *Communism and Revolution,* Princeton University Press, Princeton, N.J., 1964, relates modernization specifically to communist revolution.

2. *Modernization in the West*

Robert Redfield, *Peasant Society and Culture,* University of Chicago Press, Chicago, 1956, is an excellent introduction to the nature and conditions of traditional peasant societies. See also Robert Redfield, *The Primitive*

World and Its Transformations, Cornell University Press, Ithaca, N.Y., 1953. The coercive aspects of civilization, and the underlying search for power which created modern civilization, are brilliantly demonstrated in Lewis Mumford, *The City in History,* Harcourt, Brace & World, New York, 1961, the most complete historical analysis of the city, which is defined as the functional institution of civilized society.

The internal, and almost inescapable, logic by which political authority has become increasingly centralized and ubiquitous in modern society is traced and analyzed in Bertrand de Jouvenel, *On Power,* translated by J. F. Huntington, Viking Press, New York, 1949.

The way in which our modern economic system was imposed on unwilling peasants, and the degree to which it rests on discipline, regimentation, and the search for power, have never been more completely or brilliantly studied than in the classic by Lewis Mumford, *Technics and Civilization,* Harcourt, Brace & World, New York, 1963. Another perceptive study of the devastating impact of economic modernization is Karl Polanyi, *The Great Transformation,* Beacon Press, Boston, 1957. On social modernization, see Karl Deutsch, "Social Mobilization and Political Development," *American Political Science Review,* September 1961, vol. 55, no. 3. Karl Deutsch and William J. Foltz (eds.), *Nation-Building,* Atherton Press, Prentice-Hall, New York, 1963, consists of a collection of essays on the process of nation-building in the European and American past, as well as in the present world of emergent nations.

The coercive, brainwashing dimension of modern education, the establishment pressures to turn educational institutions into training schools of cultural conformity, and the debilitating impact of these pressures on our society, are a continuing source of concern in all the works of Paul Goodman. Among numerous books debunking our educational myths, see *Compulsory Mis-education,* and *The Community of Scholars,* Vintage Books, New York, 1966.

3. *Communism and Peasant Mobilization*

The classic work is Chalmers Johnson, *Peasant Nationalism and Communist Power,* Stanford University Press, Stanford, Cal., 1962, which demonstrates convincingly that communism, in China, was a form of peasant nationalism, as well as a process of social mobilization of peasants confronted with problems of overwhelming magnitude. Stuart Schram, *Mao Tse-tung,* Simon & Schuster, New York, 1966, reinforces Johnson's work by demonstrating that Mao Tse-tung's political career was a direct response to the needs of peasant nationalism and peasant mobilization in China. See also

Jack Belden, *China Shakes the World,* Monthly Review Press, New York, 1970, a long forgotten account of the convulsions of China in the 1940's, recently reprinted, by a man who was willing to face the Chinese experience without the ideological blinkers of a professional anti-communism.

The same process of peasant nationalism, peasant mobilization, and peasant communism can be seen in the activities of other revolutionary leaders in the emergent world confronting conditions analogous to those of China in the 1930's and 1940's. The following biographies should be particularly useful. Herbert Matthews, *Fidel Castro,* Simon & Schuster, New York, 1969, is probably the best study of Castro in English, by a sympathetic observer, long acquainted with Cuba, who understands how Castro's attitudes were determined by the objective conditions he confronted, rather than by ideological preconceptions. The national peasant roots of Yugoslav communism are well illustrated in Fitzroy Maclean, *The Heretic,* Harper & Bros., New York, 1957, written by a man who has no conceivable ideological affinity for communism, but is very sympathetic to Tito's communist mobilization of the peasants in Yugoslavia. David Gordon, *The Passing of French Algeria,* Oxford University Press, New York, 1966, analyzes the struggle for Algerian independence against France, and examines in detail the nature of the FLN leadership. C. Heinz and H. Donnay, *Lumumba,* translated from the French by Jane Clark Seitz, Grove Press, New York, 1969, is a journalistic account of the Congolese national leader's overthrow, imprisonment, and death; somewhat superficial and sensationalistic, but valuable because of the absence of those conditioned anti-communist reflexes which mar so much American journalism.

Luis Taruc, *Born of the People,* International Publishers, New York, 1953, is a first-hand account by the leader of the Filipino Huks of how he became a communist in response to conditions in the Philippines analogous to other peasant revolutionary situations in the emergent world. His second work, *He Who Rides the Tiger,* Praeger, New York, 1967, was written after he had surrendered to the Filipino authorities, and abjured communism. It is in some ways an even more convincing document, since it is written out of an avowedly anti-communist bias, yet constantly reveals, even if unconsciously, the objective logic which turned Taruc into a communist.

4. *The Telescoped Revolution*

Barrington Moore, *Social Origins of Dictatorship and Democracy,* Beacon Press, Boston, 1966. A very important theoretical study which attempts to explain and categorize the nature of modern societies by examining the nature of their modernizing experience.

Louis Hartz, *The Liberal Tradition in America,* Harcourt, Brace & Co., New York, 1955, is an attempt to demonstrate that the success of liberalism and the open society, in the United States, was due to unusually fortunate circumstances.

Frantz Fanon, *The Wretched of the Earth,* translated by Constance Farrington, Grove Press, New York, 1963, is the great classic on the need for revolutionary violence in the liberation of the emergent world.

K. M. Pannikar, *Asia and Western Dominance,* George Allen & Unwin, Ltd., London, 1953, shows us the history of one major area of the emergent world as seen from the perspective of the emergent world itself. Pannikar, an English-trained professor, and a radical Indian political figure, emphasizes the exploitative nature of past Western domination, and defines the task of the emergent world partly as the overthrow of the burden of the white man. Eric Williams, *From Columbus to Castro,* Harper & Row, New York, 1970, makes essentially the same kind of survey for the Caribbean area. Williams, a native political leader, and former Prime Minister of Trinidad and Tobago, also emphasizes the struggle of the emergent world against the burden of the white man.

John Kautsky, "An Essay in the Politics of Development," in John Kautsky (ed.), *Political Change in Underdeveloped Countries,* John Wiley & Sons, New York, 1963, is an excellent study of the problems of leadership in the emergent world, and the strong likelihood of what Kautsky calls the totalitarianism of the intellectuals. Another excellent study is Edward Shils, "The Intellectuals in the Political Development of the New States," *World Politics,* April, 1960, vol. 13, no. 3. René Dumont, *False Start in Africa,* translated by Phyllis N. Ott, Praeger, New York, 1969, in which the famous French agronomist presents a sharp criticism of the tendencies of some leaders to substitute revolutionary posture and rhetoric for the hard work of rational and positive construction needed in the emergent societies.

5. *The Struggle for Economic Development*

Benjamin Higgins, *Economic Development,* W. W. Norton & Co., New York, 1968, is a monumental compendium, which includes a wealth of empirical information, yet never degenerates into a merely "statistical" or "technical" study. Jonathan Levin, *The Export Economies,* Harvard University Press, Cambridge, Mass., 1960, is a structural study of the international economic system, and the necessarily inferior role played in that system by the emergent societies.

Latin America has been the region where the new economic imperialism associated with the United States has been most pronounced. Donald Dozer, *Are We Good Neighbors?*, University of Florida Press, Gainesville, Fla., 1959, answers his own question in the negative. Although the author maintains a broadly tolerant view of United States policy, and does not attempt a polemical indictment, he demonstrates that we have failed to genuinely help the Latin American nations in their struggle for development. A much more biting and specific indictment is William A. Williams, *The United States, Cuba, and Castro*, Monthly Review Press, New York, 1962, which seeks to demonstrate how United States policy not only helped to produce the Castro revolution, but drove it into a radical, communist, pro-Soviet stance.

The point that economic development in the emergent world must mean a challenge to Western economic domination is also made in O. Edmund Clubb, Jr., "The Second World Revolution," *The Progressive,* June, 1965, vol. 29.

Dudley Seers, (ed.), *Cuba*, University of North Carolina Press, Chapel Hill, N.C., 1964, is a study of the revolutionary transformation of Cuba under Castro. Presented objectively and without recriminations, clearly pointing out the weaknesses and failures of this revolutionary experiment, it never takes these deficiencies as evidence of the "evil" nature of the Castro regime.

Robert Heilbroner, *The Great Ascent*, Harper & Row, New York, 1963, is a popular study of all the problems of economic development, presented with insight and understanding by a writer who has a knack for explaining complicated problems in simple terms.

Walter Webb, *The Great Frontier*, University of Texas Press, Austin, Texas, 1951, is the classic work outlining the role played by the availability of inexpensive, surplus resources in the overseas world in the development of Western capitalism. Theodore W. Schultz, *Transforming Traditional Agriculture,* Yale University Press, New Haven, Conn., 1964, surveys the problems confronting traditional societies in the throes of development. The chief such problem, Schultz argues, is discovering how to tremendously increase the productive capacity of their agriculture.

6. *The Ideology of Revolution*

Paul Sigmund (ed.), *The Ideologies of the Developing Nations*, Praeger, New York, 1967, is a compilation of some of the ideological responses of the emergent world, drawing directly upon the words of its leaders. The editor concludes that the problems of the emergent world tend to create certain common denominators in the ideological responses of this leadership. These common denominators parallel the characteristics defined in this essay as communism. See also Edward Shils, *Political Development in the New States,* Mouton, The Hague, 1968.

Irving L. Horowitz, *Three Worlds of Development,* Oxford University Press, New York, 1966, is one of the great theoretical works on the sociology of development. Horowitz argues that the needs of undeveloped societies militate in favor of authoritarian regimes, where the concepts of Western liberalism are seen as sources of internal divisiveness in a collective struggle for development.

Irving L. Horowitz, *Revolution in Brazil,* E. P. Dutton & Co., New York, 1964, is a survey of the conditions producing revolution in that great Latin American country. Horowitz analyzes the revolutionary movement of Francisco Juliao, and seeks to relate that movement to genuine social and national goals, for which communism is a means rather than an end. Peter Nehemkis, *Latin America,* Alfred A. Knopf, New York, 1964, makes an interesting contrast, for Nehemkis rejects communism as a legitimate form of political expression.

Lee Lockwood, *Castro's Cuba, Cuba's Fidel,* Macmillan Co., New York, 1967, is an eye-opener. The author, a correspondent for *Life* magazine, presents the result of a personal visit to Cuba. Writing without ideological preconceptions, Lockwood is obviously dismayed by the pernicious hostility and deliberate misunderstanding exhibited by this society toward the courageous and enormously difficult task of overcoming Cuba's backwardness. Equally revealing is Jose Yglesias, *In the Fist of the Revolution,* Pantheon Books, New York, 1968, a first-hand account of a sojourn in a country town in Cuba in 1967, by an American writer of more or less middle-class Cuban origins.

Lucian Pye, *Politics, Personality, and Nation-Building,* Yale University Press, New Haven, Conn., 1962, is a theoretical study of leadership in the emergent world. The author seeks to relate the individual leader's struggle for his own personal identity to the larger struggle of the society to build itself into a modern nation. See also Richard Harris, *Independence and After,* Oxford University Press, London, 1962, an analysis of leadership in the emergent world, caught in the dual struggle to escape outside political domination, and to build modern societies. Gwendolen Carter, *African One-Party States,* Cornell University Press, Ithaca, N.Y., 1962, surveys African politics, and attempts to explain the conditions which militate against an open, multi-party political system in Africa.

7. *Containing Communism: A Formula for Frustration*

Richard J. Barnet, *Intervention and Revolution,* World Publishing Co., New York, 1968, provides the basic structural framework for this topic. It is the best analysis of the way the struggle between the advanced world, particularly the United States, and the emergent nations, presents itself to the antagonists themselves. Conor Cruise O'Brien, "Contemporary Forms of Imperialism," in Arthur I. Blaustein and Roger R. Woock (eds.), *Man Against Poverty,* Random House, Vintage Books, New York, 1968, is less comprehensive and more polemical. It is primarily an indictment of the role of the advanced nations, particularly the United States, in the struggle for development of the emergent world. Arnold C. Brockman, *The Communist Collapse in Indonesia,* W. W. Norton & Co., New York, 1969, is written from an opposite viewpoint, assuming that the struggle to destroy communism in the emergent world is a valid one, and pointing to the defeat of the communists in Indonesia as evidence that the policy of what Barnet calls the National-Security Manager is viable.

Lucian W. Pye, *Guerilla Communism in Malaya,* Princeton University Press, Princeton, N.J., 1956, illustrates once more the shortcomings of a theoretical framework which views communism as an alien conspiracy. This excellent study of Malaya tends to deny the relevancy of its own evidence, since the success or failure of communism in Malaya is separated from functional needs. The same kinds of theoretical inadequacies are illustrated in Douglas Pike, *Viet Cong,* M.I.T. Press, Cambridge, Mass., 1966, where the wealth of data cannot be related meaningfully to any functional interpretation of the Viet Cong, the success of which is interpreted solely in terms of "technique." The real nature of "containment" is cruelly exposed in the works of Jonathan Schell, *The Village of Ben Suc,* Knopf, New York, 1967; and Jonathan Schell, *The Military Half,* Knopf, New York, 1968. Writing in purely objective terms, without ideological interpretations, Schell describes in chilling terms the horror of "pacification" for the recalcitrant peasant population of Vietnam.

William A. Williams, *The Tragedy of American Diplomacy,* Dell Publishing Co., New York, 1962, analyzes United States foreign policy since 1898 in the context of the struggle for development in the emergent world and recommends "an open door for revolution." Bernard Kiernan, "The Limitations of U.S. Policy Toward the Underdeveloped World," *The American Scholar,* Spring, 1962, vol. 31, no. 2, also embodies a recommendation for our support of left-wing revolution, specifically in reference to the United States and Castro's Cuba.

The clearest and most succinct summary of the argument that Soviet foreign policy does not have a special ideological dimension not found in the behavior of "normal" states is Samuel Sharp, "National Interest: Key to Soviet Politics," in *Problems of Communism*, March-April, 1958, vol. 7. The opposite point of view is presented in Kurt London, "Soviet Foreign Policy: Fifty Years of Dualism," in Kurt London (ed.), *The Soviet Union*, Johns Hopkins Press, Baltimore, 1968.

8. *Prospects for the Future*

Marvin Kalb & Elie Abel, *Roots of Involvement*, W. W. Norton & Co., New York, 1971, illustrates some of the problems in seeking to interpret recent changes in United States Vietnam policy. Earl C. Ravenal, "The Nixon Doctrine and Our Asian Commitments," *Foreign Affairs*, January, 1971, gives less reason for optimism. The author analyzes the Nixon Doctrine for Asia, and finds its greatest weakness in the continued assumption that the containment of Communist China is the chief goal of the United States in the Far East.

Lewis Mumford, *The Pentagon of Power*, 2 vols., Harcourt, Brace & Jovanovich, New York, 1970, is the summa of Mumford's work, the final and most complete statement concerning the power fantasies and compulsory delusions on which so much of modern civilization is based. Kenneth Boulding, *The Meaning of the Twentieth Century*, Harper & Row, New York, 1964, presents a somewhat more hopeful picture of the possibilities of modern civilization, although Boulding also sees civilization as an essentially coercive process of regimentation, and argues for a post-civilized transcendence of these disciplines.

Bernard Kiernan, "Eastern Europe and the Problem of Modernization," *Vidya*, Spring 1969, no. 3, discusses the problems of communism in eastern Europe and argues, among other things, that the experience of the communist countries of eastern Europe provides hope that communism and Marxist ideology are not a permanent bar to the development of social democracy.

Notes

1. Communism: The Revolution of Modernization

1. Douglas Pike, *Viet Cong*, M.I.T. Press, Cambridge, Mass., 1966, p. 33.

2. As quoted in *The New Republic*, March 19, 1966, p. 8.

3. T. H. Von Laue, *Why Lenin? Why Stalin?*, J. B. Lippincott Co., Philadelphia, 1964, p. 16.

4. Wolfgang Sauer, "National Socialism: Totalitarianism or Fascism?" *American Historical Review*, December 1967, pp. 418–419. John Kautsky speaks of "fitting the Russian Revolution into the broad historical pattern of the nationalist revolutions in the underdeveloped countries." "An Essay in the Politics of Development," in John Kautsky (ed.), *Political Change in Underdeveloped Countries*, John Wiley and Sons, New York, 1963, p. 70.

5. Raymond Aron, *The Century of Total War*, Doubleday & Co., Inc., New York, 1954, p. 165.

6. Von Laue, p. 50.

7. As quoted in Adam Ulam, *Expansion and Co-Existence*, Praeger, New York, 1968, p. 405.

8. As quoted in Frederick Barghoorn, *Politics in the USSR*, Little, Brown and Co., Boston, 1966, p. 29.

9. W. W. Rostow, *The Stages of Economic Growth*, Cambridge University Press, Cambridge, England, 1960, p. 106.

10. Barbara Ward, *The Rich Nations and the Poor Nations*, W. W. Norton & Co., New York, 1962, pp. 60–61.

11. George Lichtheim, *Marxism*, Praeger, New York, 1963, p. 368.

12. William E. Griffith, "European Communism, 1965" in William E. Griffith (ed.), *Communism in Europe*, M.I.T. Press, Cambridge, Mass., 1966, v. 2, p. 7.

2. Modernization in the West

1. Barrington Moore, *Social Origins of Dictatorship and Democracy*, Beacon Press, Boston, 1966, p. 506.

2. Robert Redfield, *Peasant Society and Culture*, University of Chicago Press, Chicago, 1956, p. 112.

3. Cyril Black, *The Dynamics of Modernization,* Harper & Row, New York, 1966, p. 26.

4. Karl Marx, *The Eighteenth Brumaire of Louis Bonaparte,* International Publishers, New York, 1963, p. 125.

5. John Kautsky, "An Essay in the Politics of Development," in John Kautsky (ed.), *Political Change,* p. 16.

6. Irwin T. Sanders, *Balkan Village,* University of Kentucky Press, Lexington, Ky., 1949, p. 144.

7. Shepard B. Clough, *A History of the Western World,* D. C. Heath & Co., Boston, 1964, p. 8.

8. Melville J. Herskovits, *Dahomey,* J. J. Augustin, New York, 1938, vol. 1, p. 55.

9. Lewis Mumford, *The City in History,* Harcourt, Brace & World, Inc., New York, 1961, p. 30; see also pp. 39–54.

10. Moore, *Social Origins,* p. 467.

11. Mumford, *The City in History,* p. 46.

12. Herman Weilenmann, "Nation and Personality Structure," in Karl Deutsch and William J. Foltz (eds.), *Nation-Building,* Atherton Press, Prentice Hall, New York, 1963, p. 50.

13. Kautsky, "An Essay," p. 92.

14. Jack C. Fisher, *Yugoslavia—A Multinational State,* Chandler Publishing Co., San Francisco, 1966, p. 19.

15. Black, *Dynamics,* p. 13.

16. James S. Coleman, "Nationalism in Tropical Africa," *American Political Science Review,* June 1954, vol. 48, no. 2, p. 405.

17. George Lichtheim, *Marxism,* p. 388.

18. Nicolas Spulber, "Economic Modernization," in Robert F. Byrnes (ed.), *The United States and Eastern Europe,* Prentice Hall, Englewood Cliffs, N.J., 1967, p. 57.

19. See Charles Tilly, *The Vendee,* Harvard University Press, Cambridge, Mass., 1964.

20. As quoted in C.B.A. Behrens, *The Ancien Regime,* Harcourt, Brace & World, New York, 1967, p. 44.

21. David Brandenburg, "Early Modern Economics," in Clough (ed.), *A History of the Western World,* p. 473. "Mercantilism . . . was the economic counterpart of the political processes by which the national states were being built up." S. B. Clough and C. W. Cole, *Economic History of Europe,* D. C. Heath, Boston, 1952, p. 197.

22. Clough and Cole, p. 197.

23. Benjamin Schwartz, *Chinese Communism and the Rise of Mao,* Harper, New York, 1951, p. 199.

24. Black, *Dynamics,* p. 24.

25. "Talk of the Town," *The New Yorker,* July 18, 1970.

26. Peter Gay, *The Enlightenment,* vol. I: *The Rise of Modern Paganism,* Random House, New York, 1966, p. 141.

27. Paul Sigmund (ed.), *The Ideologies of the Developing Nations,* Praeger, New York, 1967, pp. 173–179.

28. Kenneth Boulding, *The Meaning of the Twentieth Century,* Harper & Row, New York, 1964, p. 16.

29. "Le pilote tient la barre, l'équipage fait la manoeuvre, le devoir des passagers est de rester à leur place." *L'Express,* February 9, 1962. My translation.

3. *Communism and Peasant Mobilization*

1. David Mitrany, *Marx Against the Peasant,* University of North Carolina Press, Chapel Hill, N.C., 1951, p. 25.

2. Karl Marx and Frederick Engels, "The Communist Manifesto," in *Selected Works,* International Publishers, New York, 1968, p. 39.

3. Robert Redfield, *Peasant Society and Culture,* p. 137.

4. Gunnar Myrdal, *Beyond the Welfare State,* Yale University Press, New Haven, Conn., 1960, pp. ix, 139, 210 etc.

5. Peter Nehemkis, *Latin America,* Alfred A. Knopf, New York, 1964, p. 4.

6. Dan Jacobs and Hans H. Baerwald (eds.), "Introduction," *Chinese Communism,* Harper & Row, New York, 1963, pp. 3–4.

7. Chalmers Johnson, "The Japanese Role in Peasant Mobilization," *Peasant Nationalism and Communist Power,* pp. 31–70.

8. Johnson, p. 2.

9. Johnson, p. 5.

10. Johnson, p. 157. Robert Tucker makes the same point and includes as examples China, Yugoslavia, Albania, and Vietnam. "Paths of Communist Revolution, 1917–1967," in Kurt London (ed.), *The Soviet Union,* Johns Hopkins Press, Baltimore, p. 23.

11. Johnson, *Peasant Nationalism,* p. 5.

12. Johnson, pp. 156–157.

13. David A. Wilson, "Nation-Building and Revolutionary War," in Deutsch and Foltz (eds.), *Nation-Building,* p. 86.

14. R. V. Burks, "Eastern Europe," in C. E. Black and Thomas P. Thornton (eds.), *Communism and Revolution,* Princeton University Press, Princeton, N.J., 1964, p. 98.

15. Rostow, p. 111.

16. Johnson, pp. 180–181.

17. Stuart Schram, *Mao Tse-tung,* Simon & Schuster, New York, 1966, p. 52.

18. Schwartz, *Chinese Communism,* p. 187.

19. Ramon Ruiz, *Cuba,* University of Massachusetts Press, Amherst, Mass., 1968, p. 19.

20. Herbert Matthews, *Fidel Castro,* Simon & Schuster, New York, 1969, p. 183.

21. R. V. Burks, "Eastern Europe," p. 96.

22. Fitzroy Maclean, *The Heretic,* Harper & Bros., New York, 1957, p. 195.

23. Maclean, p. 365.

24. R. V. Burks, *The Dynamics of Communism in Eastern Europe,* Princeton University Press, Princeton, N.J., 1961, p. 129.

25. As quoted in William E. Smith "Julius K. Nyerere," *The New Yorker,* October 23, 1971, p. 52.

26. Irving L. Horowitz, *Three Worlds of Development,* Oxford University Press, New York, 1966, p. 31.

27. Frantz Fanon, *The Wretched of the Earth,* trans. by Constance Farrington, Grove Press, New York, 1963, p. 73.

28. K. S. Karol, *China,* Hill and Wang, New York, 1967, p. 102.

29. Johnson, p. xi.

4. *The Telescoped Revolution*

1. Cyril Black, "Revolution, Modernization, and Communism," in Black and Thornton (eds.), *Communism and Revolution,* p. 23.

2. Karl Deutsch, "Social Mobilization and Political Development," *American Political Science Review,* September 1961, vol. 55, no. 3, p. 498.

3. W. W. Rostow, p. 17.

4. Ibid.

5. "Comme un chef d'état révolutionnaire. La décision de réaliser une révolution profonde m'est venue avec la certitude qu'un pays comme le nôtre doit brûler les étapes pour accéder à la technologie moderne et à un niveau de vie supérieur." As quoted in *L'Express,* June 8, 1970, p. 31. My translation.

6. Hugh Seton-Watson, *Nationalism and Communism,* Praeger, New York, 1964, p. 39.

7. Lucian Pye, *Politics, Personality and Nation Building,* Yale University Press, New Haven, Conn., 1962, p. 9.

8. Pye, *Politics,* p. 8.

9. William A. Williams, *The Tragedy of American Diplomacy,* Dell Publishing Co., New York, 1962, p. 93.

10. Melville J. Herskovits, *The Human Factor in Changing Africa,* Knopf, New York, 1962, p. 127.

11. Fanon, p. 41.

12. René Dumont, *Types of Rural Economy,* trans. by Douglas Magnin, Methuen and Co., Ltd., London, 1957, pp. 23–24.

13. As quoted in Christopher Thorne, "The Shanghai Crisis of 1932," in *American Historical Review,* October 1970, vol. 75, no. 6, p. 1626.

14. As quoted in K. M. Pannikar, *Asia and Western Dominance,* George Allen and Unwin, Ltd., London, 1953, p. 36.

15. As quoted in Donald M. Dozer, *Are We Good Neighbors?,* University of Florida Press, Gainesville, Fla., 1959, p. 200.

16. W. R. Crocker, *Self-Government for the Colonies,* George Allen & Unwin, Ltd., London, 1949, p. 89.

17. Jean Paul Sartre, "Preface," in Fanon, p. 15.

18. Quoted in Dozer, p. 254.

19. W. R. Crocker, *Self-Government for the Colonies*, p. 8.

20. Crocker, p. 40.

21. "Cuba découvre aujourd'hui que l'enthousiasme révolutionnaire ne remplace ni l'organisation ni la technique, et que les lois de rendement industriel sont implacables." "Cuba: la Fin des Illusions," in *L'Express*, July 20, 1970, pp. 25–28; my translation.

22. David A. Wilson, "Nation Building and Revolutionary War," in Deutsch and Foltz, p. 88.

23. David Apter, *Some Conceptual Approaches to the Study of Modernization*, Prentice-Hall, Englewood Cliffs, N.J., 1968, p. 35.

24. Kautsky, "An Essay," p. 55.

25. Kautsky, p. 39.

26. Arslan Humbaraci, *Algeria*, Praeger, New York, 1966, p. 31.

27. David Gordon, *The Passing of French Algeria*, Oxford University Press, New York, 1966, p. 100.

28. Pye, *Politics*, p. 5.

29. Kautsky, "An Essay," pp. 106–113.

30. William J. Foltz, "Building the Newest Nations," in Deutsch and Foltz (eds.), *Nation-Building*, p. 123.

5. *The Struggle for Economic Development*

1. Benjamin Higgins, *Economic Development*, W. W. Norton & Co., New York, 1968, p. 268.

2. Report by the Secretary General of the United Nations Conference on Trade and Development, *Towards a New Trade Policy for Development*, United Nations, New York, 1964, pp. 11–19.

3. Dozer, pp. 262–263.

4. Dudley Seers, "The Economic and Social Background," in Dudley Seers (ed.), *Cuba*, University of North Carolina Press, Chapel Hill, N.C., 1964, pp. 3, 19.

5. Higgins, p. 284.

6. Hla Mynt, *The Economies of the Developing Countries*, Praeger, New York, 1965, p. 148; see also Robert Heilbroner, *The Great Ascent*, Harper & Row, New York, 1963, pp. 125–128.

7. Brian Crozier, *Morning After*, Oxford University Press, New York, 1963, p. 77.

8. Williams, *Tragedy*, p. 2.

9. André Bianchi, "Agriculture," in Seers (ed.), *Cuba*, p. 98.

10. William A. Williams, *The United States, Cuba and Castro*, Monthly Review Press, New York, 1962, p. 16.

11. Dozer, p. 341.

12. Gerald Clark, *The Coming Explosion in Latin America*, David McKay Co., Inc., New York, 1962, p. 272.

13. Edward Behr, *The Algerian Problem*, W. W. Norton & Co., New York, 1961, p. 36.

14. "on . . . a vu . . . les fonctionnaires français s'efforcer de guider les investissements algériens vers des productions qui ne feraient pas concurrence aux industriels français." As quoted in *L'Express*, November 30, 1970, p. 23. My translation.

15. Higgins, *Economic Development*, p. 298.

16. Ellen Hammer, *The Struggle for Indo-China*, Stanford University Press, Stanford, Calif., 1954, p. 91; see also pp. 72–74.

17. Richard J. Barnet, *Intervention and Revolution*, World Publishing Co., New York, 1968, p. 38.

18. Edmondo Flores, "Latin America: Alliance for Reaction," *The Nation*, June 21, 1965, vol. 200, no. 25, p. 661.

19. Raul Prebisch, "Towards a Dynamic Development Policy for Latin America," in Sigmund (ed.), *The Ideologies of the Developing Nations*, pp. 369–370.

20. Jonathan Levin, *The Export Economies*, Harvard University Press, Cambridge, Mass., 1960, p. 157.

21. O. Edmund Clubb, Jr., "The Second World Revolution," *The Progressive*, June 1965, vol. 29, p. 16.

22. As quoted in David Gordon, pp. 18–19.

23. Williams, *Tragedy*, p. 88.

24. Lee Lockwood, *Castro's Cuba, Cuba's Fidel*, Macmillan Co., New York, 1967, p. 282.

25. Crozier, *Morning After*, p. 43.

26. René Dumont, *False Start in Africa*, trans. by Phyllis N. Ott, Praeger, New York, 1969, p. 70.

27. Guy Wint, *The British in Asia*, Institute of Pacific Relations, University of British Columbia, Vancouver, Canada, 1954, pp. 115, 192, etc.

28. Rupert Emerson, *From Empire to Nation*, Beacon Press, Boston, 1960, p. 38.

29. "Nous ne voulons plus que l'Algérie soit considérée comme un satellite de l'économie française. L'essentiel, pour nous, est que la France admette que l'Algérie est devenue majeure . . . si la France n'admet, dans une certaine mesure, qu'une Algérie dépendante, alors, il vaut mieux trancher." *L'Express*, November 30, 1970, p. 25. My translation.

30. Walter Webb, *The Great Frontier*, University of Texas Press, Austin, Texas, 1951, pp. 13–28.

31. Webb, p. 13.

32. Webb, p. 16.

33. Webb, pp. 182–191.

34. Webb, p. 13.

35. Higgins, p. 296.

36. Kautsky, "An Essay," p. 22.

37. Kautsky, "An Essay," p. 78.

38. John P. Hardt and Carl Modig, "Stalinist Industrial Development in Soviet Russia," in Kurt London (ed.), *The Soviet Union,* p. 302.

39. As quoted in William E. Smith, "Julius K. Nyerere," *The New Yorker,* October 30, 1971, p. 53.

6. *The Ideology of Revolution*

1. Edward Shils, *Political Development in the New States,* Mouton, The Hague, 1968, p. 67.

2. Emerson, *Empire to Nation,* p. 370.

3. Dozer, p. 307.

4. Prebisch, "Toward a Dynamic Development Policy for Latin America," p. 376.

5. William G. Carleton, "The New Nationalism," *Virginia Quarterly Review,* Summer 1950, vol. 26, p. 438.

6. Rostow, *Stages,* p. 25.

7. Prebisch, "Toward a Dynamic Development Policy for Latin America," p. 368.

8. Emerson, *Empire to Nation,* p. 367.

9. Shils, *Political Development,* p. 67.

10. Horowitz, *Three Worlds,* p. 20.

11. In Sigmund, p. 237.

12. For a summary of Nyerere's views on the need for unity in an emergent nation, see the article by William E. Smith, "Julius K. Nyerere," in *The New Yorker,* October 16, 23, 30, 1971.

13. As quoted in Harold Isaacs, *The Tragedy of the Chinese Revolution,* Atheneum, New York, 1968, p. xi.

14. Ch'en Tu-hsiu, in *La Jeunesse,* as quoted in Karol, p. 44.

15. Barnet, p. 275.

16. For an incisive survey of Latin America, as seen from the perspective of a radical left committed to change, development, and modernization, see Irving L. Horowitz, Jesue de Castro, and John Gerassi (eds.), *Latin American Radicalism,* Random House, New York, 1969.

17. See James S. Coleman and Carl G. Resberg (eds.), *Political Parties and National Integration in Tropical Africa,* University of California Press, Berkeley, Calif., 1966; Gwendolen Carter, *African One-Party States,* Cornell University Press, Ithaca, N.Y., 1962; Rupert Emerson and Martin Kilson (eds.), *The Political Awakening of Africa,* Prentice-Hall, Inc., Englewood Cliffs, N.J., 1965.

18. Barnet, p. 275.

19. Horowitz, *Three Worlds,* p. 227.

20. Emerson, *Empire to Nation,* p. 371.

21. As quoted in William E. Smith, "Julius K. Nyerere," in *The New Yorker,* October 30, 1971, p. 53.

22. Heilbroner, p. 160.

23. Higgins, p. 809.

24. Lee Lockwood, *Castro's Cuba, Cuba's Fidel,* Macmillan Co., New York, 1967.

25. Marshal D. Shulman, *Beyond the Cold War,* Yale University Press, New Haven, Conn., 1968, p. 107.

26. Emerson, *Empire to Nation,* p. 373.

27. John Plamenatz, *German Marxism and Russian Communism,* Longmans, Green and Co., New York, 1954, p. 318.

28. Tucker, "Paths of Communist Development," p. 9.

29. Karol, p. 18.

30. "L'esprit révolutionnaire conduit sans doute finalement au parti unique (donc à la réduction de la démocratie) à la réforme agraire (donc à l'expropriation des colons français) et aux nationalisations (donc à une transformation des relations économiques et surtout financières.)" Jean Daniel, *L'Express,* March 22, 1962. My translation.

31. Lichtheim, *Marxism,* p. 372.

32. Matthews, *Fidel Castro,* p. 318.

33. Edward Shils, "The Intellectuals in the Political Development of the New States," *World Politics,* April 1960, vol. 13, no. 3, p. 344.

34. Merle Fainsod, "Summary and Review," in Cyril E. Black (ed.), *The Transformation of Russian Society,* Harvard University Press, Cambridge, Mass., 1967, p. 230.

35. Les K. Adler and Thomas G. Patterson, "Red Fascism," in *American Historical Review,* April 1970, p. 1062.

7. Containing Communism: A Formula for Frustration

1. Fanon, p. 65.

2. Luis Taruc, *He Who Rides the Tiger,* Praeger, New York, 1967, p. 59.

3. Edward Behr, *The Algerian Problem,* pp. 73-74.

4. The first figure was quoted by Colonel Ouamrane, of the Algerian Army of Liberation, to Arslan Humbaraci, a Turkish journalist who was a close and privileged observer of the Algerian war of independence, and who comments that the figure "is certainly not far from the truth." Arslan Humbaraci, *Algeria,* pp. 34-35.

5. Edward Behr, *The Algerian Problem,* p. 69.

6. Crocker, *Self-Government for the Colonies,* p. 27.

7. Crocker, p. 41.

8. *L'Express,* October 11, 1971, p. 26.

9. Pannikar, *Asia and Western Dominance,* p. 105.

10. Johnson, p. 186.

11. Brian Crozier, *The Rebels,* Beacon Press, Boston, 1960, p. 12.

12. Crocker, p. 123.

13. As quoted in *The New Yorker,* October 6, 1962.

14. Crocker, p. 124.

15. Johnson, *Peasant Nationalism,* p. 187.

16. Barnet, pp. 23-26.

17. Barnet, pp. 3-19.

18. Barnet, pp. 36–46.
19. Barnet, p. 23.
20. Barnet, p. 24.
21. Barnet, p. 31.
22. Pye, *Politics, Personality, and Nation Building*, pp. xvii-xviii.
23. Barnet, p. 33.
24. Saul Bellow, *Mr. Sammler's Planet*, Viking Press, New York, 1969, p. 147.
25. Franz Alexander, *American Journal of Orthopsychiatry*, October 1941, vol. 11, in William Ebenstein (ed.), *Modern Political Thought*, Holt, Rinehart, & Winston, Inc., New York, 1960, p. 85.
26. Barnet, p. 33.
27. Barnet, p. 34.
28. Pike, p. 32.
29. Lucian Pye, *Guerilla Communism in Malaya*, Princeton University Press, Princeton, N.J., 1956, pp. 40–45.
30. Barnet, p. 29.
31. Williams, *Tragedy*, p. 295.
32. Taruc, p. 33.
33. Dozer, p. 323.
34. As quoted in Smith, "Julius K. Nyerere," *The New Yorker*, October 23, 1971, p. 100.
35. Ruiz, p. 5.
36. Gordon, p. 65.
37. "Toute aide est bienvenue. Même de la part des communistes." As quoted in *L'Express*, October 4, 1971, p. 26. My translation.
38. Thomas T. Hammond, "The Origins of National Communism," *Virginia Quarterly Review*, Spring 1958, vol. 34, no. 2, p. 277.
39. Kurt London, "Soviet Foreign Policy," in London (ed.), *The Soviet Union*, p. 345.
40. Samuel Sharp, "National Interest: Key to Soviet Politics," in *Problems of Communism*, vol. 7, March-April 1958, p. 18.
41. Sharp, p. 18.
42. Jeremy Bernstein, *The Analytic Engine*, Random House, New York, 1963, p. 97.
43. Kurt London, "Soviet Foreign Policy," in London (ed.), *The Soviet Union*, pp. 327–363.
44. The phrase is borrowed from William A. Williams, *The Tragedy of American Diplomacy*, pp. 296–297.

8. *Prospects for the Future*

1. Frederick Barghoorn, "Prospects for Soviet Political Development," in London (ed.), *The Soviet Union*, p. 90.
2. H. Gordon Skilling, "The Party, Opposition, and Interest Groups in Communist Politics," in London (ed.), *The Soviet Union*, p. 144.

Index